# TUPPERWARE

Smithsonian Institution Press
Washington & London

Alison J. Clarke

# TUPPERWARE

The Promise of Plastic
in 1950s America

TUPPERWARE is a registered trademark of Dart Industries Inc.

Copy editor: Joanne Reams
Production editor: Deborah L. Sanders
Designer: Chris Hotvedt

Library of Congress Cataloging-in-Publication Data
Clarke, Alison J.
Tupperware : the promise of plastic in 1950s America / Alison J. Clarke.
p.    cm.
Includes bibliographical references and index.
ISBN 1-56098-827-4 (cloth : alk. paper)
1. Tupperware (Firm)—History.   2. Plastic container industry—United
States—History.   3. Tableware industry—United States—History.
4. Plastic tableware—United States—History.   I. Title.
HD9662.C664T863   1999
338.7′668497′0973—dc21      99-16972

British Library Cataloguing-in-Publication Data available

Manufactured in the United States of America
06  05  04  03  02  01  00  99    5  4  3  2

♾ The paper used in this publication meets the minimum requirements of the American National Standard for Information Sciences—Permanence of Paper for Printed Library Materials ANSI Z39.48-1984.

For permission to reproduce illustrations appearing in this book, please correspond directly with the owners of the works, as listed in the individual captions. The Smithsonian Institution Press does not retain reproduction rights for these illustrations individually, or maintain a file of addresses for photo sources.

The objects pictured on pages ii and iii of this book are details of the photograph on page 37. Tupper, Earl S. Kitchen containers and implements. 1945–56. Photograph © 1999 The Museum of Modern Art, New York.

*Tupperware: The Promise of Plastic in 1950s America* is not sponsored or endorsed in any manner by Tupperware Worldwide / Dart Industries Inc.

For Constance Loadwick White, with love.

## Contents

# Contents

# Acknowledgments

Without the insight of Tupperware dealers, hostesses, and managers from the 1950s to the present day in the United States and United Kingdom, this book could not have been written. I thank the many people who contributed time in relaying their oral histories concerning the product and corporation. Several of the past executives from the company were enthusiastically supportive of the research and genuinely interested in the product's cultural history. I am particularly grateful to Elsie Mortland, Joan Jackson, Joe Hara, and the Flaherty family.

Fellowships at the Smithsonian Institution's National Museum of American History proved invaluable in supporting archival research. There I benefited from the expertise and encouragement of numerous staff members and Smithsonian fellows, including Katherine Ott, Steve Lubar, Anne Serio, Barbara Clark Smith, Bill Yeingst, Rodris Roth, Tom Bickley, Mimi Minnick, John Fleckner, Charlie McGovern, Fath Ruffins, Reuben Jackson, Vanessa Simmons, Meg Jacobs, Shelley Nickles, John Hartigan, Scott Sandage, Pete Daniel, and Mary Dyer. I acknowledge the efficient and inspired help of my summer research intern, Jenny Chun. I also thank the library staff at the National Museum of American History, especially Stephanie and Jim, and all the staff of the Archives Center and the Division of Domestic Life.

Big thanks to Dick Hebdige, Jeffrey Meikle, James Horn, Ann Smart Martin, Dell Upton, Penny Sparke, Roger Horowitz, Gary Kulik, and colleagues at the Royal College of Art for thoughtful advice at the early stages of my research. I am particularly grateful to Professor Christopher Frayling for his initial encouragement of my "Tupper Magic" pursuit.

Research supported by a grant-in-aid at the Center for the History of Business, Technology, and Society at the Hagley Museum and Library, Wilmington, Delaware, in the summer of 1996 provided vital supplementary details regarding plastic manufacture. Similarly, for background information concerning contemporary sales companies Elizabeth M. Doherty at the Direct Selling Association, Washington, D.C., generously offered the organization's library and resources for my use.

Numerous kind colleagues and friends have offered constructive criticism of this research over the lengthy period of its completion and endured endless "Tupperized" ranting. I thank Matthew Hilton, Maria Blyzinsky, Clayton Harris, Michael Carroll, Jeremy Eaton, Deborah Ryan, Judy Davies, and Carolyn Corben. Without the generous hospitality and banter of Noah Steinberg and Josh Cohen my stay in D.C. would have been far less enjoyable; thanks, you two. Many thanks also to Rachel Fincken and Mr. Williamson for sharing, in different ways, the more sociable and spiritual dimensions of research and life in Washington, Brighton, and New Orleans.

Special thanks to Daniel Miller for his patience, wit, and inspiration and to my kind and insightful acquisitions editor, Mark Hirsch, for showing sustained support and enthusiasm for this project. I am most grateful for the conscientious work of Joanne Reams, Deborah L. Sanders, and the Smithsonian Institution Press's anonymous reader.

Paul Foster and the Clarke family have shared the project, in some form or another, from its initiation through to its completion, and I owe them all much more than thanks for their love and unerring support. I dedicate this book to them and to my grandmother, the redoubtable, fun-loving Constance White.

# TUPPERWARE

# Introduction

A Tupperware party takes place somewhere in the world every 2.5 seconds, and an estimated 90 percent of American homes own at least one piece of Tupperware. Since the mid-1990s, around 85 percent of Tupperware sales have been generated outside the United States in countries as diverse as South Africa and Japan.[1] Artifacts ranging from Wonder Bowls to Ice-Tup molds, fitted with the patented Tupper airtight seal, have equipped the kitchens of millions of households since their inception in 1940s America. An icon of benign suburban living, described by one commentator as being as "all-American as the stars and stripes," Tupperware remains inextricably bound to the sociality of the "party plan" direct sales system that has been appropriated across the world.

Although competitors such as Rubbermaid use conventional retailing and advertising methods (distributing most of their plastic containers through supermarkets and hardware stores), Tupperware relies ostensibly on word-of-mouth recommendation and practical demonstration techniques of a specialized dealer. In a modern consumer culture premised on increasing standardization, self-service, and efficiency, the Tupperware party (which gathers a predominantly female group for a product demonstration in a convivial atmosphere) defies the logic of contemporary marketing strategies. The majority of Tupperware dealers have no professional sales qualifications or experience. Instead the company relies on the entrepreneurship of individuals paid on commission and brought together

1

through a cohesive corporate culture. The product cannot be purchased "off the shelf," yet in 1997 Tupperware's worldwide net sales reached $1.2 billion, and nearly 118 million people attended a Tupperware demonstration.[2]

When an amateur inventor and designer named Earl Silas Tupper first invented Tupperware around 1942 (from a refined version of polyethylene that he referred to as "Poly-T: Material of the Future"), he envisaged the total "Tupperization" of the American home.[3] Throughout the Depression Tupper had persevered in his endeavor to become a commercial inventor and transform his economically precarious life from rags to riches. Women's lives, he believed, would be considerably enhanced by his new labor-saving, flexible, lightweight containers; no more spills and odors in the refrigerator, no more wasted leftovers. By 1947, home magazines such as *House Beautiful* hailed Tupperware designs as "Fine Art for 39 Cents" with gorgeous textures reminiscent of jade and mother-of-pearl, but American housewives remained largely unimpressed. Department store displays and newspaper advertisements promoted Tupperware as the answer to the dreams of the modern homemaker, but still sales dwindled.

Then, in the early 1950s, Brownie Wise, a middle-aged housewife and impoverished single mother living in Detroit, initiated the Tupperware party. Wise had sold Tupperware as an independent door-to-door salesperson to pay her young son's medical bills and Earl Tupper, astonished by her sales figures, demanded to know her secret; it was, she responded, "the Tupperware party." By 1951, convinced by the success of direct selling, Tupper agreed to withdraw Tupperware products from all department stores and retail outlets. The Tupperware party became the company's exclusive form of distribution. Wise was awarded the position of vice president leading the newly formed Tupperware Home Parties Incorporated (THP). She began her amazing transition from housewife to leader of a multimillion dollar enterprise, appearing in women's magazines and business journals across the land.

By the mid-1950s, the Tupperware party (at which women gathered in the home of a volunteering "hostess" for lively product demonstrations) had become a cultural hallmark of postwar America. While Earl Tupper continued to expand his product range, inventing cocktail shakers and hors d'oeuvre dishes for a newly affluent population, Brownie Wise recruited Tupperware dealers in droves. In 1954, she became the first woman to grace the front cover of *Business Week* with her adage, "If we build the people, they'll build the business." The accompanying editorial described her quirky and outlandish sales and recruitment techniques. Poly, a piece of black polyethylene slag insured for $50,000, accompanied her on nationwide trips to dealer and distributor sales rallies. As the inspiration behind Earl Tupper's first injection-molded Tupperware tumbler, the molten lump became a potent Tupperware talisman: "I tell [dealers]," Wise informed *Business Week,* "to shut their eyes, rub their hands on Poly, wish, and work like the devil, then they're bound to succeed." That same year, Wise buried thousands of dollars worth of prizes, including diamond rings, mink coats, and toy Cadillacs (exchangeable for the full-scale models) in the grounds of Tupperware headquarters in Orlando, Florida.[4] As Tupperware women avidly began to "Dig for Gold!" a preacher spoke of Tupperware as a "bulwark against communism."

Despite the astounding success of the Tupperware enterprise, which received constant press coverage and design and business accolades, Tupper and Wise held widely differing approaches to the business. Tupper despised large gatherings of people and refused to attend the annual sales rallies known as Homecoming Jubilees, but Wise reigned over her Tupperware dealers with increasingly flamboyant displays of charisma. While Tupper led the design development of ketchup funnels and cake domes at the Tupper Corporation factories in Massachusetts, Wise gave away items from her personal wardrobe — lavish evening dresses, coordinating hats and accessories — to her sales elite (the "Vanguard") in Orlando. At the height of Tupperware's success in the 1950s, Tupper furnished his home in the restrained style of traditional New England good taste. Wise's Florida home, filled with contemporary artwork, rattan furniture, and flamingo pink upholstery, was described by one journalist as being more like "the lobby of a swank beach hotel." On the one hand, Tupperware taught thrift and containment; on the other, excess and abundance. These contradictions were indicative not merely of biographical and gender differences, but of a historical shift from the Depression economy to a postwar boom.

The Tupperware story defies simplistic theories of market economics or modernist design dicta expounded by most scholarly treatments of the phenomenon. Internationally renowned exhibits from the Museum of Modern Art, New York, to the Victoria and Albert Museum, London, display Tupperware as a reputed artifact of distinctive design, its commercial success ensured by its streamlined, functional appeal to a discerning, rational consumer. However, Tupperware's significance as a twentieth-century artifact is better explained by references to the iconic status of the product in popular culture from the 1950s to present day, ranging from sitcoms and cartoon strips to cult magazines and Hollywood films.

In an episode of the American NBC sitcom *Seinfeld,* for example (renowned for its satirization of the mundane happenings of everyday urban life), one of the main characters, obsessive neighbor Kramer, makes a gift of leftover Chinese food, sealed in Tupperware, to a homeless person in the neighborhood. Because the container is authentic Tupperware, as opposed to a store-bought imitation, it is lent under the assumed pretext that it will be emptied and promptly returned. However, on returning to collect his Tupperware, Kramer is met with a disgruntled response; the indignant homeless person insists the container was a gift. Kramer, affronted by the incredulity of such a suggestion (nobody gives away real Tupperware!), turns from charitable gesture to near physical assault in an attempt to retrieve his precious vessel. Tupperware, the proceedings suggest to the amusement and recognition of millions of 1990s American viewers, might rationally be construed as a functional plastic food container. Yet, absurdly, in a society that disposes of billions of plastic food receptacles every day, Tupperware remains inexplicably sacrosanct.

This book offers a cultural history of Tupperware and explores the processes by which objects of mass consumption are appropriated as meaningful artifacts of everyday life and, more specifically, why certain objects come to matter more than others do. How can Tupperware be at once mundane and extraordinary? Why might a sitcom dealing with the minutiae of everyday social relations and things reveal a more acute understanding of material culture than scholarly museum exhibits? In the case of Tupperware, there is a notable gulf between its academic status as a simple, uncluttered functional design, born of the modernist ethos "Form Follows Function," and its sociocultural significance as material culture deeply embedded in the intricacies of social relations, domestic habits, and rituals of consumption.

The Tupperware party, a phenomenon less easily explained by theories of utilitarianism, originated according to corporate anecdote as an expedient way of showing bewildered 1950s housewives how to fit the Tupperware seal securely on their polyethylene containers. The notion of "bewildered" housewives, ambling from bridge party to Tupperware party, compounds the notion of the all-consuming postwar American woman, capable of accomplishing little more than attending coffee hours, shopping (under the influence of corporate advertising), and nursing junior (with the guidance of childcare expert Dr. Benjamin Spock). Even the term "Tupperware burp," used to describe the expelling of air from the Tupperware container after application of the lid, seems to extend a metaphor equating women's faculties solely with a predisposition for nurturing and domesticity.

Depictions of "Tupperware ladies," swapping recipes and dreamily fondling plastic refrigerator dishes, have substantiated the stereotype of 1950s women as domestic, quiescent victims of corporate capitalism. However, this study considers mass consumption and Tupperware (an arguably conservative aspect of feminine culture) as wholly valid aspects of women's history. For Tupperware, as product and party, thrived on the changing and frequently contradictory social and economic roles of women and consumption in the late twentieth century.

Much of the initial research for this book was based on the oral histories of women, in the United States and Great Britain, who were involved with Tupperware as hostesses lending their homes for parties or as dealers seeking a full or supplementary income. Like many historians (whose debates are outlined in Chapter 5) I initially associated the immediate postwar period in which the Tupperware party boomed with the oppressive homogenization of corporate culture and the rise of conservative domesticity. This form of sales, which so neatly exploited women's networks and resources in a period of limited opportunities, was undoubtedly a "form of organizational parasitism," as one feminist critic of the party plan writes, "analogous to that form of colonialism which extracted taxation by utilizing the existing tribal structure rather than developing its own grass roots system of administration and collection."[5] Despite the validity of this description, however, the women interviewed frequently spoke of their involvement with Tupperware not just as a means of circumventing the limitations of their domestic and economic situations but as a positive and self-determining experience. Of course, millions of women attended Tupperware parties as a matter of course and as little more than obligation to neighbors or friends. But on another level the Tupperware corporate culture offered an alternative to the patriarchal structures of conventional sales structures, which many women, completely alienated from the conventional workplace, wholeheartedly embraced. Despite the ingenuity of the airtight container, it was Tupperware's appeal to sociality and the valorization of women's domestic lives, in its objects, sales system, and corporate culture, that led to its success.

This book traces the Tupperware phenomenon from its initial design to its worldwide mass consumption. Technological progress, business acumen, and the "logic" of market economics did not ensure the success of this commodity. Rather it achieved its iconic status through a process of social and cultural mediation inseparable from broader histories of technology and business. In this context, Chapter 1 explores the designs and inventions of Earl Tupper, who in the midst of the American Depression was striving to become a commercially successful designer. It places the practice of design within the context of a broader domestic economy and illuminates the social and economic conditions that led to Tupper's understanding of aesthetics and modernity. Chapter 2 considers Tupperware as an icon of modernism, which, though popularly defined as such by the contemporary design press and establishment, bore little relation to women's motives for attending Tupperware parties or purchasing Tupperware designs. Chapter 3 considers the initial attempts to market Tupperware, its appeal to changing social customs and aspirations, and its significance as a gift and novelty, rather than a purely utilitarian commodity. Chapter 4 places the Tupperware party in a historical context of direct sales concerns such as Fuller Brush and Stanley Home Products. It emphasizes the shift, in a period of increasingly alienated commercial activity, toward direct sales as a form of exchange that maximized social interaction and the increasingly prominent role of women as consumers and salespeople. Chapter 5 considers the Tupperware party in the context of North American suburbanization and the growth of postwar mass consumption, and the party plan's relation to women's social and economically disenfranchised roles and prominence of an "ideology of domesticity." Chapter 6 charts the ascent of Brownie Wise as a highly successful 1950s businesswoman, her use of positive self-help philosophies that aided Tupperware's appeal to women precluded through ethnicity, class, and social status from mainstream economic and cultural activities. Chapter 7 describes the lavish gift-giving ceremonies and award schemes of THP that turned commodities into highly potent gifts and indirectly led to Wise's dismissal as vice president of THP in 1958. It considers consumption in its historical context, as a pro-active rather than passive pursuit as articulated through the activities and philosophies of Tupperware and Wise herself. Chapter 8 summarizes Tupper's sale of the Tupperware enterprise and its expansion to a global market from 1958 onward, and it also considers the enormous influence of the Tupperware party plan on successive direct sales ventures aimed at women.

# Introduction

Tupper's inventions were not the result of formal drawing-board exercises executed in a professional industrial design office, but of observations and understandings of domestic rural life in New England. He combined the vernacular of amateur mechanics with the popularized images of 1930s futurism. Much as Tupperware parties prospered through their grass roots appeal to localized meanings (a party in a Mormon home in Utah differed widely from a party in the affluent New Orleans garden district), Tupper's designs responded to the specifics of everyday problems and social relations. These observations, as the following chapter outlines, proved crucial to the creation of Tupperware as an icon of modern domesticity.

# "To Be a Better Social Friend"
## Designing for a Moral Economy

The streamlined form of the classic Tupperware Wonder Bowl
brings to mind the modernist maxim (suggestive of machine-born
simplicity and rationalism), "Form Follows Function." Yet despite
Tupperware's streamlined aesthetic and its emergence in a period associated with the rise of the American industrial design profession, in fact the
object could not be further removed from the culture of corporate design. Household goods and office machinery of the 1930s and 1940s un-
derwent major restyling by "design heroes" such as Raymond Loewy,
who in 1949 was featured on the cover of *Time* magazine and lauded for
his part in reversing the downward trend of Depression consumer sales by
increasing demand through design.[1] Tupperware belonged to an alternative
form of entrepreneurial and design endeavor rooted more firmly in a nineteenth-century context of engineering and invention, and in the early-
twentieth-century role of the "jobber" and merchandiser, than the 1930s
fashion for corporately sponsored industrial design.[2]

Earl Silas Tupper, born in Berlin, New Hampshire, in 1907, struggled
throughout the Depression years, along with his wife, Marie, to secure an
adequate standard of living for his family. His designs were based on an
acute understanding of everyday domesticity and moral economy.[3] They
originated from the ideals of social reform and utopianism (which in Tupper's vision melded progressive aspects of technocracy with the conservatism of the 1930s colonial revival) rather than the highbrow aesthetics of

formal modernism or the ardent commercialism of professional industrial design.[4] Writing in his invention notebooks in the late 1930s, Tupper observed the importance of progressive invention: "To invent useful and successful inventions, those with inventive minds should take up individual advanced work and study along some worthwhile line. One should not be afraid to look far, far into the future and visualize the things that might be. . . . Remember, the things which are so commonplace today would have been the ravings of a fanatic a few years ago."[5] His design antics were clearly fired by entrepreneurial zeal, but as personal documents reveal, this was by no means the sole motivation of his frequently obsessive and frenetic contrivances. Tupper viewed design and invention as a contemporary practice with a transformative power to enhance the lives of "the masses." As historian of technology Joseph Corn suggests, some inventors have "resembled less the rational and purposeful economic man of scholarly theory than what we might call the visionary man, a kind of dreamer who imagines that his mechanical contrivances could solve social problems."[6] This description of the visionary inventor perfectly encapsulates the figure of Earl Tupper, who from his New Hampshire small farm combined the physically arduous labor of his struggling tree surgery business with his endeavor to transform society through the creation of new product designs. Fastidiously documenting his activities, Tupper worked from home using borrowed and salvaged materials to develop prototypes for household gadgets and fancy goods. This self-taught, informal design process came to fruition when, in 1937, he found casual employment as a sample maker working under license with the Du Pont chemical supply company for the Doyle Works in Leominster, Massachusetts. In 1939, after two years' immersion in the techniques and processes of plastic manufacture, Tupper established his own concern, the Tupper Plastics Company.

The biographical profile of Earl Tupper as a dependable Yankee inventor proved crucial to the company's promotional campaigns for "Poly-T: Material of the Future" from which Tupperware, the innovative polyethylene container, was derived in the early 1940s. "The whole philosophy of the man and his institution," read a 1949 advertisement, is embodied in the Tupperware product. "Not a product hastily conceived, hastily produced and recklessly recommended," the copy continued, but a design born of intensive research and the highest quality manufacturing.[7] Despite the mythologizing bent of the company's advertising copy, Earl Tupper's role in the creation of Tupperware could hardly be exaggerated. Although by the 1950s the corporate use of biography (exemplified, for

Earl Silas Tupper, designer, inventor, and custom molder, demonstrating the unique features of his polyethylene, injection-molded invention, the Bell Tumbler, fashioned from "Poly-T: Material of the Future," ca. 1942. Author's personal collection.

example, by the fictitious image of the ideal homemaker Betty Crocker of packaged cake mix fame) had become a familiar commercial device, from its inception as a revolutionary household item Tupperware was genuinely conceived, overseen, and promoted by its original inventor.[8] Protection of the reputation and provenance of the product, an embodiment of Tupper's ideals of Protestant conservatism, social reform, and technological progress, became paramount; his refrigerator dishes were, he believed, destined to change the lives of American citizens and help dispel the discontentment of a wasteful consumer society. While his competitors might happily apply their plastic technology to the production of cheap and garish knick-knacks and dog dishes in the pursuit of a quick buck, Tupper envisioned a world utterly transformed through the appropriate application of polyethylene.

Tupper's desire to be "a better social friend" through "relentless drive" in invention and design encapsulated the intrinsic sense of modernity invested in his products.[9] The story, then, of Tupperware's popularity is not simply one of technological ingenuity and marketing success, but rather an example of the historical specificity of material culture and the mediation of related social relations and cultural beliefs. Profane as a dog dish, sublime as a sandwich box, Tupperware's indispensability, as the following chapter explores, derived as much from a moral, as a market, economy.

From the onset, Tupper's self-proclaimed mission was to act as a twentieth-century "super-coordinator" inhabiting an "observatory and workshop high above this world," from which he could "observe general trends i.e. form, streamlining, jazz, health, food, exercise, sunlight, then invent, not too radically to be accepted by a conservative audience, the next logical step in each trend."[10] Throughout the 1930s he maintained diaries, sketchbooks, and invention notebooks to record, in minute detail, the conception and development of each of his ideas. Most notably his formal studies of design remained inseparable from his day-to-day labor, domestic life, and relationships. Pages titled "Thoughts and Plans . . . Conversations and Letters" sought to document and protect his progress as an illustrious inventor and "super-coordinator." Under headings dedicated to specific didactic pursuits, such as "How to Invent," "How to Realize An Invention," "Observe This Procedure to Establish Date of Conception," and "On Protecting an Invention," Tupper devised methods to optimize his chances of success and to ensure copyright and patent security.

Self-conscious analysis of his goals and direction, encapsulated by journal entries titled "The Purpose of My Life," reveal a persistent striving toward self-betterment. Though it exhibits the technical rigor of a professional engineer or inventor's notation, the journal is also indicative of the diaries of New England Puritan testament.[11] Tupper's diaries, notebooks, and journals were not restricted to the musings of the inner self; rather they were intended as public statements of intent. Despite the frequently personal and self-revelatory nature of Tupper's writings, it is significant to note that in his absence his wife Marie completed journal entries as a matter of course, inserting her own detailed observations of the day's proceedings. The journal thus belonged, in a sense, to the household rather than to Tupper as an individual and charted an imaginary trajectory toward "success" and social mobility as a modern form of spiritual atonement.

As a young man Tupper worked in the small commercial nurseries belonging to his parents in Shirley, Massachusetts. He consistently encouraged his parents to expand their business but was constantly disappointed by their disinclination toward entrepreneurial activity. Frustrated by his own hand-to-mouth existence, he began to immerse himself in a relentless campaign to improve his situation. "One must keep on trying," he steadfastly pledged, "until recognized and until attainment of success."[12]

Self-discipline and self-determination, which he considered natural elements of his New England Protestant upbringing, manifested themselves
at an early age. In 1923, at the age of sixteen, Tupper committed himself
to a strict dietary and exercise regime in an attempt to imitate the posture
and anatomy he so admired in the pages of the popular magazine *Physical
Culture*. Using photographs and short biographical descriptions, the publication featured semiclad male and full-dressed female "specimens"
chosen for their "physical perfection" and "harmonious symmetry." Awestruck by the physical prowess of one particular male "specimen," Tupper
went to the lengths of contacting the journal to ascertain more biographical information, so that he could strive for a comparable standard of self-
discipline and physical control.[13] Throughout the 1930s Tupper continued to record details of his height, weight, exercise regime, and diet as he
charted his progress toward the balance of his inner moral state and physical well-being. In March 1933, left with little more than "two nickels to
rub together" and tormented by his parents' reluctance to "fufil their
promises" and lend some "readies" for one of his utopian ventures, Tupper
consoled himself with the pursuit of bodybuilding and intensive reading.[14]

Tupper's potent mixture of Protestant work ethic, positive thinking,
and utopianism was indicative of a rhetoric of the American dream that
adapted to the historically specific transition from the prosperity of the
1920s to the devastation of the 1930s. In the face of social injustice and
economic decline Tupper believed in self-determination and the democratic role of capitalism: "Destiny thru the subconscious mind," he wrote
in the midst of the mass unemployment of the Great Depression, "finds a
successful future for every open minded thinking individual who earnestly
gropes for his destined work."[15]

## "Cosmopolitan Utopian"
### Commerce, Culture, and Social Democracy

Earl Tupper's belief in the power of amateur entrepreneurialism, tacit
business acumen, and self-education proved vital to his own design ideology and, ultimately, to the immense success of his marketing ventures.
This began in 1932, when as part of an ambitious self-improvement program, Tupper signed up for a correspondence course in business and advertising.[16] Recently married and father of a baby son, he desperately
sought to better his financial and living situation with all the vigor of a

moral crusade. This endeavor epitomized contemporary rags-to-riches narratives of entrepreneurial success that, given the harsh social and economic realities of the Depression, shifted from an emphasis on strength of character to a stress on the power of personality and self-help.[17] "Let the job seeker sell himself like he would a machine—as something which can produce desirable things which the other 'machines' cannot," wrote Tupper in his first correspondence course exercise. The "machine," he suggested, should be constantly maintained, developed, and engineered to perfection by its "operator," geared up to effectively take on any new and profitable task.[18]

The use of such a metaphor—a well-oiled machine primed to produce desirable articles aimed at a competitive mass market—encapsulates the 1930s ethos of mass production. Tupper, a self-consciously constructed "man of his times," firmly believed in the social and economic benefits of a mass productive economy. Determined to pursue a livelihood beyond his rural existence, he embarked on a course that might open up the world of advertising and manufacturing to him, culminating in work as an agent or marketer.

Advertising, promoted by the industry as the elixir for Depression ills, held a new currency in the popular imagination. Throughout the 1920s and 1930s publications with exemplary titles such as *A Theory of Consumption* (1923), *The Mind of the Buyer: A Psychology of Selling* (1921), and *Consumer Engineering* (1932) typified the contemporary pseudoscientific confluence of economic theory and popular psychology.[19] Many of these works, indicative of the direction of a new science-led advertising, were littered with references to "conspicuous consumption," "intelligent buying," and "emulation theory." Others even borrowed anthropological structures and cross-cultural analogies to explain how "the meaningless vestiges of former customs" could hinder the modern consumer's pursuit of utility.[20]

Just as mass production presented a solution to the growing social and economic ills, so too did mass consumption. A prominent commentator, pioneer of the department store chain, and author of *Successful Living in This Machine Age* (1932), Edward Filene advocated abandoning class hierarchies and liberating the masses through increased wages, lower prices, a shortened workday, and the plentiful availability of goods. The increasingly professionalized advertising industry, equipped with a range of new-fangled psychological theories, facilitated the relationship between mass production and mass consumption: "Depression times demanded a new breed of engineer: the 'consumption engineer'. The new consumption engineer would complement the production engineer through aggressive marketing activities, especially advertising. He would manufacture customers."[21]

Despite the professionalization of the industry, Tupper's chosen correspondence course promised its students the opportunity to circumvent expensive and overly theoretical education by encouraging applicants to consider "back-door" entry into the advertising world. By focusing their initial advertising attempts on local merchants and manufacturers, prospective students might accrue invaluable experience; and "though work may not always be had for the mere asking," the introductory course literature reassured, "the missionary efforts put forth in showing people proof of ability . . . [is] more impressive with future employers than mere claims."[22] Fashionable consumer psychology and economic theory were overlooked in favor of lengthy, detailed accounts regarding the integration of advertising into established workings of everyday commerce. A particularly fecund area for development, the course literature remarked, was the mail-order business, which used a network of agents receiving "attractive premiums." "A great variety of such commodities as fancy goods, poultry seeds, live stock, rustic furniture, hardware specialties, books, curios, dyes, jewelry," they advised, were "sold to customers by mail-order methods." This method of advertising and merchandising, though potentially profitable, had its drawbacks. "It is important to select a good specialty, to be patient, and to experiment carefully in order to find the most effective and economical way of selling," the course tutors warned.[23] This grass roots approach to advertising and marketing defied the rationalization and theorization of an increasingly formalized industry.

Although Tupper was a keen follower of modern literature and contemporary ideas, the no-nonsense localized approach to promotion and marketing advocated by the correspondence course appealed to his sense of pragmatism far more than the newfangled ideas of consumer psychology. Indeed the rather crude advice of the correspondence course, which predated the introduction of Tupperware products through mail-order catalogs and premium incentive schemes by more than a decade, later defined the direct sales initiatives used by Tupper in the 1940s as the first attempt at distributing Tupperware through the party plan selling scheme. The party plan scheme, which came to define the Tupperware phenomenon, also relied on a workforce made up of individuals operating with little formal business training or advertising qualifications.

In a more general context, as a rapidly expanding professionalized force in modern America during the 1920s and 1930s, advertising shifted from an emphasis on the properties of the product to emphasis on the consumer's needs and anxieties. As historian Roland Marchand argues, this led to a range of newly articulated and sophisticated advertising styles: "In their efforts to win over consumers by inducing them to live through experiences in which the product (or its absence) played a part, advertisers offered detailed vignettes of social life."[24]

The "detailed vignette," which later became a pivotal device in marketing strategies aimed at securing the cultural assimilation of Tupperware in 1940s America, formed the basis of Tupper's earliest attempts at copywriting. In a hypothetical advertisement to promote advertising courses offered by correspondence schools, Tupper constructed a moral story featuring two classmates, Bill and Paul. By inverting contemporary middle-class wisdom regarding the primacy of formal education and the appropriate pathways to success, Tupper's vignette glorified the aptitudes of the layperson and celebrated the value of everyday know-how. In this scenario, Bill, the less-privileged, lower-middle-class underdog, succeeds through enthusiasm and the development of social skills. Paul, financially dependent on his wealthy parents, graduates from "artificial college life" with debts of $30,000 and finds himself unprepared to earn a living. Bill entrenches himself in a steady, going concern that fosters his "practical everyday sense" and supplements his tacit knowledge with an education gained through a correspondence school. The development of Paul's personality and character is restricted, rather than furthered, by four years of college instruction (his mind full, according to Tupper's copy, of "obsolete bookisms"). Consequently he graduates to a life of unemployment and bewilderment at "how ridiculous his position is." In contrast, Bill is a successful correspondence school graduate, socially skilled and versed in the realities of commerce, and becomes a happy, accomplished, well-balanced, and productive citizen. He marries the boss's daughter and buys a little roadster, which, on returning from the wedding trip with his "starry eyed bride," he parks by his little brown bungalow. Considering Bill's self-made success, "Would you want to be Paul?" concludes Tupper's practice copy.[25] As a self-educated man, who spent evenings reading literature ranging from Balzac, Conrad, and Dumas to *Reader's Digest* and *Popular Mechanics,* Tupper showed a contempt for the cosseted "college pampered person," admiring instead the self-made pioneer of American cultural mythology.[26]

Commerce, culture, sociality, and self-determination could, according to Tupper, create a perfect and harmonious future. His visions of an advertising utopia revolved around an ideologically conservative notion of communal prosperity that would be enabled, quite literally, through capitalist democracy and highly efficient marketing campaigns. Retailers, for example, could eradicate "stiff formality" by keeping records of their customer's birthdays, anniversaries, and special events and presenting gifts according to "the percent of profit made on goods sold them during the year."[27] Crass materialism and wanton consumption (exemplified by Tupper's vitriolic tirades against lottery-playing, barhopping men and cigarette-smoking women) were juxtaposed with a utopian vision of America's future, in which commerce and social relations blossomed. A world driven by the engine of advertising and enhanced by the social democracy of consumption would fund mass education and advance the project of modernity. Hankering after sentimental renditions of the preindustrial past held no appeal for Tupper: "No matter how poets and song writers play up the pagan existence and medieval civilizations," he wrote in 1932, "I'll still take modern civilization (so called) and ultra modern civilization—the more advanced the better, I'm for it."[28]

In his hypothetical plans for a theme park, Cosmopolita World, Tupper outlined a corporate utopia suggestive of the visions espoused by advocates of technocracy, such as Howard Scott and Harold Loeb, who upheld science and technology as the determining forces of future societies, their values, arts, and cultures.[29] Featuring "a daily pageant review of the world from extreme primitive [*sic*] to ultra modern," Cosmopolita World was devised by Tupper as the showcase for a publication concept, a newspaper called *Cosmopolitan Utopian*. The paper acted as both a commercially oriented, profit-driven publication and a communal space for discussion and debate, with weekly prizes awarded to winners of a competition for "200 word summaries of what the week's advertisements have done for the writer."[30] Subscription to the weekly newspaper was set at five cents, less than the actual cost of producing one copy. "But," wrote Tupper, "the concerns who advertise in this magazine pay us enough to make up the difference." The newspaper, he continued, would be used "to educate the folks in things that are ordinarily neglected in preparing people to better meet the things of everyday life"; advertisers could enhance the lives of consumers by informing them of forthcoming innovations, such as stores featuring the only "doors in the world that open and close as customers approach or leave" and "the most sanitary restrooms," operated by foot.

In this modern utopia, everything—social reform to sanitary restrooms, pageantry to material abundance—came together through the interrelation of technological progress and corporate control. Tupper's fantasy echoed the technocratic movement's utopian drive for efficiency and the notion of democracy secured through science-led politics, culture, and commerce.[31]

Advertising, then, would sponsor this temple of modernity, the font of all knowledge, fully accessible to the average American citizen; through advertising, Tupper dreamed, minds would be broadened and goods would be sold. Visitors to the educational and friendly Cosmopolita World would benefit from a central Information Bureau, which offered complete access to and advice on how to acquire knowledge. "Whatever happens in the wide world," read Tupper's slogan, "you'll get details or see it first at Cosmopolita World. If we can't have the actual thing then we will have a duplicate, or the best pictures and most complete and reliable information."[32]

The notion of a corporate utopia, in which technology and corporate structure enable democracy and a stabilized economy, had been outlined by the famous inventor-businessman King C. Gillette in his book *The People's Corporation* (1924). Gillette's background was strikingly similar to Tupper's; raised in a small Wisconsin town in the late nineteenth century, he combined invention—devising the first disposable safety razor—with business acumen in pursuit of utopian ideals. He envisioned a world in which "inventors, scientists, businessmen, companies, states and nations" formed "one coherent and unified human organization."[33] Although, like Gillette, Tupper admired the "ultra-modern" he was also drawn to the sentimentalized vision of America's colonial past outlined by manufacturer and social commentator Henry Ford in *My Life, My Work* (1922). As the instigator of the factory assembly line, Ford combined his belief in scientifically managed production with a nostalgic vision of pastoral life. In 1924, as an experiment in social reform, Ford installed a dam at his farm in Dearborn to create a hydroelectric plant. In contrast to his massive factories in Highland Park and River Rouge, Ford created idyllic workers' communities in the form of small villages consisting of ten or eleven houses clustered around the plant. More an exercise in aesthetics than philanthropy, Ford's vision was part of a broader contemporary conflict between modernity and tradition. This conflict underpinned Tupper's visions and informed everything from his discourse on "wasteful" consumption to his romanticized descriptions of "motherly old fashioned" ladies working serenely at their spinning wheels.[34]

Despite his grandiose capitalist and corporate aspirations Tupper expressed a genuine interest in social change. In 1933 he commented, for example, on the ingenuity of the communist paper *Daily Worker*. Though he considered the communists' "efforts toward their goal futile," he added, thoughtfully, "There must be a tremendous reform in many ways before we can truthfully call this era one of civilization."[35] The ideas espoused by the *Daily Worker* led Tupper to ponder the conscience-raising dimensions of lengthened economic hardship, concluding that another five years of the Depression might actually "awaken the mass to activity" for the benefit of world civilization.[36]

Throughout his writings Tupper meditated on striving toward social justice and minimizing suffering in general, proudly presenting to the Humane Society, in 1937, an invention for a cruelty-free animal trap. In accordance with the grander schemes of modernism he placed an inordinate amount of faith in the advancement of modern science, empirical research, and the eradication of human misery. But his model of humanitarian commitment cast free enterprise and capitalist profit making as the "natural" outcome of social evolution.

In May 1937 an emergency appendectomy left Tupper confined to a hospital bed. "So much contact with bodily ills," he commented excitedly, "has left me thinking about bodily inventions."[37] Within days of his painful operation Tupper had devised several medical contraptions including a "dummy patient with rubber intestines, colon, and appendix" with which he could demonstrate his revolutionary instrument for nonsurgical "appendix removal thru [the] anal opening" to the medical profession.[38] Further scientific medical and surgical research, he envisioned, would be sponsored through the receipt of a 5 percent royalty on each appendix removed. Less ambitious but highly perceptive and even prophetic medical observations were inspired by Tupper's contempt for the inadequate health and safety measures in the industrial workplace. Witnessing the amputation of a fellow worker's finger by a "half trained punk of a doctor," Tupper became convinced that modern surgery had the potential to repair rather than destroy partly severed limbs.

Tupper's musings over politics and social democracy proved inherently contradictory. In the same year that he devised his trap for the Humane

Society and complained of industrial health and safety conditions, he sketched designs for the "Tupper Bomb," which exploded and discharged $CO_2$ gas on impact. This might prove particularly useful, he noted, for industrial leaders in dispersing disgruntled striking workers.[39] For despite a passing admiration of President Franklin Roosevelt, observing that the nation would benefit "socially and materially" from his intelligence, Tupper's utopian ideals were perhaps more attuned to Frank Capra's populist vision of Shangri-la (depicted in the film *Lost Horizon,* which he viewed in 1937) than the political realities of the New Deal.[40]

## "To Be a Better Social Friend"
### Invention as an Ethical Pursuit

In 1933, although Tupper had failed to gain permanent employment in the advertising industry, he resolved "to develop [himself] mentally, physically and spiritually, and thus make worthwhile contacts."[41] His correspondence course studies proved invaluable in solidifying his entrepreneurial endeavors as an inventor and designer. In the following three years Tupper labored as a tree surgeon and the tenant of a small farm and tended his parents' commercial greenhouses. His evenings were spent pursuing issues of invention, including the study of business theory, copyright law, popular technology, and classic literature.[42] Despite the restriction of a limited and irregular income Tupper subscribed to a wide range of publications, including *American Home, Printer's Ink, Red Book, Reader's Digest,* and *Literary Guild* to familiarize himself with current affairs, consumer trends, and modern lore.[43]

Tupper's visionary insights, utopian ideals, and commercial fantasies were sharply juxtaposed with his life as a rural homestead dweller and manual worker. Surrounded by an extended family and operating within a complex system of informal economy, the Tupper household relied on ostensibly traditional values: thrift, reciprocity, respect for elders and "social betters" and the honoring of established customs. Bartering labor for loans, exchanging goats for land, procuring paid work though social affiliation, swapping seasonal canned vegetables, and accessing equipment and transport through reciprocal arrangement were transactions that formed the fabric of everyday life and the basis of the fight against economic hardship. Gifts and exchanges of labor and homemade goods linked households in this New England community in a way that was simultaneously enabling and constraining. For the Thanksgiving of 1934, for example, Tupper killed several of his own turkeys and constructed oak boxes for their presentation as gifts to local businessmen, such as a Mr. Sheedy who frequently advised Tupper on ways and means of pursuing his design ideas and obtaining loans.[44] Similarly employment with the Doyle Works in Leominster in 1937 was the direct result of his brother's earlier involvement with another local manufacturing concern, the Viscoloid plastic factory (a highly innovative plant owned by Du Pont), and the recommendations of local contractors. Word-of-mouth endorsement won Tupper contracts for his early tree-surgery business, but as he only sporadically owned an automobile, much to his chagrin, he relied on the generosity and reliability of friends and relatives to transport him to and from his work. It was this lack of independence and his constant frustration with individuals less motivated than himself to better their situation that fired Tupper's ambition. But this integral and formative understanding of domestic economy, social relations, and moral obligation formed the basis of the revolutionary polyethylene Tupperware designs marketed to the rural homesteader of the 1940s as thrifty containers ideal for bulk storage and the preservation of homemade goods. Tupper's earliest mailorder catalogs focused on the household and its customs and "decorum" as the bedrock of civil living. And the potential of Tupperware items as gifts as well as domestic aids guided the promotion and design process from their inception to their present-day consumption at Tupperware parties.

Self-sustaining rural lifestyles and the concept of decentralization had gained credence during the Great Depression as an expression of the idealized "simple life." Social critic Ralph Borsodi's *This Ugly Civilization: A Study for the Quest of Comfort* (1929) epitomized a contemporary romanticization of rural dwelling and a condemnation of urbanization and massscale mechanization. By the late 1930s, the "agrarian dream," a familiar tenet of American culture, manifested itself in the publication of the *Free America* journal and the creation of the "school for living," which taught subsistence living and the value of domestic economy as the elixir for the ills of American civilization.[45] Although figures such as Borsodi echoed the turn-of-the-century critique of the excesses of Victorian vulgarity and a contempt for industrialization (embodied in the aesthetics of the American Arts and Crafts movement), his original aim was to meld the quality of rural life with the virtues of modern labor-saving appliances. To quote historian David Shi in *The Simple Life: Plain Living and High Thinking in American Culture,* Borsodi's principal idea was to "'domesticate' the machine and mechanize the homestead, to synthesize the pastoral urge and the technological fact in a literal sense. If bringing the machine into the garden could enable the 'quality-minded' to enjoy greater economic independence, satisfying and varied work, and a life of beauty, then doing so posed no necessary threat to one's dignity or freedom."[46]

Similarly, Tupper's admiration for the simplicity of rural living did not preclude technological advance or a passion for the paraphernalia of modern consumer culture.[47] Despite his precarious financial situation, which culminated in the bankruptcy of his landscaping and tree-surgery business in 1936, the family made numerous visits to nearby towns to window-shop and fantasize about potential household furnishings. The longing for security and comfort was punctuated by a series of comparatively extravagant purchases from local department stores and the Sears and Roebuck catalog. During a twelve-month period spanning September 1933 to October 1934, the Tupper household purchases included a new, noiseless portable typewriter at $70, a fountain pen and pencil set ("its the latest thing out, a $4.25 article"), a radio at $12.98, a briefcase and gloves, a dictionary, an imitation sharkskin Gladstone suitcase, a made-to-measure suit, a Ford Touring Car (later part-exchanged for a Ford V8 black sedan with red wheels for $552), a gun, and the family's first telephone.

Though the price of peanut butter had risen, Tupper complained, because of inflation "from seven and a half to fifteen cents," his larger purchases, accoutrements of modern living, were major investments in the procurement of a better future rather than an indulgent escape from a miserable present.[48] With the exception of the occasional fantasy, including a journal entry describing efforts to summon forth a 1933 Ford Cabriolet "using telepathy and auto-suggestion," consumption during this period focused almost exclusively on Tupper himself. As the household's formal breadwinner he required the socially appropriate accessories to enable him to seek business as a modern "industrial inventor and designer."

Popular literature of this period questioned the wholesale materialism of the American dream in preference to a newly spiritualized version of self-actualization. Despite his own less-than-frugal consumer habits, Tupper denounced the practices of individuals who chose "to dissipate their energies" via inappropriate pursuits of popular culture and mass consumption. These individuals were merely paving the way "for their own ruination" by wasting the "opportunity to search themselves, find themselves, express their own creativity and contribute priceless gems to civilization," he protested.[49] Unlike the all-consuming masses, Tupper justified his pursuits and indulgences for articles of modern design (noiseless typewriters, sharkskin Gladstone cases, "the latest thing" fountain pens) within the broader moral economy of the Tupper household. There were, however, moments of perceived moral weakness, in which Tupper's loathing of excess turned inward and led him to condemn his own consumptive desires. On Christmas Day 1934, after a lavish dinner and a surfeit of chocolates, Tupper (even at this socially sanctioned time of excess) sought redemption for what he perceived as his family's cultural decline: "Marie and I have resolved to feed our eyes, minds and souls by going places, doing and seeing things, rather than eating . . . on future holidays."[50] The extravagance of gift giving, he added, should in future be confined only to those young enough to believe in Santa Claus.

Mental fortitude, rather than the Protestant ethic of unadulterated hard work, came to the forefront as an antidote to disillusion in an era that, according to many American historians, harbored no hint of radical ideology. In this context, the rise of positive thinking epitomized by Dale Carnegie's *How to Win Friends and Influence People* (1936) and Frank Welsh and Frances Gordon's *Thinking Success into Business* (1932) defied the "realities" of social inequity by refocusing attention on the inner life of the individual and the capacity, against the odds, to succeed. Certainly Tupper's relentless self-motivation embraced the doctrine of positive thinking, born of a desire to counter the negativity and apathy of the Depression: "Boy!" he exclaimed in one diary entry, "I feel more stranded than Robinson Cruso [*sic*] ever could have felt—being broke in a world depressed with pessimists, *is being broke!*"

Foreign cultures and their value systems were explored in widely read volumes such as *The Importance of Living* (1937) by Lin Yutang, which considered the spirituality taught by Eastern mysticism. *Lost Horizon,* the story of an idyllic land of eternal youth and harmony, written in 1933 by James Hilton, was made into a highly successful epic film directed by Frank Capra in 1937, which Tupper made a gleeful diary note of seeing at his local cinema on September 4 that year. Shangri-la, the utopian civilization central to the narrative, featured architecture combining the simplicity of the International Style and the poetic lavishness of Xanadu's pleasure dome. Like Tupper's ideals of democratic consumption and well-mannered living, Shangri-la, nestled among the Himalayas, espoused a religion of moderation and courtesy. Rather than pursuing wanton material accumulation, at the expense of abandoning knowledge and culture, Shangri-la boasted a self-sustaining economy based on fair exchange as opposed to the exploitative processes of buying and selling. Though a naturally abundant gold supply optimized the occasional transactions with the outside world, candle makers, blacksmiths, weavers, and potters joyfully pursued their crafts in an idyllic and productive environment that promised a secure future; peace, security, harmony, and beauty eradicated the drive toward greed and materialism. Although Shangri-la depicted a basically noncapitalist utopia, like Tupper's Cosmopolita World (which embraced modernity, commerce, and technology) it shared a vision of a productive and cultured civilization, enabled by a sustainable economy and the production of appropriate material culture.

By 1939 the spectacle of the New York World's Fair depicting "The World of Tomorrow," which Marie and Earl Tupper avidly visited, portrayed a tangible version of a design utopia that, like Shangri-la, seemed to beckon forth a golden age. Using streamlined futuristic designs informed by the literary utopias of the late nineteenth and early twentieth century, the organizers aimed to show "how the United States could maintain democracy in the face of growing threats of communism and fascism, redress the alienation between individual and the community, and provide plenty for all."[51] Although Tupper's visit must have included at least one of the top designer's exhibits (the fair was a showcase for new professional industrial designers such as Henry Dreyfuss, Norman Bel Geddes, and Walter Dorwin Teague), his diary entry makes no mention of particular exhibits or designers. For despite his enthusiasm for the fair (he made a return visit a little more than a week later), Tupper found himself keener to "do business on his [plastic coat] hangers," showing them to potential retailers during his stay in New York City, than to muse on the delights of the spectacular streamlined showcase.[52]

## Design for Living
### The Ingenuity of the "Amateur" Inventor

Earl Tupper's designs and inventions stemmed from a relentless pragmatism and an unyielding idealism rather than from formal aesthetic training. "I wish I were doing inventing, in which my heart is, rather than tree work which I do not care deeply for," he lamented in 1933.[53] In his quest for economic security in a time of scarcity and social upheaval, he invested in the contemporary material culture his visions of individual self-actualization and social optimism. Although he viewed his relative poverty and laboring work as a hindrance to his true vocation, his persistent (at times obsessive) drive to transform and improve the daily chores of rural and domestic life formed the basis of his inspiration. His earliest designs centered on the problems and activities associated with his agricultural labor. The "Knee-Action" Agricultural Harrow and the "Gypsy Gun" (a creosote spray pump for the eradication of gypsy moth eggs from trees) arose from a dictum, gleaned from *Popular Mechanics,* that warned would-be inventors to "focus . . . effort on the problem and not entirely on the device."[54]

From its initial publication in 1902 as a trade journal (aimed at mechanics and skilled shopworkers), *Popular Mechanics* shifted emphasis to the homeowner and the handyman and by 1910 boasted a quarter million circulation. Throughout the next three decades the publication expanded its popular appeal (by 1950 it had become a mass-circulation magazine) by addressing, with an easy-to-read style and diagrams illustrating technical information, a readership of do-it-yourself enthusiasts, hobbyists, and amateur designers. With the growth of technical hobbies and the rise of consumer-related magazines in the 1930s, *Popular Mechanics* "instructed readers how to construct built-in furniture for the dining room, repair cracked china, wire a door bell or garage door opener, and carry out any of the thousand other maintenance and improvement projects necessitated or suggested by the modern technology-filled home."[55] Novices were guided in easy-to-follow steps how to construct household items, such as wastepaper baskets, from scrap materials or turn their hand to the creation of wooden toys as Christmas presents for the children.

During the 1930s, an era of sporadic employment for many men, "the hobby" provided an acceptable form of domestic activity, which, with its emphasis on skill and technique, did not undermine accepted gender roles.[56] As a leisure pursuit that fostered skill and invention, the hobby had the potential of being applied outside the domestic sphere in the pursuit of formal work or as a sideline to accrue extra income (making bird feeders for neighbors or mending bicycles, for example).[57] "How-to" texts, which proliferated in the 1920s, had similarly acknowledged the rise of the novice as the flip side of the new emphasis on expertise. However, as one historian of technology notes, as "the line between novice and expert, amateur and professional, became more defined, a growing number of novices sought to acquire the specialized information that would enable them to cross it."[58] Certainly Earl Tupper's scrutiny of journals ranging from *Popular Mechanics* to *Printer's Ink,* his completion of an advertising correspondence course, and his familiarity with copyright law and patent procedure (gleaned from research trips to local libraries) show his self-conscious attempts to move from amateur hobbyist to professional designer.

Tupper made concerted efforts to pursue the commercial viability of many of his homemade goods. In 1937, he made a streamlined sled for his son Ronnie, the prototype for which he took promptly to a novelty shop in nearby Leominster, where the proprietor Mr. Green agreed to display the design at a forthcoming toy show. This particular design, based on his experience as an active parent, later won the approval of Sears and Roebuck as a mass-produced article. However, in the early years of Tupper's inventions his tireless perseverance rarely proved so fruitful.[59]

His astute observations and drive toward the popularization of technological innovation, the crux of his design procedure, often failed to take account of broader manufacturing changes and shifts in consumer taste. In June 1933, his invention of a rumble seat top — a cover for the open seat situated to the rear of early automobiles — was inspired by Tupper's perception of increased demand for streamlined silhouettes in modern cars. He experimented with the device at home on his own Ford roadster and, using a prototype made by Marie, sought the advice of prominent local business people to ascertain its potential as a patented item. Despite numerous ambitious but futile attempts to contact Henry Ford (whom he simultaneously admired but feared might steal his ideas), Tupper persisted in his informal marketing research inquiries. Unfortunately, however, the National Automobile Chamber of Commerce indicated that although a small segment of the market desired open cars, "the stream line car of the future will be a closed car," thus undermining drastically the usefulness of the rumble seat top.[60] After lengthy home experiments and prototype testing, Tupper's seemingly promising invention was overtaken by technological and stylistic change as rumble seats began to be phased out of automobile production.

Despite the numerous setbacks and rejections by local manufacturers and businesses of his design and marketing ideas, Tupper persevered. Ambitious and desperate, he compared himself directly to the archetypal Renaissance man Leonardo da Vinci. "I too am strapped for money, and have notebooks full of sketches and a house full of models and inventions," he lamented dramatically in 1933.[61]

Throughout this intensive period of experimentation in the 1930s, family and domestic life featured prominently as the underpinnings of

Tupper's greater mission "to be a better social friend." In popular literature of this period, "family life," writes historian Charles R. Hearn, "took on more importance because it was viewed as one specific value which might compensate for the growing disillusionment with the pursuit of economic success."[62] Certainly much of Tupper's personal writings were records of commonplace details of family life, from the delights of the children's first teeth and growing vocabularies to the mundane minutiae of household maintenance. Although Tupper fastidiously recorded the arduousness of his given tasks, noting the amount of time spent laboring each day, or the lengthy distance walked to reach the destination of each tree surgery job, and even the number of pages read in a book completed, it is only in his absence, when Marie completed the diary entries, that the full extent and relevance of her labor is made visible. A typical entry reveals her day beginning at 4:00 A.M., when she traveled to work at her parents-in-law's greenhouses, returning home at 8:00 A.M. to begin washing clothes and finally completing her child care and chores by midnight.[63] Marie tried to supplement the family's income by making hand-painted gift cards to sell in local gift shops, and she constantly supported Tupper (practically and inspirationally) in his applications as an inventor.[64] The intricacies of domestic economy, family life, and consumer culture bolstered Tupper's inventions and design processes, which he eventually applied in a formal context during his appointment as a sample maker in a plastics factory, an appointment that led to his involvement with custom molding and ultimately to the "discovery" of Tupperware.

## The Du Pont Alliance
### Tupper's First Experiments with Plastic

In 1937, Earl Tupper transferred his skills as an amateur inventor to the design department of a small Massachusetts manufacturing company known as the Doyle Works in Leominster. He knew of the Doyle Works through a contact who had lent workshop space to him in the past, and after familiarizing himself with the factory managed to secure a casual position as a sample maker working on behalf of the Du Pont chemical supply company. In a burgeoning plastics industry, sample makers were responsible for researching and prototyping potential products, mainly through trial and error. Using relatively unknown materials they experimented with product forms and manufacturing techniques and, in Tupper's case, relayed this information directly back to the chemical supply company. It was in the interests of manufacturers and plastic chemical companies alike to pursue product development and expand the use of plastic in the consumer market, and the tacit knowledge of enthusiastic sample makers proved invaluable in this process.

The plastics industry of the 1930s did not rely on a simple equation of supply and demand. Rather, as cultural historian Jeffrey Meikle emphasizes, "The development of new plastics occurred within a complex world of international corporate rivalries, parallel processes, cross-licensing (sometimes among three or four firms), informal exchanges of information among the industrial chemical fraternity, and agreements that traded rights to one plastic for those to another."[65] The Du Pont chemical company stood at the forefront of plastic innovation during this period, investing capital and human resources (from chemical engineers to public relations managers) in intensive research and experimentation. Whereas in the nineteenth century plastic offered itself as the perfect material of imitation and substitution, by the twentieth century the notion of the "perfect plastic" was abandoned. Instead companies such as Du Pont embraced plastic as a substance of "endless variety" and "infinite versatility," and coupled with the rise of a mass consumer market, "[a] function for every plastic and a plastic for every function became the goal."[66]

Historically renowned for the production of novelties, toys, optical frames, buttons, and combs, Leominster (known locally as "Comb City" since the turn of the century) and the surrounding area relied on the economic success of its plastics industries, which, during the 1920s, had been geared almost exclusively to the fabrication of celluloid.[67] The custom molder or "jobber," who used the sample maker to devise prototypes, formed an integral relation between production and consumption by fielding changes in consumer taste and introducing unfamiliar articles to reticent retailers. In the 1920s, the local plastics industries of Leominster, almost solely dependent on the fabrication of ornamental hair accessories, suffered mass unemployment and financial loss, ostensibly because of the changing fashion for bobbed hair. Consumer whims and stylistic changes had immense consequences for an industry geared to the specialization of a new retail market. With the introduction of automated production technology in the 1930s, injection molding brought Leominster once again to the forefront of plastic production. Its tentative relation with retail merchandising made the roles of sample maker and custom molder ever more significant.

The relatively ad hoc employment agreement between Du Pont, the Doyle Works, and Tupper illustrates how amateur inventors and entrepreneurial custom molders (who operated without professional training in marketing, chemistry, engineering, or design) stood at the forefront of major innovations in product design and plastics development of this period. "The custom molder . . . between the wars," to quote Meikle, "was an independent businessman, of working class origin, who had started out in rubber processing, in celluloid fabrication, or in fields such as jewelry, comb, or toy manufacturing that later adopted plastic materials."[68] Such ventures relied on the amateur inventors' and sample makers' ability to produce specialized components and attractive consumer items. Tupper, for example, received a 10 percent commission on any idea "conceived to save or make money" for the Doyle factory. Besides paying him for his everyday tasks of putting together prototypes and machining dyes, the Du Pont chemical company sponsored his plastics experimentation with a ready supply of materials. This arrangement, typical of the burgeoning plastics industry during this period, reduced Du Pont's liability as an employer while maximizing the company's development potential in the manufacturing industry. Tupper used his own unpaid time to devise patentable products, which the Doyle Works informally agreed to manufacture if they were deemed appropriate or financially viable.[69] This mutually beneficial arrangement was devised to increase manufacturing output at the Doyle Works and expand and develop the use of plastic materials made by their suppliers, the Du Pont company. Although Tupper spent most of his time working as a sample maker, initially concentrating on fairly mundane Viscoloid prototypes, his unrestricted access to machinery, methods, and materials allowed him to realize his ambition to act as a freelance "Industrial Inventor-Designer: Custom Inventing, Designing and Manufacturing."[70]

During this period Du Pont embarked on a campaign to increase their profile in the manufacture of consumer goods and counter negative public opinion generated by criticisms regarding the company's profiteering through munitions supply during the First World War (in the period 1915–18, Du Pont's profits swelled from $5 million to $60 million).[71] The advertising company Batten, Barten, Durstine and Osborn's slogan "Better Things for Better Living . . . through Chemistry" came to encapsulate Du Pont's drive to impress the modern consumer with its designs for everyday living. In order to conceive and engineer markets for their goods the company relied on a rigorous, if informal, understanding of the nuances of consumer trends.

In this context, building upon the invaluable experience gained from his work at the Doyle factory, Tupper acted as the company's emissary, collating information regarding competitors' products, retailers' buying policies, and stylistic trends. He was sent to local trade fairs and reported on them directly to the Doyle management, with detailed advice on product development and outlines for the requirements for more advanced machinery. At Brockton Fair, September 1937, Tupper recorded the outstanding innovations of each exhibit, from novel inventions for an orange juice pitcher to "watch charms" made by the Waltham Watch Company. "I believe," he commented excitedly, "the waterproof plastic [Lucite] watch case of mine can be made and sold to jewellers to fit all makes and sizes of works." Inspired by the designs for "watch charms," later that day he devised a double ring "to be worn on adjoining fingers. One ring having a dog the other a dog house."[72] Access to waste materials, reputedly the basis of his first polyethylene experiments, proved to be an added bonus of the job. After completing his assigned sample making Tupper worked on his own inventions, including, for example, a self-standing toothpaste and shaving cream dispenser with self-closing cap, which saved shelf space and time. Sometimes he eradicated material costs altogether: "I can get hold of 'reject' Bakelite industrial speciality for nothing, and then convert them to flower pots, etc. and sell at good prices," he noted in his invention diary.[73]

Tupper compiled information from counter girls and merchandising displays to assess the vitality and directions of specific markets, noting, for example, a typology of available plastic baby rattles on which he might improve. On a typical window-shopping trip to the small town of Fitchburg, he recorded comb designs manufactured by Japanese competitors, lamenting the improbability of Du Pont's ability to undercut them in price or copy them in sophistication of design.[74] Such excursions formed the basis of his designs, most notably his acknowledgment of a gift and premium market aimed at a specifically gendered audience. Casual marketing research inquiries led him to the realization that an array of modern consumer items were purchased specifically as trinkets, gifts, or tokens of affection. Thus his design for the Sweetie Picture Buckle belt, intended for retail gift sale or use as a premium, consisted of a series of linked transparent plastic segments in which snapshots of loved ones could be inserted; this was particularly effective as a premium, as consumers might receive a new segment with each purchase of a given commodity, such as breakfast cereal, until they completed their own customized belt. With the addition of saints and holy images, the belts, he noted, would prove especially popular "in the south."[75]

This empirical approach to design research extended to Tupper's social and familial relations, to the extent that his success as an inventor depended as much on the labor and initiatives of friends and family as on his individual genius. An elaborate network of female kin provided practical help in making prototypes, devising instruction leaflets, offering design ideas, and suggesting product modifications.

## Fancy Knitting Needles and Slip-Proof Garter Hooks
### Design and Domestic Economy

With the procurement of work at the Doyle factory from 1937 onward, Tupper's absence from home increased; according to one journal entry made by Marie, "Earl left at 6.30 [A.M.] and didn't get back until 9 [P.M.]."[76] In the evenings his work for Du Pont and on his own inventions extended into home life. Marie and female relatives and friends acted as informal consultants and product testers for Tupper's latest designs. Eyebrow dye shields, garter hooks, knitting needles, egg peeling clamps, flour sifters, and dish rack draining pans were all inspired and developed by women's cultural practices and experiences of domestic economy. The shields for dying eyebrows, a contemporary cosmetic practice, were tested on sisters Gladys and Eunice, who offered very specific suggestions for design alteration: "Both said there had been no combs or shields out, and they liked the idea," noted Tupper. "They suggested that the row of teeth be shorter since it is used crosswise."[77] Similarly designs for garter hooks were tested on Marie's stockings, and prototypes were reworked from his mother's and sister's existing examples. On devising knitting needles of "modern tasteful appearance," in colors women could coordinate with the item they happened to be knitting, Tupper used female networks as focus groups to gauge the success of his inventions. "I put five sets of the new knitting needles into my brief case to take home for Marie, and for several women who knit at sewing circles, to try out and give me their reactions."[78]

Designs for domestic objects, such as this dish rack with drain pans (1937), were informed by Tupper's observations of everyday domestic labor and by the suggestions of female kin. Sketchbook and invention journal, Tupper Papers, series 2, box 4, Archives Center, National Museum of American History, Smithsonian Institution, Washington, D.C.

Some of Tupper's designs for women, which failed to reach the patent application stage, proved less commercially appealing to say the least. In May 1937, he began work on an "instrument for starting menstruation in women who have delayed monthlies or are pregnant." The design failed

In 1935, Tupper applied the contemporary design ideal of "streamlining" to women's torsos with the invention of a rigid corset incorporating metal or wood plates. Sketchbook and invention journal, Tupper Papers, series 2, box 4, Archives Center, National Museum of American History, Smithsonian Institution, Washington, D.C.

to progress beyond its initial inception but several months later Tupper made sketches for an equally controversial design: a "Slave Necklace" and "Egyptian Slave dancing girl Waist Ring," composed of two plastic circles linked by a chain. "About 2 A.M. I awoke with the conception of a new

feminine necklace and belt . . . in semblance of old Egyptian Slave dancing girl rings that were put on to restrict fatness," he noted in his invention diary.[79] Although the design, in terms of its overtly constraining features, was eminently risqué, it drew on the enduring themes of
Egyptology popularized in advertising images since the turn of the century and reinterpreted in the 1920s and 1930s as a manifestation of the
modern, exotic sexuality of the New Woman.[80]

Another constraining device designed in accordance with contemporary women's fashions and referred to in sketches as "Corsets with Cross
Muscles" consisted of "wide flat strips of wood, metal or other material"
strapped to the abdomen to create a "flat appearance." A suggested merchandising campaign included targeting "young girls and undeveloped fe-
males" and placing advertisements in "Movie magazines, Lonely Heart
magazines, and Sunday Paper sections," publications popularly consumed
by working-class women and adolescent girls.[81]

More practical innovations such as a flour sifter, dish rack pans, and a
tampon case came directly from Marie's suggestions. Likewise, in the factory, female workers provided a constant stream of advice and ideas for
Tupper's designs. Nail motifs and designs, which as Marie had pointed out
few women could afford to have applied by a professional manicurist,
were made by Tupper from celluloid and demonstrated on enthusiastic female co-workers at the Doyle Works. After fellow workers Blanche,
Mary, and Jenney praised the innovation, it was further refined at home
with Marie: "We agreed that red, black, blue, yellow even green and pink
would be good colors, as well as gold or silver — and perhaps pearl," Tupper commented.[82] After consulting female shop clerks he devised "a kit
having suitable nail ornaments for all occasions (shamrocks, hearts, valen-
tines, etc.)," including personalized initials added by department store
shop assistants in accordance with a sweetheart's name. "The initials," he
imagined, "would presumably be the customer's and her boyfriend's."[83]

Women in the Doyle factory frequently decorated Tupper's designs by
hand and in some cases even wrote the accompanying literature and instruction manuals for his products.[84] A typical item, given to Marie as a
birthday gift, included the work of a woman who frequently added finishing touches to Tupper's designs: "Tonite gave Marie a purple mirror,
one of three new 'suspension' mirrors designed and made up. . . . Custom
built and exclusive with a free-hand painted iris on the back put on as a
special favor by Audrey Wye."[85] Tupper's inventions formed an integral
part of the household's moral economy and material culture. Tools to im-

prove his engineering and sample making were deemed by Tupper as the only acceptable and useful gifts that Marie might give him.[86]

Unfortunately, despite his acute observation and analysis of commonplace items and their uses, Tupper failed in his attempts to make his products, even his most ingenious or useful items, appeal to female consumers. Sure Stay hairpins, tested by Marie and patented by Tupper in 1937, genuinely solved a number of familiar problems, but attempts to market the product appealingly in a culturally meaningful context proved more problematic as Tupper's clumsy advertising attempt reveals: "Many women wear more or less false hair. Wigs cost good money, and romance or social prestige often hangs by the hair's of one's head." The copy concluded abruptly, "A good 'Sure-Stay' hairpin is needed."[87] The ability to make new goods appeal to the consumer (particularly to women) would prove, along with a dogged and persistent belief in the power of invention, paramount to Tupper's eventual commercial success. "When an inventor or advertiser doubts his ability . . . he has only to compare his work with the 'masterpieces of yesterday', and remember that while those masterpieces seem, to the ordinary mind of today, crude . . . they represent the best efforts of the recognized experts of the day," Tupper reassured himself.[88] Indeed, the success of his most famous design, Tupperware, relied almost exclusively on the extent to which his product could progress from origin to sale. Marketing was at least as important as an item's actual usefulness. As previous experiments (such as the rumble seat top ) had revealed, the reception of new technology and design was a far from predictable process. Despite the intentions of the inventor or manufacturer, the "modern consumer" often proved unresponsive to so-called innovations.

By 1940, the Earl S. Tupper Company (formed by Tupper in 1939) of Leominster, Massachusetts, offered a small selection of fancy goods and gift articles using the novelty appeal of modern plastics. The *Merchandiser,* a retail magazine catering to cheaper hardware, novelty, and gift shops, featured a cellulose-acetate nautical necktie rack, the "latest hit" that "attaches anywhere in [the] home." Designed in the form of a spoked ship's wheel and molded with a decorative anchor motif, the rack held up to thirty-six ties. Available in imitation metal finishes of "aluminum, bronze and gold," the "nautical but nice" storage device could also be used for feminine accessories such as ribbons and belts. The necktie rack was available in an assortment of colors ("blue, pink and green") meant "to harmonize with room decorations and to please feminine taste." Under the heading "New Uses Illustrate Plastics' Potentialities for '5 & 10' Items," the "Kamoflage comb," another Earl S. Tupper design (a combination nail file and comb disguised as a fountain pen, which men could discreetly wear in their top pockets), was featured alongside a Lucite Illuminated Tongue Depressor manufactured by a rival manufacturer.[89]

Around 1942, after producing a number of these barely successful plastic novelty household gift items, Earl Tupper produced a flexible, injection-molded polyethylene bell-shaped container that formed the basis of his revolutionary, generic kitchenware. The result of lengthy experiments with raw polyethylene during World War II material shortages, the containers were manufactured at Tupper's own molding factory, Tupper Plastics Incorporated (known after 1947 as the Tupper Corporation). As well as devising its own consumer items, the newly formed Tupper company relied on work performed under subcontract to Du Pont; despite resin shortages, the business thrived through defense contracts, for example, molding parts for gas masks and naval signal lamps.[90] In 1949, the patent for his ingenious "Tupper seal," an airtight lid available in assorted sizes to fit the expanding range of Tupperware polyethylene stackable containers, was finally granted. Also that year, a diary entry revealed a new resolve: to focus attention on particular rather than diverse design ventures and acknowledge the importance of marketing considerations. "Beautiful design & good functional design will enable us to outsell our competitors . . . we shall correct weaknesses in our current designs, project trends and anticipate needs, then *sell aggressively!*"[91] At last, Earl Tupper had successfully patented a commercially viable product. After engineering an endless array of contraptions and gadgets, from self-sharpening scissors to underwater mirrors, Tupper created a design combining his utopian visions and free-market convictions. Despite the skepticism of the Bakelite Division, Union Carbide and Carbon Corporation (from which the Tupper Corporation received many of its raw materials during this period of severe shortages and which advised Tupper to limit his manufacturing efforts to producing cosmetic tubs) Tupper pursued his vision of the total "Tupperization" of American homes and by 1956 found his utilitarian wares bottom-lit like objets d'art in the display cabinets of New York's Museum of Modern Art.[92]

t w o

• • •

Tupperware
The Creation of a Modernist Icon?

I n 1956 curators at the Museum of Modern Art, New York, chose a
number of Tupperware kitchen containers and implements for a national exhibition of outstanding twentieth-century design. The selection criteria of the MOMA exhibit centered on the aesthetic rather than
the commercial merit of the objects. With its streamlined injection-
molded forms, Tupperware embodied the machine aesthetic of a technologically determined, functional form. Based on this modernist rationale,
Tupperware items were judged "uncluttered" and "carefully considered
shapes . . . marvelously free of that vulgarity which characterizes so much
household equipment."[1] This accolade was the culmination of a decade of
representation that cast Tupperware's designer at the forefront of a narrative of American modernism whereby industrial designers harnessed the
technologies of wartime innovation to reinvigorate the postwar consumer
economy.

Invented in the early 1940s, the first Tupperware object was a 7-ounce
(200-gram), injection-molded, milky white container that challenged
many of the limitations associated with contemporary domestic plastics.
Called a "bell tumbler" because of its conical shape, it was fashioned from
a substance trademarked "Poly-T: Material of the Future," a refined version of basic polyethylene, a synthetic polymer that was nontoxic, odorless, flexible, and lightweight. The potential of polyethylene, used primarily for insulation purposes in industrial and aviational contexts, had

The "carefully considered shapes" of Tupperware selected by curators at the Museum of Modern Art in 1956 for display. Designer: Tupper, Earl S. Kitchen containers and implements. 1945–56. Translucent flexible plastic. Manufacturer: Tupper Corporation, U.S.A. The Museum of Modern Art, New York. Gifts of the manufacturer. Photograph © 1999 The Museum of Modern Art, New York. AD28 Barrows 3201-58.

yet to be fully explored in the production of domestic commodities. Although Tupper Plastics Incorporated utilized other plastic types, including styrene, styron, and acetate, Earl Tupper aligned himself specifically with the development and augmentation of polyethylene as an uncharted material. He frequently used analogies of wartime upheaval in his promotion of polyethylene and positioned himself as the guardian of this new material. "With the end of the war [polyethylene] was another young veteran that had accelerated from childhood to a fighting job," he espoused in 1949. "It had done its job well but like all young vets returning from the wars it had never had civilian adult experience."[2]

Commercial, quantity production of polyethylene began in the United States in 1943, although the material in its most basic form was developed in Great Britain at the beginning of the 1930s. The Du Pont and Bakelite chemical companies used the substance, by itself and in combination with other materials, to serve various purposes including extruded insulation for small precision instruments, radar, and radio equipment.[3] As a comparatively chemical-resistant thermoplastic it was made into industrial washers, gaskets, packing, linings, and chemical tubing. "Unusually form-stable at temperatures approaching its softening range," it bridged the gap between categories of rigid and nonrigid plastics, retaining toughness and flexibility at extremely low and comparably high temperatures.[4] As early as 1946, *Bakelite Review* featured the tumblers and bowls of Tupper Plastics Incorporated as unique plastic items resistant to cracks, chips, and peeling "even under the most severe strain." Beneath the slogan "For Lasting Service!" the housewares appeared as the fortuitous consequence of wartime technology: durable, reliable, practical, and serviceable. The promotional image showed a regimented lineup of identical, mass-produced containers poised on the kitchen shelf, ready for domestic action, thrifty in both material and function, an "enviable combination of usefulness and beauty." The editor reiterated that kitchen cabinets stocked with these polyethylene items would protect the homemaker from an endless "drain on the household budget" through efficient storage and the prevention of "costly breakage in houseware."[5] As a product concept born of the shortages of the Great Depression and wartime rationing, Tupperware perfectly embodied the *Good Housekeeping* plea that "Leftovers Can Be Tasty!"[6]

Polyethylene could be made in a variety of colors, surface decorated with imprinted inks, and readily formed using mass-production injection, compression, and blow-molding techniques. In 1947, with the patent pending for the "Tupper seal" (an air- and liquid-tight flexible cover made for injection-molded tumblers), the potential of polyethylene's unique features was maximized and Tupperware was transformed into a distinct product: "vermin and insect proof . . . unspillable . . . the first and only such articles the housewife has ever had." By 1948 all Tupperware canisters and refrigerator bowls became "standard equipped" with seals.[7] As the linchpin of the product's success, the seal utilized the flexibility and molecular memory of polyethylene's properties to create a snugly fitting cover based on an inversion of a paint can lid; it was the direct result of Tupper's observations of the objects and mechanics of everyday living. From the onset, the Tupper seal, as an excerpt from the Tupper Corporation's correspondence reveals, transformed the product from a flexible plastic bowl to a patentable technological form. Using stern tones the ad-

Trade publications such as *Modern Plastics* showed this thrifty, modern, postwar housewife of 1946 transferring leftovers to a Tupperware Wonder Bowl for refrigeration. Such images epitomized Earl Tupper's vision of the total "Tupperization" of American homes. Tupper envisioned Tupperware becoming a national generic brand, like the Coca-Cola poised in the open refrigerator. Tupper Papers, series 3, box 6, Archives Center, National Museum of American History, Smithsonian Institution, Washington, D.C.

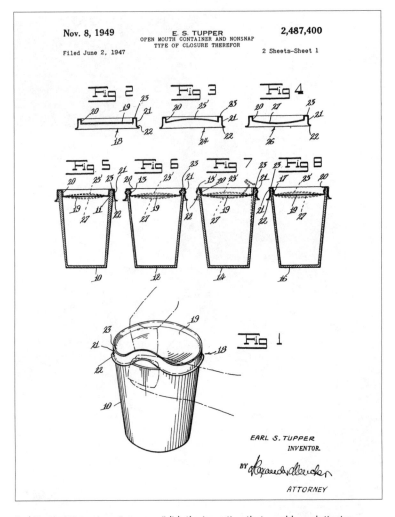

Earl Tupper's ingenious "nonsnap" lid, the invention that would revolutionize kitchen storage. These drawings accompanied his patent application in 1947. Tupperware Patent Records, Tupper Papers, series 2, box 4, Archives Center, National Museum of American History, Smithsonian Institution, Washington, D.C.

vertising manager reprimanded a reputable houseware journalist for misrepresenting the invention: "I realize the necessity for editorial writers using their own nomenclature in describing products fully . . . but there is one thing that gets our goats here. That is, to have these Patented Seal Cover Combinations termed 'lids.'"[8] Indeed, the seals differed enormously from "snap-on-and-off" closures typically used for food and beverage containers, as one newspaper, reporting on the patent, observed: "In contrast with prior constructions, Mr. Tupper has devised an improved non-snapping and noiseless closure that is attachable to the lip of a container by a simple hand manipulation and is removable therefrom by a peeling-off procedure."[9] This "simple hand manipulation," whereby air is expelled as the polyethylene lid is eased over the sides of a container's aperture, became famous as the "Tupperware burp."

The Tupper Corporation displayed an immense protectionism toward their newly conceived commodity as did the industry from which it sprang. In 1948 the *Modern Plastics Encyclopaedia* included a tea set manufactured by the Tupper Corporation as the exemplary domestic polyethylene form, indicative of the plastic's essential properties: flexible, waterproof, lightweight, and functional in a wide range of temperatures. Versatility and durability formed a rare combination in the broader context of plastic's ambiguous reputation during this period, and polyethylene appeared as the plastic that had "come of age."

Although plastic was once dubbed the "miracle material," by the 1940s utopian beliefs in its transformative powers had waned, with indiscriminate mass production and the widespread misapplication of materials. For a consumer public that commonly encountered disintegrating, combustible, and odorous plastic products, disillusionment formed a crucial part of the "plastic experience." Confusion abounded regarding definitions of what actually constituted "plastic" and the extent to which it should be considered a boon or a curse. Cultural mythology, substantiated by the manufacturers' oversimplified scientific explanations, frequently described the plastic-making process in terms of beguiling alchemy. The first snow-white, featherweight Tupperware item, according to corporate accounts, came from a lump of black, recalcitrant chemical waste product referred to as "slag." Through an act of genius and alchemy, Earl Tupper summoned forth a divine creation to benefit humanity. "He looked deep into the material," declared a promotional film, "and found Tupperware." The corporate representation of Tupper's invention typified the veiled and romanticized marketing ploys of many plastics producers who promised miracles to American homemakers.

But all plastic was not perfect. Despite the marvelous claims of manufacturers, everyday products such as plastic shower curtains disintegrated into sticky, useless sheets and apparently sturdy baby baths cracked, split, and peeled. Many fabricators preempted public misgivings by highlighting and counterpoising potential problems; a typical advertisement read, "This unique salad bowl . . . molded of Bakelite polystyrene [has] resistance to vinegar (acetic acid) and vegetable oils," obviously implying that most plastic products did not. A burgeoning mistrust and incredulity made the domestication of plastic a tentative process. In 1944 Walt Disney Studios released a satirical cartoon, "The Plastics Inventor," which featured Donald Duck attempting to transform household waste, using a cooking pot and an oven, into a plastic-molded, fully operational airplane. The aviation design acknowledged the public perception of plastic as a heavy-duty, wartime material and deliberately juxtaposed it with the thoroughly domestic understanding of plastic (and its disappointments). Inevitably, Donald's "invention" disintegrates during the airplane's first exposure to the elements, offering as cultural historian Jeffrey Meikle concludes "a cautionary tale on the folly of blindly trusting scientific experts" and their exaggerated claims.[10]

## Flying Saucers and "Fine Art for 39 Cents"

In 1947 *House Beautiful* featured polyethylene kitchen containers manufactured by the Tupper Corporation, under the grandiose title "Fine Art for 39 Cents." Used effectively, polyethylene (the article suggested) defied these nightmarish visions of plastic as a disposable, faddish entity easily molded to the excesses and foibles of mass consumption. Tupperware accrued status far exceeding the banality conferred on most utilitarian household goods or plastic wares, borrowing instead the luxuriant terms of decorative arts connoisseurship. The bowls were praised for their "fingering qualities of jade" and likened to smoothness and iridescence of alabaster and mother-of-pearl. Though the refrigerator bowls received functional acclaim for their "fitness for purpose" and "truth to materials," editor Elizabeth Gordon focused her product appraisal on tactility, sensuality, and desire. "Does it satisfy our aesthetic craving to handle, feel and study beautiful things?" she asked rhetorically.[11] She concluded that the artifacts, fashioned from the Tupper Corporation's trademarked substance "Poly-T: Material of the Future," exceeded any measurable, rational, or functional criterion for assessment. "Above all else," she announced, "the bowls have a profile as good as a piece of sculpture." As icons of modern

In 1947 *House Beautiful* featured Tupperware under the title "Fine Art for 39 Cents," promoting the containers as everyday works of art ideal for the discerning, middle-class consumer. Reprinted by permission from *House Beautiful,* copyright © October 1947. The Hearst Corporation. All rights reserved.

artistry they provided "shining points of interest as soup or berry bowls, or condiments dishes."

This special edition of *House Beautiful,* a reputable home interiors magazine, resulted from collaboration with the trade association, the Society of the Plastics Industry, which sought to encourage women to view plastics as a noncontentious and increasingly domesticated feature of the 1940s middle-class American home. Traditional housewares and furnishings, from silverware to curtain hangings, operated within their own complex system of stylistic rules and meanings, but plastic, as a newcomer, occupied a thoroughly ambiguous position. Several editors of the magazine agreed to compile information and research (initiated by their visits to the second National Plastics Exposition of 1947), to assist bewildered consumers in understanding the significance of plastics in postwar life. With fifty pages devoted to "Plastic . . . A Way to a Better More Carefree Life," this edition of *House Beautiful* served as a consumer handbook describing the relation of plastic to the intricacies of modern homemaking. The potentially alienating aspects of the new materials, unfamiliar in texture, density, and form, were countered by revelations regarding their labor-saving, wipe-clean features. Tupperware, "Fine Art for 39 Cents," conjured up a far more elaborate set of cultural meanings.[12]

Through the development of his material culture, Earl Tupper aimed to tell the story of polyethylene. When in 1949 he confidently introduced his range of "revolutionary" containers to potential mail-order consumers, using the newly devised brand-name "Tupperware," he fostered an image of total "Tupperization," the widespread rationalization of American homes through the use of Tupperware: "Now let's not think of Tupperware, fashioned from the 'material of the future' as a vogue, a novelty, a passing fancy. Instead, think of it as having taken its rightful place with other fine table furnishings . . . silver, linen, china. . . . Tupperware is here in a most substantial way . . . its position is assured."[13]

Although the product received widespread media attention in journals and houseware sections of national and local newspapers, the process of Tupperization had made little headway, and its position in the American home was far from assured. The Tupper Corporation rented a prestigious showroom on New York's Fifth Avenue to encourage potential retail and wholesale buyers to study the revolutionary houseware first hand. The search for exclusivity continued. In 1947, Tupperware courted the British royal seal of approval when Princess Elizabeth received a collection of dinnerware as a prenuptial gift under the press caption "'Flying Saucers' for Princess Elizabeth." Dignitaries such as King Ibn of Arabia and the Maharaja of Ender also enjoyed Tupperware presentations, which were flown for collection to prearranged destinations by Trans World Airlines. "Initial collections of the 'Flying Saucers,'" wrote a journalist of the

*Boston Post,* "took off last night" as TWA also chose to equip their carriers with the "brand new dinnerware designed especially for airline use."[14] As well as being an important adjunct to the modern kitchen, the Tupperware "flying saucers" were enhanced by borrowing the stylish cosmopolitanism suggested by international air travel. On a more mundane level, a rigorous public relations campaign, supported by the larger chemical companies Bakelite and later Du Pont, depicted Tupper products as trustworthy household items, commodities with "a rightful place" among the accoutrements of the respectable home. In stark contrast to Earl Tupper's durable and superior "Material of the Future," and his concerted efforts to upgrade the image of plastic with a New York City showroom and *House Beautiful* feature, the popular consumption of plastic artifacts during this period continued to revolve around their appeal to frivolity, fashion, and novelty.

Chemical companies continued to battle the consumer's and manufacturer's misuse and misunderstanding of plastics. By the 1940s they promoted their raw materials to manufacturers and consumers alike by generating a specific understanding of the properties of plastic through nominated products. "Better Things for Better Living . . . through Chemistry," read the Du Pont axiom, which introduced manufacturers and investors to polyethylene as an ideal means of creating new products or restyling established ones. In 1948 Du Pont sponsored full-color advertisements for Tupper's tumblers, under the Du Pont trademark and slogan; they appeared in *Modern Plastics, Modern Industry, Product and Engineering, Fortune, Business Week, U.S. News,* and *Machine Design* and described polyethylene as a chemically inert, flexible, low-density plastic that "floats on water!" Other manufacturers, it advised, were "using many of these properties to advantage in products as diverse as refrigerator bowl covers, insulation for television cables and — baby pants."[15] Numerous competitions exhibited Tupperware as a winning product; in September 1948 *Plastics World* announced the winners of the Modern Plastics Competition, which included a major award for the Tupper Corporation's "Millionaire Line" of housewares utilizing Du Pont materials. The previous year Tupperware had been overall winner of the General Housewares category, one of several winners associated with Bakelite polyethylene. Although Tupperware had yet to secure a proven or extensive consumer market, it had become a crucial part of a corporate campaign to culturally mediate plastic in the postwar period. The February 1948 edition of *Modern Plastics,* under the heading "Precocious Plastics," described polyethylene as "only an infant in years" but holding the promise of great success in the future and featured Tupperware as the representative polyethylene product. And so the genesis of a new generic plastic product had begun with the interchangeability of the terms "polyethylene" and "Tupperware."

## "Lovely-to-Look-at Party Accessories" or "Modern Functional Forms"?

"Better by Far than Can or Jar!"—Tupper Poly-T canisters may not have provoked "love at first sight" in homemakers, as one promotional plea claimed, but they did offer the consumer a genuinely innovative product at a comparatively affordable price.[16] In 1947 a three-piece Wonder Bowl set retailed at $1.39, and a pack of six 9-ounce (266-milliliter) tumblers cost 99¢ with matching coasters at 5¢ each. A standard covered refrigerator bowl, 3.25 inches (8.25 centimeters) high, 4.5 inches (11.5 centimeters) in diameter, tapering to 2.5 inches (6.35 centimeters) at the base, cost 39¢. Air- and liquid-tight Tupper seals were sold as additions to the other containers in the range, at a maximum of 25¢ each according to size. Although items such as a utility bowl that was "heat-resistant, practically unbreakable, alcohol proof, fireproof and readily washable," manufactured from an inflexible plastic by Wolfe Products Company for 75¢, were featured side-by-side with Tupperware in houseware pages, there were no directly comparable products. A "Tiny-Tot's" segmented "lustrous" plastic food bowl, complete with feeding spoon and tumbler, sold at $1.49 and was manufactured by a picnic dinnerware company of New York City, but none of these items offered a waterproof seal or nonodorous, translucent properties. In terms of comparable food storage items, plastic refrigerator bags, sealed using the heat of a domestic iron, provided disposable airtight storage. Zippered polyethylene bags, "transparent, waterproof, greaseproof, stainproof, and mildewproof," available in department and hardware stores, were recommended for refrigeration storage and for storing clothes and "other valuable articles" and cost $1.98 for three "envelopes."[17] Neither of the plastic-bag storage methods proved popular. Despite the plethora of synthetic goods available to the public, manufacturers themselves had yet to fully distinguish one material, and its potential uses, from another. Because plastic was a material so tainted by ambiguity, the Tupper Corporation avoided the term altogether, referring instead to the brand names "Poly-T," "Material of the Future," or "Tupperware." Similarly commentators, including female journalists dealing with issues of consumption in the postwar home, ignored technical details in preference to appeals to popular feminine concerns and the reality of housework chores. In particular they emphasized the tactility, sensuality, and decorative features of Tupperware rather than its technical or chemical specifications.

"There's a 'new look' to refrigerator containers," declared housewares journalist Harriet Jean Anderson of the *Herald Tribune* in 1948. "Selecting a wardrobe for a refrigerator which after all is such a prosaic and inanimate thing," she continued, "may not seem very interesting" until fashionable and stylish additions such as the Tupperware container added panache to the mundanity of cold storage. But Tupperware also solved a readily recognizable refrigeration problem caused by attempts to keep appropriate foods as fresh as possible. The ice generated by use of a "humidor"—a small box at the bottom of the refrigerator to which moisture was added to freshen salad and vegetables—caused particular concern. The escaping moisture from the compartment formed into "big kegs of ice and icicles . . . all over everything."[18] Tupperware's promise of "sealed in freshness" usurped the humidor, the saucer over the bowl, and all the other ineffectual refrigeration storage devices. On the whole, despite the growth in domestic refrigeration, utensils adhered to traditional forms and materials. At the time of Tupperware's launch the Sears and Roebuck catalog offered, for example, "white porcelain enamel dishes" and Aqua-Satin "food fresh" covers (made from "extra heavy pure processed silk") for refrigerator storage.[19]

Tupperware items far exceeded the utilitarian features of comparable products and were described as ideal "lovely-to-look-at party accessories" filled with popcorn, pretzels, potato chips, or ice cubes.[20] The Wonder Bowl, available in three graduated sizes, stood as the archetypal Tupperware object for storing food, meats, eggs, fruit, or vegetables. Smaller refrigerator bowls were useful for leftovers and prepared sauces and desserts. Wonder Bowls, as their nomenclature suggests, encapsulated the distinctive and revolutionary features of the newly defined plastic category. Available in nested trios, the bowls were "pliable but unbreakable," soft and resilient, useful for mixing, storing, and serving. A thermal version, with double walls forming an insulating cavity, functioned as an ice bucket.

Canisters provided a more utilitarian facet to the range; their shapes echoed the more traditional forms of glass, tin, and ceramic. Under the title "Subject to Change," one houseware journalist juxtaposed Tupperware with tea caddies and hinged metal coffee containers. Their flexibility contributed to their labor-saving, easy-to-clean capabilities: "If food sticks to them, you do not scrape it away but flex the bowl to loosen it"; otherwise they happily coexisted with condiments of "your mother's generation."[21] Unlike the dilettantism of style commentators, houseware journalists, aware of the physicality of housework, acknowledged the ergonomics and sensuality of Tupperware designs. The tactility of Tupperware radically challenged the rigidity of rival plastic products; they were "light and easily handled." Houseware editors frequently chose to photograph the containers in poses where a woman's hand squeezed the bowl to create a pouring spout.[22] Flexible Poly-T tumblers, available by 1947 in a range of pastel colors advertised under the slogan "For Lasting Beauty and Utility," offered safe alternatives to glass and ceramic tumblers, with their "bounce-back" properties. They were ideal for leisurely outdoor entertaining, bathroom usage, and diligent parenting.

Poly-T products were consistently promoted as objects to be distinguished from the riot of cheap ornaments, inane gifts, and second-rate housewares offered by the rapidly expanding and exceedingly profitable plastics industries. In an internal corporate memorandum to his advertising manager in 1949, Earl Tupper reflected on the short marketing history of Tupperware and acknowledged the immense significance of consumption, and the motives behind consumer choice, in creating a worthy product: "We were not discouraged by those buyers who said our colors were not gaudy enough . . . we directed our energy to education of the public. We avoided greed for quick dollar returns. At great immediate loss to ourselves we refused applications that could have paid us well at that time. Our product was so new as to be instantly recognizable. The association of that product in its first appearances would create lasting impressions. We undertook to make these impressions favorable."[23]

As flying saucers, royal gifts, or fine art for thirty-nine cents, from its onset Tupperware generated a product profile that accentuated the extraordinary and sublime. Yet throughout the postwar period, art and design experts, predominantly men, persisted in using the form for ammunition in a contentious battle over taste, consumption, and social mobility; their appraisal of the product, unlike that of female houseware journalists, played down the fashionability and sensuality of Tupperware, construing it instead as a revered "machine formed" industrial product design.

# The Creation of a Modernist Icon?

## "Ubiquity Made Visible"
### The Perfect Commodity

By 1956 the elitist curators at MOMA, who hailed the utility and beauty of Tupperware and lamented the "vulgarity" of other household equipment, admired the product as a shining beacon of hope in a period defined by an unprecedented rise in mass consumption and a perceived decline in mass consumer taste. For advocates of "good design" it defied the fecklessness of a motley plastics industry and the ostentatious frippery of brightly colored, overdesigned gadgetry. Increased affluence, conspicuous consumption, and class mobility defined postwar America, according to one commentator, as the site of "one of history's great shopping sprees."[24] Contemporary household appliances, available in a myriad of colors and styles, exemplified the stylistic move toward "populuxe," a term used retrospectively to describe a newly defined consumer democracy through which "each householder was able to have his own little Versailles along a cul-de-sac."[25] In this context, Tupperware represented the elusive modernist ideal of a tasteful, restrained, and mass-produced artifact, free of inauthentic decoration and gratuitous ornament.

The modernist predilection for "humble," everyday objects inverted the appreciation of fine and decorative arts, placing instead the prosaic commodity on the pedestal. According to this doctrine, the truly sophisticated and educated consumer could distinguish between the authentic and the inauthentic artifact irrespective of its origins; in this way taste was preserved as a manifestation of "cultural capital" rather than the gauche expressions of a newly affluent social group. In 1949 *Life* magazine published a pictorial chart illustrating the hierarchies of taste operating among new cultural groups pursuing particular American lifestyles. A popular article written by Russell Lynes, describing the impact of "the tastemakers," formed the basis of the satirical piece. According to Lynes, new social groupings that operated beyond conventional, production-led definitions of class stratification signaled social change in postwar America. Taste, manifest in "brow" levels ranging from low, lower middle, and upper middle, to high, made apparently trivial choices of consumption (clothes, drinks, furnishings, etc.) highly potent. The highbrow tastemaker, on the one hand, confidently mixed a deep admiration for a "decanter and ashtray from [a] chemical supply company" with the purchase of named designer furniture of Charles Eames, the lighting of industrial designer Kurt Versen, and a taste for ballet. The lowbrow tastemaker, on the other hand, considered a decorative, embroidered "balsam-stuffed pillow" as a "Useful Object" and favored a mail-order "overstuffed" chair and a re-production fringed lamp; preferred lowbrow entertainment took the form of American popular culture, namely Western movies, rather than Euro-pean arts.[26] Lowbrow taste relied on limited forms of knowledge (the convenience of mass-circulated, mail-order catalogs and a passé reliance on comfort, tradition, and display expressed through "stuffed" and "fringed" reproduction furnishings); highbrow taste revolved around demonstrations of highly specialized expertise and an aesthetic sensibility premised by ideological rather than practical or sentimental desires. In comparison with the "balsam-stuffed pillow," either a crude homemade product or (even more degrading) a mass-produced nostalgic imitation, the glass decanter and ashtray made by a chemical supply company dis-played the simple honesty of a functional, everyday commodity.

Tupperware, then, epitomized this notion of the authentic commodity. It tapped into a lengthy intellectual debate established in the 1920s and 1930s regarding modernism, mass culture, and the tension between moral and aesthetic concerns. Notions of "highbrow" and "lowbrow," outlined in an essay by cultural critic Van Wyck Brooks as early as 1915, formed the basis of a critique in the 1930s of mass culture and consumption. New York intellectuals and the Frankfurt School critical theorists considered cultural forms as manifestations of an advanced capitalist economy bent on manipulation of the masses through "inauthentic" forms of cultural production, which perpetuated a state of "false consciousness" through their blatant appeal to the "lower" senses of human endeavor.[27] In con-trast, an object that was simply useful could appeal to the masses through its straightforward function rather than sentimentality and the unenlight-ened desire for escapism. In the ideal commodity, machine and art were united for the benefit, rather than the delusion, of the masses. In 1949 the Detroit Institute of Arts displayed an array of household products under the title "An Exhibition for Modern Living," which included several stacks of Tupperware canisters and bowls, severe stainless steel bread boxes, plain aluminum nesting saucepans, and alarm clocks with simple faces.[28] As in the MOMA exhibit, the curators selected objects they rec-ommended as legitimate commodities, rather than recognized as genu-inely commonplace household goods; novelty egg timers, fancy oven gloves, and floral toaster covers were not permissible in this vision of modern living, despite their popularity in the real marketplace. The 1954 publication of *Industrial Design,* authored by Van Doren, a leading modernist designer of the 1930s, also included Tupperware in its account of contemporary design. The volume showed Tupperware containers set against a stark, black background and casting their own dramatic shadows to demonstrate the commanding vision of a technocratic democracy. "Eminently representative of good design taking the fullest advantage of an inexpensive machine-molding process. . . . [A]ll Tupperware," concluded the caption triumphantly, "is designed to sell at low prices."[29]

Twenty-five years later, in a historical survey of design and mass production, also titled *Industrial Design,* the reductionist analysis of modernism prevailed. The author, John Heskett, accounted for the phenomenal success of Tupperware using the phrase "very functional, with a clever air-tight lid."[30] As a twentieth-century commodity Tupperware expressed an evolutionary logic whereby market economics and technological progress combined to create an ideal aesthetic and functional form for mass consumption. Significantly none of these accounts mentioned the Tupperware party, although this method of direct selling, which formed a crucial dimension of the product's sales during the 1940s, had by 1951 become the exclusive retail distribution method for Tupperware items. The authenticity and integrity of the Tupperware modernist object seemed uncomfortably compromised by the gendered sociality and quirkiness of the Tupperware party, with its appeal to consumption as a social rather than rational practice.

To contemporary art curators and design commentators, the elevation of Tupperware to a position as modernist icon and a "design classic" precluded the convoluted trappings of the Tupperware party. Unlike many of the elaborate appliances of the postwar consumer culture, with their built-in style obsolescence and inconsequential design features, Tupperware represented a pure commodity. For the self-determining, rational consumer it offered measurable function and use-value. Most importantly, according to the formal analysis, it expressed the essential concept of the ideal twentieth-century commodity: an identical, alienable, mass-produced form. From a modernist standpoint, the neutrality of Tupperware products expedited their circulation as commodities operating in an objectively driven market economy.

According to many cultural critics, plastics provided the lowest common denominator of the commodity world. Indicative of this stance, writing in the aptly titled book *The Waste Makers,* Vance Packard equated plastic with the manipulative strategies of the manufacturing industries and the foibles of the postwar consumer: "Plastics have appealed to producers not only because they are usually cheaper than metal but also because their built-in colors help promote selling on the basis of style and impulse."[31] For design reformers and advocates of the "good design" movement, Tupperware utilized plastic as a purposeful and tasteful aesthetic choice rather than a cheap and flippant gimmick.

Injection molding, which spawned products in a matter of seconds with no visible human intervention, perpetuated the notion of plastic as an effortlessly formed, promiscuous substance, which like mass consumption itself contributed to an advanced state of alienation. Roland Barthes's essay, "Plastics," written in the late 1950s, describes the injection molding process thus: "At one end, raw, telluric matter, at the other, the finished, human object; and between these two extremes, nothing; nothing but a transit, hardly watched over by an attendant in a cloth cap, half-god, half-robot." Plastic, "ubiquity made visible," is ever pliable and transmutative. Ultimately Barthes concludes, "Objects will be made for the sole pleasure of using them."[32] His essay casts the substance simultaneously as the symptom of rampant consumer capitalism and a symbol of its democratic progress: "It is the first magical substance that consents to be prosaic." Injection molding transformed plastic from its bourgeois, capitalist origins as an imitative luxury material (mock tortoiseshell, pseudoprecious stones, and other trappings of artifice), which, according to Barthes, belonged "to the world of appearances, not to that of actual use." Through this method of production "plastic has climbed down," he declared. "It has become a household material."[33]

Injection molding did increase the capability for cheaper, high-quantity production. But the molds themselves, designed, crafted, and highly maintained, required major capital investment. The high cost of machine molds encouraged simplification of design because they required smooth, polished surfaces (to enable the easy removal of molded pieces) and minimal detail (to prevent expensive finishing processes). These technical requisites cohered perfectly with popular images of modernistic, aerodynamically streamlined creations.[34] Despite modernist assertions of technological determination, however, the majority of plastic designs continued to rely on imitative and derivative forms, much to the disappointment of increasingly discerning consumers. "Imitative plastics of the postwar era," comments Meikle, "gave themselves away as if the makers could not be bothered with the effort necessary to carry off the effect. One did not have to be a modernist champion of 'truth to materials' to grow tired of the charade and to prefer 'the real thing' when it was available at an affordable price."[35]

Tupperware adhered to a functionalist aesthetic, which according to a modernist depiction consisted of a core of "classic" shapes in the form of Wonder Bowls, canister sets, refrigerator bowls, and tumblers, along with their ingenious airtight Tupper seals. This aesthetic lent an authenticity to plastic, a material notoriously geared toward the deceptions of mass consumer society. The coffee/tea service (a coffee or tea pot, creamer, sugar bowl, cups, and saucers) revealed the extent to which polyethylene offered a feasible alternative to traditional materials without being wholly derivative. The coffee cup, injection molded in one piece from a single mold, was revered as a prime example of form following function. Manufactured in a single process, the hollow handle jutting out as an extension of the cup's recess, this technologically derived design "not only solved the problem" of incorporating a handle, it also "added volume" and provided "excellent stacking possibilities."[36] For advocates of modern design it epitomized the sculptural, machine aesthetic that defined plastic as a legitimate material within its own right. From the onset this item proved to be exceptionally popular with design critics and, with the implementation of the Tupperware party in the 1950s, a growing number of consumers. Yet according to oral histories (and logical deduction), the design was intrinsically flawed; on tipping the cup toward the lips, liquid escaped as efficiently from the hollow handle as from the main recess of the cup.[37] Despite claims to the contrary, rational functionality and utility were by no means the sole determinants of Tupperware's immense commercial success. Some Tupperware forms may have coalesced with a modernist aesthetic but, as the plethora of Econo-Canisters covered with hand-painted floral patterns and whimsical motifs suggests, certain less-austere versions of the Tupperware range (excluded from the professional design press and the exhibits of elitist museums) more aptly fulfilled the desires of many a nonrational 1940s consumer.

The modernist framework typically invoked to look at objects of twentieth-century design reveals a paucity of cultural and historical analysis. The construction of "great individuals such as Raymond Loewy and Norman Bel Geddes . . . as the creators of modern mass consumer culture," as one critic has commented, leads to "a study of the industrial artifact which quite ignores the consumer."[38] Invention and design, according to Tupper, were born of the ultimate potentiality of human resources.

In this context, everyday consumer products were the result of "imagination, inspiration, gifted genius, plus reasoning logic, instinctive knowledge, cosmic knowledge, experience." It is revealing to note that whereas modern design figureheads of the 1930s and 1940s remained entirely absent from Tupper's discourses and notes, the entrepreneurial inventor and the Renaissance man loomed large. Although according to numerous historical accounts, industrial designers were shaping the forms, functions, and popular visions of the twentieth-century United States, Tupper failed to acknowledge or make even passing reference to their apparently high-profile achievements.[39] Indeed, modernity and its projects, according to entrepreneurs and inventors such as Tupper, were more appropriately manifest in the guise of the Renaissance man. Popular historical characters such as Thomas Jefferson, Leonardo da Vinci, and Thomas Edison, true visionaries who had transformed civilization with their "inventive, intuitive and trained mind[s]," stood in sharp contrast to the league of superficial industrial designers acting as little more than stylists employed to create cosmetic changes according to the vagaries of fashion and maximization of corporate profit.[40] As a "super-coordinator" dedicated to "progress by steps so [as] not to be too jarring with harmony [and] our habits and things around us," Tupper spurned the superficiality of corporate stylists who offered little in the way of genuine technological innovation or accessible design for the masses. His more ambitious endeavor was to proffer his inventions as gifts to humanity and "to live widely and fully . . . to try to understand the true purpose and intent of everything that has inherent usefulness to humanity and posterity."[41]

As the following chapter explores, the creation of Tupperware as a generic household item involved a complex process of cultural mediation in which the product's objectively defined features, such as its "very functional" streamlined form and "clever air-tight lid," paled into comparative insignificance. Despite its acclaim as an icon of the machine aesthetic and American mass production, by the late 1940s Tupperware had failed to secure any stable consumer base. As an exemplary polyethylene product Tupperware received the backing of Du Pont's public relations strategies, which helped ensure its prominence in an array of magazines and newspapers from *House Beautiful* to the *New York Times*. With an 80 percent increase in home refrigeration in the decade beginning in 1941, Tupperware offered a genuinely unique and innovative alternative to traditional methods of food storage and presentation; furthermore, it had no direct competitors.[42] Yet poised between established markets in fancy goods, utilitarian hardware, gift articles, and luxury housewares, the item remained a mere passing fancy for the modern consumer. Although the Tupper Corporation desperately sought to locate its product in the contemporary domestic sphere, through advertising campaigns and distribution efforts, ultimately it was shifts in gender relations and consumption practices that identified Tupperware as the ideal accoutrement of modern living.

three

• • •

# "Poly-T: Material of the Future"
## A Gift of Modernity

t is a truth of the marketplace that there is no one reason or logic behind the success of one product over another. As anthropologists Mary
Douglas and Baron Isherwood remark, "Goods arrive in the shops
today: some of them will become tomorrow's necessities. What is the direction and power that selects among the modern luxuries and procures
that shift in status so that from being first unknown, then known but dispensable, some goods become indispensable?"[1] Despite the rational explanations of contemporary design commentators of the immediate postwar
period, regarding the utility and aesthetics of the Tupperware objects,
functionalism fails to explain the cultural significance of this range of
polyethylene containers. Tupperware did not evolve as the natural outcome of technological innovation and capitalist entrepreneurialism but as
the result of a dynamic process between production and consumption. As
Claude Fischer, sociologist of technology, asserts, "Mechanical properties
do not predestine the development and employment of an innovation.
Instead, struggles and negotiations among interested parties shape that
history. Inventors, investors, competitors, . . . customers, agencies of
government, the media, and others conflict over how an innovation will
develop."[2]

As a product derived from wartime experiments in plastics technology
and the competition between chemical supply companies (namely
Bakelite, Du Pont, and Dow) to secure domestic markets in a period of

government-imposed rationing, the production of Tupperware was clearly a contested process. Inseparable from this aspect of business history, however, was Tupperware's relation to the changing definitions of the postwar household, consumption practices, and gender roles. The polyethylene innovation turned from an obscure gimmick to a generic product within a decade. And although marketing ploys and advertising campaigns initiated by the Tupper Corporation were an integral part of this process, the shift in Tupperware's status ultimately derived from its reinterpretation and appropriation according to the consumer's response. Earl Tupper consistently mediated consumer reactions to his products and redesigned and marketed his products accordingly. Eager to generate consumer familiarity with the brand but reluctant to jeopardize the reputation for high quality that he envisaged for his product in the long term, Tupper agreed to link up with reputable household brands and use Tupperware as incentive premiums ("giveaways" tied to other branded products). By 1949 Earl Tupper operated as a corporate president overseeing the Tupper Corporation in Farnumsville, Massachusetts, and the sister Tupper plant in Cuero, Texas. Under the sales slogan "Utility Plus Art" the New York showroom promoted the respective wares using the trademarks Millionaire Line, Tupperware, Poly-T, and Tupper-Seal. With the support of John Healy, advertising manager, and Frank Fisher, production manager, Tupper continued to personally oversee the promotion of Tupperware designs throughout his tenure as president in the 1940s through to the late 1950s. These designs and their advertising campaigns manifested the cultural contradictions and urgencies of modern life and its altering values. Despite referring to Tupperware in overtly technological terms, promotional literature generally avoided references to mass production, chemical compounds, or technical details. Instead it sought to locate Tupperware in the everyday lives of modern Americans, bridging the gulf between traditional customs and the newly formulating manners of the postwar home. A *Herald Tribune* houseware editorial of 1948 recommended "feather weight, pliable" Tupperware as the ideal and unusual gift for the fashionable June bride. "The hostess-to-be has a flair for informal entertaining and an eye for modern design," read the feature, and Tupperware, along with "new As-You-Like-It table cloths," was bound to "please young moderns."[3] The quest for an understanding of the female consumer, as a bride-to-be or a "young modern," remained a prerequisite of Tupper's earliest experiments in design and advertising.

## "The Decorum of Things"
### Material Culture and Modern Manners

In his first marketing attempt aimed solely at the domestic consumer, in 1949 Tupper published a mail-order catalog illustrated with product settings in his own New England home and featuring a range of twenty-two standardized Tupperware items. Combining detailed illustrations and copious amounts of instructive text, it read as a manifesto advocating Tupperware as the panacea for modern domestic problems from cocktail mixing to child rearing. As the culmination of Tupper's tacit research into domestic economy and modern manners, the catalog plotted the cultural significance and specificity of objects in every area of the home. Product types were divided loosely into interdependent categories (tableware, food preparation and storage, entertainment and leisure) serving prominent areas of homemaking. As well as offering a range of polyethylene bowls and canisters with flexible, airtight seals, the catalog featured "accessories" (cocktail stirring spoons and poker chips) and gadgets such as the Vacu-Mixer pancake-batter shaker. The Wonder Bowl, a simple container formed from one rounded mold, proved particularly versatile; it was suitable for table use, food preparation and storage, and entertainment and leisure pursuits. Ultimately, design critics and housewares journalists would identify the Wonder Bowl (still in production at the cusp of the twenty-first century) as the exemplary Tupperware article.

Introduced as the revolutionary new material, Poly-T, Tupperware complemented the role of established materials such as china, glass, pottery, silver, and crystal. The products' radically modern look and feel were juxtaposed with the orthodoxy of the traditional domestic sphere, yet the items were carefully mediated using a series of didactic table settings and highly detailed descriptions of their uses. The maintenance of manners, social relations, and domestic rituals associated with such conventional tableware prevailed. "This material is so clean and wholesome of itself that it lends that feeling to the whole table when it is placed there," read one promotional plea.[4] Tupperware might slip reassuringly into the honored position of a floral china dinner or tea service and establish itself as a new form of tableware. "That their design is as modern as the material from which they are fashioned," explained a catalog caption, "yet conforming to the basic principles of good taste, is interesting." It was not a wholly unreasonable proposition that Poly-T might become a generic form of tableware, considering the general decline of the

"Young moderns," a new consumer group identified by postwar houseware editors, had an "eye for modern design" and a preference for informal living. Tupperware's versatile pastel containers were the ideal accoutrement for contemporary entertaining, given the changes in gender roles. Promotional image, ca. 1946. Photo 87.255. Courtesy of Hagley Museum and Library, Wilmington, Delaware.

postwar formal, fine china market, attributed to the resistance of American consumers to "accept modern china for formal dining and entertaining."[5] As an embodiment of the "war-effort," from which polyethylene was derived, it also acted as a symbol of national victory and an expression of patriotic military endeavor and mass production turned to civilian use.

Most significantly, reference to appropriateness and good taste did not revolve around the understanding of the artifacts as ideal, useful, and aesthetically minimalist modernist forms but as the accoutrements of respectable middle-class living. Modernity was proffered in terms of Tupperware's capabilities in "contributing to the gentility of the table and convenience in the kitchen" rather than its ability to bolster the house as a place of rational home economy. Despite Poly-T's promotion as "the material of the future," direct reference to the technology or chemistry

A Tupperware tea service, fashioned from Poly-T, is juxtaposed with the traditional fireside setting of a New England home. The promotion of Tupperware involved the careful negotiation of overtly modern forms among the established material culture and rituals of the American home. Tupper Papers, series 3, box 10, negative 94-13716, Archives Center, National Museum of American History, Smithsonian Institution, Washington, D.C.

of the products was consciously avoided. Instead descriptions alluded to precedents of natural beauty—the organic, mouth-watering assortment of "Soft Glowing Pastel tones—Orange, Lemon, Lime, Raspberry and Plum"; the precious mineralogy of "Frosted Crystal, Ruby, Amber and Sapphire Blue," all found in the wonderment of nature. Later color variations were, according to oral histories, inspired by Earl Tupper's observations of delicate shades of Florida's native orchids.

Similarly, product descriptions making direct editorial reference to aesthetic distinction, such as "simple good taste," related less to the technocratic ideals of modernism and more to the ascetic restraint of Protestantism. References to "chaste lines," "restrained dignity," "clean, graceful paring," and "values of decor" implied that the designs embodied the comfort of moral fortitude. This synthesis of materiality and morality is at the crux of what historians have described as "the Puritan aesthetic"—a notion, some have argued, crucial to the formation of both American history and mass consumption. Similarly the Puritan belief in the potency of icons and the power of material forms underpinned the notion of Tupperware as a humble yet sublime entity, a manifestation of "God's work" in the everyday domestic sphere.[6]

The New England Protestant kitchen held particular resonance in America's cultural history. Throughout the nineteenth century local fairs and international expositions exhibited reproductions of colonial or "olde tyme" kitchens as didactic curiosities and exemplars of Old World domestic values. Kitchens formed the focus of the "Sanitary Fairs" organized as fund-raising events by women's committees to support the Sanitary Commission (a central relief agency and forerunner of the Red Cross). The Brooklyn Fair of 1864, the committee of which was dominated by native New Englanders, featured such an exhibit, of which a local commentator said, "We also have a New England Kitchen, in deference to the powerful and respectable element in our midst, which hails from New England."[7] By the late nineteenth and early twentieth centuries colonial kitchens, with all the moral implications of their cultural origins, became staple facets of permanent museum exhibits as the period room became a common means of representing America's cultural past.[8]

The use of the New England home and kitchen throughout the product catalog, replete with colonial furnishings and traditional household implements, acted as a counteraesthetic to Tupperware's overt modernity. For Tupperware, advertising copy and images suggested, contributed both conceptually and materially to domestic stability and a refined sensibility. It readily assimilated the rituals of etiquette and socialization associated with food and entertainment within the home. According to one catalog description, "Early indoctrination in the fundamentals of gracious living sets a pattern that will endure for years and form a natural feeling for the niceties of life. So, the mother who does not permit even the partaking of midday luncheon by the children in other than an orderly and pleasing manner, uses her Tupperware."[9]

Tupperware was portrayed not as an occasional household implement but as a device to substantiate and expand the values of everyday civility. The home as a site of morality and religious sanctity is a familiar tenet of nineteenth-century American cultural history.[10] The tradition of nineteenth-century domestic reform, led by activists such as Catharine Beecher and Ellen Richards, was carried forward and combined in the twentieth century with ideas of scientific management expounded by an increasingly professionalized body of home economists. Like Tupper, home economists believed in the material transformation of social worlds and "envisioned an ideal consumer society in which producers manufactured high-quality goods for healthful ways of living."[11] But although Tupperware Econo-Canisters and refrigerator bowls seemingly embraced "an ethic of rational consumption," novelty items, such as the Silent Partner Poker Chips and the Tupperware Place Card Holder (a receptacle with holes for cigarettes, a box of matches, and a placecard), clearly did not.[12] They were more in keeping with what Christine Frederick, author of the popular *Selling Mrs. Consumer* (1929), described as products designed to appeal to the "emotional desire for change."

Frederick, herself a prominent advocate of scientific management, signaled a newly forming alliance between manufacturers, advertisers, and home economists when she delivered a speech to the National Retail Institute, "Mrs. Consumer Speaks Her Mind: How Women Look at Your Store," encouraging manufacturers to capitalize on the intuitive desires of the female consumer.[13] Although Frederick's uncompromising involvement with commerce created controversy within her profession, by 1925 an increasing number of corporations had installed home service departments with the specific intention of using home economics to interpret and manipulate consumer activity. By 1929 numerous household manufacturers "employed graduate home economists in research, product development, sales and publicity."[14]

During this period, Corning Glass Works, the producers of the oven-proof glassware Pyrex, sought diligently to transform their product from a gift item and novelty into a staple product; in the process they relied on in-house home economists to interpret the "woman's point-of-view." Through the operations of a consumer service, test kitchen, and field service, home economists contributed directly to the redesign and representation of Pyrex ovenware. In the immediate post–World War II period, traveling home economists visited retail outlets, public utility companies, and schools to demonstrate the merits of Pyrex products and monitor consumer preference. The demonstration of electrical ranges through cooking lessons was a familiar policy of corporations advising consumers of new technologies in the 1920s. But in marked contrast the Corning field representatives of the 1940s openly "functioned as surrogate salespeople and as market researchers."[15]

The Tupper Corporation was presented with a problem similar to that of the Corning Glass Works: how to turn an innovative household product from a mere gift and novelty item to a staple or generic form. Pyrex benefited from its team of home economists to assess consumer requirements, but the Tupper Corporation relied on Tupper's tacit research and ideological preaching to control "Mrs. Homemaker's" demand for Tupperware products. Despite promotional initiatives, such as the descriptive mail-order catalog and in-store demonstrations, Tupperware sales languished until the formal instigation of the Tupperware party plan direct sales scheme in 1951. As well as providing a unique form of retail distribution, the party plan system, like the Corning Glass Works field representative demonstrations, provided a forum for market research and consumer contact that fed directly back into the design and manufacturing process.[16] This would prove far more effective than the rhetoric of mail-order catalogs and department store displays in cultivating the attention of the modern housewife. The politics of the home, however, and debates around consumption and gender embodied in the construct of the "New Woman" and later the convivial "hostess" remained pivotal to the meanings generated around Tupperware.

## Mass Consumption and the Legacy of the "New Woman"

From the rise of the department store to the propagandist role of the consumer-citizen, women have stood at the forefront of changes in capitalist consumer society.[17] Their social roles and cultural identities have been inscribed with the moral contentions and meanings of consumption. In turn-of-the-century America, for example, the term "New Woman" was coined to describe a form of modern femininity popularized through a range of interchangeable images "from the mannish reformer, professional woman, and earnest labor activist, to the free-spirited outdoor girl and sexually assertive flapper."[18] By the 1920s and 1930s, contemporary fears associated with the emancipation of women and the decline of the American character focused on the "New Woman" and her relation to new modes of consumptive activity. During the 1920s home economists and social reformers advocated the professionalization of women's roles as homemakers and consumers in response to technological, economic, and political changes. "Back to the home" campaigns sought to allay fears regarding the newly ambiguous roles of modern women. In this context the image of the "matronly shopper" acknowledged the constructive, rather than potentially subversive, aspects of the woman's role as consumer. "Ignoring the fundamental inequality of woman's economic dependence on her spouse, writers argued that by consuming correctly she [the matronly shopper] could produce more wealth, ensure family happiness, and even contribute to national well-being," writes one historian.[19]

In dramatic contrast to this "homely" feminine construct stood the all-consuming siren. A self-indulgent woman, freed from household drudgery by labor-saving devices to wile away her time in nonproductive pursuits, she shopped as an act of pleasure, self-fulfillment, and autonomy rather than household provisioning. As a familiar stereotype the siren, an icon of artificial beauty (with "ruby lips, painted nails, bleached hair, and heavily shadowed eyes") was summoned up as the specter of modern consumer culture and moral decline. This interpretation of the New Woman focused fears regarding class, gender, and ethnicity during a period when working-class women and immigrants were defining themselves through consumption as newly independent groups.[20] To quote historian Ellen Wiley Todd, "At a time when traditional masculine prerogatives seemed compromised by unemployment and the resulting inability to support a family, an energetic sexualized female figure could be interpreted as a defiant threat to masculine claims to social and economic power."[21]

The creation of feminine identities through affiliation with specific types of consumer products, it has been argued, enabled women to challenge traditionally prescribed class and social positions. In 1938, notes historian Kathy Peiss, the Volupté cosmetics firm launched two new lipsticks named "Lady" and "Hussy"—the first offered subtle tones and a "soft mat finish"; the other, the potential to shock with a bright "gleaming lustre." Hussy, it was said, outsold Lady five to one. The manufacturers of such products utilized the ambiguous history of cosmetics (just two decades before Hussy's and Lady's release, women using cosmetics had been condemned as prostitutes and social outcasts) to promote the modernity of their wares.[22] Obviously lipstick did not liberate women from their economically, ethnically, and socially bound positions, but as a morally contested product it symbolized the paradoxes of social identity in a period of shifting gender roles; in this broad sense, consumption might be viewed as a politicized act.[23]

Earl Tupper certainly recognized a market for a new female consumer and, before inventing Tupperware, devised a number of specialized products aimed at the sassy New Woman. In 1935 he invented and patented the Double Cigarette Holder, "designed to ensure the pleasure and economy of being able to smoke the entire cigarette or its parts," based on a new idea from Paris for a "cross between a cigarette holder and a Lady's pipe."[24] Similarly his paint-on nail decorations and Sweetie Picture Buckle belts courted the frivolity and frippery associated, by some critics, with the whimsical figure of the modern woman. Yet despite his enthusiastic acknowledgment of feminine popular culture, he vehemently chided what he described as the cheap and tawdry woman, "so common today" as a cigarette-smoking, bridge-playing, "useless bit of female humanity." He contrasted this worthless, all-consuming urban female with the wholesome productivity of a matronly rural woman he encountered at a local New England fair:

> The Colonial Village [at the Springfield eastern sales fair] was good, and one of the most beautiful sights was a motherly old fashioned lady who took batches of several colors of wool that had been clipped, washed and dyed. . . . Talking sweetly all of the time, explaining the whole procedure, she proceeded to spin . . . right before our eyes . . . it is hard for me to find any words . . . that are fitting to describe such a mighty thing as we had witnessed.[25]

The "old fashioned lady" at the Colonial Village signified longevity and wisdom rather than the transience of popular consumer culture and ill-conceived trends. Most importantly she represented the supremacy of the productive, white Anglo-Saxon woman, a prolific patriotic figure summoned in contrast to the all-consuming specter of the working-class immigrant masses.

During the 1930s the traditionalism of the colonial revival was epitomised by the restoration of an entire community in Virginia—Colonial Williamsburg—that was fully completed in 1935 as a testament to American colonial history. Depicted as the "Cradle of the Republic," Williamsburg benefited from $79 million of financial support from John D. Rockefeller Jr., used to demolish hundreds of post-eighteenth-century buildings and reroute a railroad in pursuit of a restored colonial atmosphere.[26] By 1932, costumed guides showed visitors around the heritage site, promoting the cultural and civic values of the colonial period, while Rockefeller claimed the restoration project "teaches of the patriotism, high purpose, and unselfish devotion of our forefathers to the common good."[27] Similarly, Henry Ford's 1930s outdoor museum, Greenfield Village, was dedicated to the entrepreneur's depiction and glorification of America's colonial past.

The colonial revival, then, captured the national popular imagination as effectively as the geometric visions of modernity proffered by the New York World's Fair of 1939, where enthusiastic visitors celebrated the experience with the purchase of souvenir salt-and-pepper shakers in the shape of the exhibit's trademark Trylon and Perisphere edifices. Despite the modern symbolism of such souvenirs, these modernist mementos were outsold by the traditional forms of ceramic mugs featuring a stream-lined profile of George Washington that lent him "the rakish air of a neo-colonial hood ornament," showing the contrived appeal of nostaligic nationalist representation.[28]

During the Depression, social experiments such as Arthurdale, funded under the auspices of the 1933 National Industrial Recovery Act, became a beacon of Roosevelt's New Deal efforts to reinstate community among dislocated rural and industrial workers. Presided over by Eleanor Roosevelt, Arthurdale, West Virginia, was constructed as a self-sufficient community modeled on nostalgic ideas of colonial homesteads. The workers incorporated colonial country crafts such as furniture making and metalworking into their daily lives. A weaving room, situated close to the community center, was built to enable women to make "coverlets, aprons, towels, place mats, napkins, draperies, belts, handbags, pillows, neckties, scarves, babies blankets, bedspreads, and rugs" for Arthurdale dwellers and for commercial sale to other states and countries.[29] Members of an organization called the Mountaineer Craftsmen's Cooperative Association produced a catalog of goods produced at the Arthurdale forge, including candlesticks, pitchers, bowls, and teapots made as authentic copies of colonial pieces under the tutelage of metalworker James Londus Fullmer.[30] The material culture of the colonial period symbolized an enduring integrity and authority that contrasted sharply with flimsy, mass-produced goods of modern consumer culture.

The inconsistencies of Tupper's own inventions and ideologies reveal the contradictions inherent in the negotiation of modernity during this period. Despite his desire to keep ahead of modern fashions, especially those emanating from the Old World cosmopolitanism of Europe (rather than the brash materialism of America), he sought to combine these influences with a traditional appreciation for vernacular handicrafts; for "unlike writing, talking or indirect day dreaming," he wrote, "handicrafts do not entertain any high flown abstractions."[31] The romanticized pragmatism of the "motherly old fashioned" woman at the spinning wheel in the Colonial Village exemplified hope "for the stability and future of the entire human race." In a 1937 diary entry Tupper lamented the human wastage through time spent over the card table, the bar, on commercialized sport and petty gambling, activities that undermined the potential of modern American citizens. But a decade after denouncing such amoral pursuits, he promoted a range of cigarette cases, Silent Poker Chips, and cocktail tumblers that blatantly celebrated these activities. By the 1940s, however, Tupper had cast their meanings in the broader terms of household provisioning, where sociality was brought back to the home rather than conducted in harshly commercial public bars and gaming rooms.

Unlike modernist stylists with their "high flown abstractions," Tupper invested his designs with a tacit wisdom and acute observation of human relations. He sought to meld conservatism and innovation in a "definite workable reality" to remedy the discontents of modern life. Mass production and big business, he believed, were wrongly blamed by the people of the United States for the "high tension, restless seemingly futile life" of contemporary experience. Rather, he asserted, it was the misuse and mismanagement of such forms of production, and the indolence of the masses, that led to widespread dissatisfaction. Hobbies, which captured the "wonderful thing, the creation of a basic product from raw materials" merged with the individuality of the producer, would give the consuming masses "an opportunity to search themselves," surmised Tupper, as a means of combining the Protestant work ethic and modern leisure. In 1937, during his earliest plastics experiments, Tupper devised a celluloid handicraft kit for boys clubs. A unisex version, "for young people to make useful articles from Du Pont plastics," included designs for a ring and bracelet, a napkin ring, initials, a horse's head, and lucky charms.[32] The handicraft kits embraced the details and iconography of mass culture and simultaneously remedied its negative ramifications of passivity and alienation. So too did Tupper's numerous designs for gifts, items that were not essentially useful but that enhanced and expanded the intricate practices and fashions of modern social relations.

Definitions of work and leisure became highly charged during the Depression, when so many people were out of work, and the New Deal created work-relief schemes. A moral debate arose regarding the detrimental effects of entertainment and mass culture on an already paralyzed society. In this context, as social historian Steven Gelber argues, "The word 'hobby' became a strategic term used less to be descriptive than to carry the weight of authoritative approval when applied to individual activities. In other words, the term 'hobby', as used in the Thirties, was more an ideological construct created to distinguish between 'good' and 'bad' pastimes, than a natural category of leisure activity."[33]

The pro-active terms of "making," "doing," "acquiring," and "learning" outlined in Earnest Elmo Calkins's influential book, *The Care and Feeding of the Hobby Horse* (1934), emphasized the importance of active participation as a measure of the appropriate use of leisure time. In their public discussions, social commentators, educators, religious figures, and government officials invested the hobby with moral legitimacy; productive pastimes might prevent individuals from turning to "carnal, physical and passive diversions, weak in philosophic merit."[34] Tupper designed commodities for the vagaries of an expanding mass culture, but his pursuits derived from the seemingly incongruous ideals of the Protestant work ethic, nostalgia of the colonial revival, and moral righteousness of social reform. He sought to combine the worthiness of hobbies and home-crafts with the benefits of mass consumer society in the form of "productive" or thrift-based products, but he also pursued the novelty market out of necessity.

If "the hobby" opened out the domestic sphere in its redefinition of masculine leisure and work, by the 1940s the notion of the "hostess," rather than the mere housewife or homemaker, transformed definitions of women's domestic labor. The term "hostess" inferred entertainment, conviviality, and increased consumption. Not the wanton, selfish consumption of "cigarette smoking, bridge playing" women but the participatory provisioning of a thoughtful hostess knowledgeable in contemporary mores and values. Opening up the previously private sphere of the home to the brand names and consumer goods of the public sphere, the hostess made the ideal accomplice for the advertisers. In the context of post-Depression culture the hostess replaced the ideal of the thrifty housewife (a woman capable of rustling up a family meal with just a box of grits) with a glamorous but equally resourceful woman geared to home entertainment and fashionable but informal gestures of hospitality.

In the 1940s, the advent of the accomplished hostess and her convivial role outlined the "home" and "housework" as expanding denotations. But her image was not confined to the pages of glossy homemaking magazines. "Mrs.-Three-in-One"—the woman who had to be guest, waitress, and cook at her own dinner parties—was described in contemporary etiquette manuals as the personification of a dilemma that left servantless middle-class housewives responsible for both the manual labor of preparation and the pleasantries of entertainment.[35] Historians discuss the transition of women's housework during this period from the realm of simple manual labor and household organization to one of emotional and moral responsibility subject to immense social scrutiny, a transition that apparently disguised the reality of women's increased labor. Consequently the practices and social foibles associated with the role of the housewife as hostess have been seen as little more than trivial and misguided responses to the repressive nature of enforced domesticity—a degenerate form of domesticity, which, according to some historians, led to the regressive and confining role of women in the 1950s. "By raising vegetables in their backyards, crocheting afghans, knitting argyle socks, entertaining at barbecues, hiding appliances behind artificial wood paneling, giving homemade breads for Christmas presents," women were guilty of merely glossing over the "proletarianization" of housework, suggests Ruth Schwartz Cowan in her seminal history of housework, *More Work for Mother*.[36] According to such accounts, by the postwar period "ideological props," such as flower arranging and homecrafts, formed part of a "backward search for femininity" that disguised the real nature of women's labor.

The image of the hostess, delineated in Betty Friedan's book *The Feminine Mystique* as "the happy housewife heroine," originated, then, in the prewar popularization of the home as an arena of aestheticized self-provisioning, entertainment, modernity, and conviviality. The depiction of the happy hostess and home entertainment certainly alluded to the niceties of middle-class lifestyles and a standard of living clearly inaccessible to the majority of American households, even during a period of increased affluence. Not only was the housewife of 1940 "expected to spend much more time with her children than her mother had spent," she was also expected to aim for the middle-class standard of living depicted in the plethora of new and expanding women's and home-oriented magazines.[37]

From 1949 onward, Tupperware catered to the modern hostess's "attention to the nicest details of entertainment" with designs such as the Tupperware Place Card Holder, the Tupper Styrene Sandwich and Food Guides (picks with labels for identifying and picking up food), and Tupper Food Spears (for impaling olives, pickles, and stuffed celery), incorporating modern technology into the minutiae of everyday rituals.[38] Appealing to the "pleasures" of modern entertaining, the catalog noted that "such accessories as these are essential to the hostess who wants all her invitations eagerly sought after. Things like these add the dash of piquancy; the 'soupçon' of gay informality and a fine sense of the 'eternal fitness of things' to an otherwise mediocre expression of intimate hospitality."[39]

Artifacts such as Tupperware Place Card Holder and the functionally defective but ultramodern-looking tea/coffee set positioned Tupperware as an indispensable accoutrement of modern life. The niceties associated with gestures of hospitality were no longer confined to the middle-class parlor; informal entertainment opened up homes across America as sites of leisure and conviviality in the post-Depression era. Events such as the cocktail party and the finger buffet defied the stark rationalism of early-twentieth-century scientific management theories that sought to reform the inefficient practices of traditional homemaking. Taylorist visions of housewives as supplanted factory operatives measuring time, motion, and money in a drive for greater productivity were contradicted by these overtly labor-intensive displays of sociality.

To link such socially aspiring scenes with widely accessible brand-name consumer goods, such as Tupperware and Coca-Cola, was to open up modern manners and rituals to women formerly precluded by social, economic, or ethnic delineation from the broader benefits of modernity. Activities such as home decoration and flower arranging valorized household labor. It is crucial to understand that considerations such as good taste and modern manners were not merely the trappings of an aspiring middle class, for, as one historian points out, "from the perspective of the poor housewife in the early decades of the twentieth century, housework was not just work; when it could be done productively, it was a ticket to a better future for her family."[40]

Just as Tupperware's 1949 catalog appealed to good taste within the home, and the integration of commodities as useful adjuncts of modern living and manners, a 1940s marketing campaign for Coca-Cola utilized the cult of flower arranging in the domestication of its "perfect refreshment."[41] As the Depression inspired a rise in hobbies and do-it-yourself home-based activities, because of the prohibitive expense of commercial entertainment and an ideological shift toward "the simple pleasures of life," so too the role of "hostess" constructed the woman as a productive consumer forging public and private spheres.[42] By the early 1940s flower arranging, which combined homemaking skills, artistry, and public and private display, played an increasing role in the modern middle-class home. In 1941, Richardson Wright, editor-in-chief of *House and Garden* magazine and chairman of the International Flower Show Committee, described how the display of flower arrangements at horticultural shows had developed an "art obscurely pursued at home" into a "nation-wide cultural interest."[43]

In a series of volumes sponsored by the Coca-Cola Corporation, brightly colored illustrations revealed the secrets of successful flower arranging to the enthusiastic hostess. Seasonal and historical themes, oriental motifs, and bridal table designs were depicted against backdrops of modern household furnishings. "Femininity personified," a posy of drooping fuschia and tightly clustered violets, made a setting with "feminine . . . Victorian accents." "Corsages for the Guests," made from camellias, gardenias, orchids, or similar flowers, included a table setting diagram to illustrate their proper positioning. As an ultimate expression of hospitality and modernity, "ice-cold bottles of Coca-Cola in heirloom silver, a kitchen pan, a glass bowl, alone in a wheelbarrow" complemented the array of floral decorations. The booklets assured that despite lavish and elaborate backdrops, social decorum would be enhanced through the obvious display of Coca-Cola as a centerpiece of home entertaining. Hostesses were instructed in the correct handling of a beverage that "gains momentum daily." Most significantly the drinks should never be served separately from the distinctive packaging of their branded bottles. "Make opening and drinking a simultaneous action, so that you lose none of the sparkle . . . the majority of people prefer the out-of the-bottle method," recommended the booklets.[44] Like Tupperware, this branded commodity demanded a specific form of etiquette that only women privy to new realms of cultural knowledge, such as the secrets of flower arranging, might learn. Women disappointed in their ability to master this form of artistry, the publications advised, should relax and console themselves with an ice-cold bottle of Coca-Cola. Corporate promotional campaigns such as these bolstered the shift from ordinary to urbane provisioning. They depicted events ranging from the Boy Scout barbecue night to the teenage party and the bridge game, in which the branded consumer goods formed an indispensable facet of modern life, "adaptable to every occasion, to every environment."[45] Mass-produced commodities, far from being at odds with the intimacies of domesticity, provided the very cornerstone upon which they were constructed. This highly self-conscious promotional strategy acknowledged the significance of the domestic sphere, and its workings, in ensuring the successful social incorporation of commodities. Though top industrial designer Raymond Loewy redesigned the Coca-Cola bottle in a bid to increase sales, the corporation's flower-arranging campaigns are far more indicative of the means by which goods "shift in status so that from being first unknown, then known but dispensable, . . . become indispensable."[46] Like the 1947 *House Beautiful* editorial by Elizabeth Gordon, which described Tupperware as "Fine Art for 39 Cents" and ideal "shining points of interest" for the guest's dinner table, the Coca-Cola flower-arranging booklets embraced the home as an increasingly public sphere requiring new forms and objects of consumption.

## A "Premium" Product
### Tupperware in a Gift Economy

"Alienable" commodities—mass produced products with no prior social ties to dictate the nature of their exchange or the relationship of their transactors—form the basis of an efficient capitalist economy. Unlike the artifacts of premodern or noncapitalist societies, commodities are the most expedient expression of the logic of capital: priced and packaged, ready to be bought and sold with maximum ease. "Inalienable" objects—those operating within the realm of social ties, such as having religious significance or the familial ties of inheritance or sentiment—counter the forces of market exchange. According to these classic anthropological definitions, the "gift" stands as the archetypal inalienable object; bounded as it is by such social ties as sentiment and reciprocity, it is commonly contrasted with the supreme exchangeability of the capitalist commodity, a mere thing with no strings attached. These once rigidly defined categories of "gift" and "commodity" have more recently been challenged as oversimplifications.[47] In this context, according to some social scientists, the role of gift giving has been systematically underestimated as a component of contemporary capitalist consumer culture; commodities are just as likely in industrial societies to take on the social meanings and significances traditionally attributed to the "gift."[48] Yet, despite the many studies in material culture asserting that artifacts cannot be separated from the context of the social relations and modes of acquisition, historians of contemporary design, like market economists, seem reluctant to acknowledge the significance of such contexts. As anthropologist John Davis observes, "When you see an advertisement that suggests goods are ideal for gifts you might consider the possibility that manufacturers, like anthropologists, know more about the motives for exchange than marketist economists do."[49]

When Tupperware was first featured in *Time* magazine, in September 1947, the article described how the product, yet to establish a secure marketing base, had first been introduced to the public as packaging and premiums (gifts).[50] Red Rooster cheese products, for example, were packed in a Tupperware Poker Chip Rack "as a most appropriate and congenial merchandising companion . . . known and approved by discriminating hostesses in every income bracket."[51] Poly-T cigarette cases acted as premiums for Camel cigarettes, and Better Brushes direct sales distributors gave away "hundreds of thousands of the pastel tumblers" as "door-openers" and gifts with designated purchases. "More than a million prospective retail purchasers of Tupperware" reported the sales concern Premium Practice, "are receiving their first Tupper products as premiums, re-use containers, advertising specialities and business gifts."[52] Under the heading "Hang Your Stocking This Christmas, Mr. Manufacturer," the Tupper Corporation offered a series of potential gift packaging. "Tupper gives your product the package that is the premium!" exclaimed the accompanying slogan.[53]

It was its significance as a gift, rather than a merely functional commodity, that secured Tupperware's first commercial market. During this period, "jobbers" (merchandisers ordering and overseeing wholesale goods to sell to retail stores) acted as crucial emissaries and instigators in the introduction of everyday plastic articles to the consumer public. Products were aimed not merely at existing markets; they were designed specifically in response to its changing and ever-expanding requirements. Trade publications such as *The Retail Tobacconist (Tobacco Products, Smokers Articles, Confectionery, Beverages, Stationery, Toys)* and *Gift Preview: The Buyer's Guide to What's New in Gifts and Decorative Accessories,* both of which contained advertisements for the Tupperware Millionaire Line of party bowls, tumblers, smoking accessories, and social sundries, kept jobbers informed of the latest developments in product gifts and novelties.[54]

Although women constituted a vital market in the consumption of novelty goods and gifts, as Tupper's earliest informal market research had shown, novelty designs also appealed to men; yet the marketing of such items adhered to notably traditional notions of male behavior and highly practical representations of the artifact's associated properties. "The shape of things to come — a telescope cigarette case," read the copy for a Tup-

In 1947 the Tupper Corporation advertised in trade publications such as *Retail Tobacconist* to reach the growing consumer market in novelties, gifts, and tobacco-associated sundries. Tupper Papers, series 3, box 7, Archives Center, National Museum of American History, Smithsonian Institution, Washington, D.C.

per King Cigarette case retailing at thirty-nine cents in a 1940s edition of the *Tobacco Jobber*. "You can throw it, drop it, sit on it, jump on it—it still won't break . . . but don't throw it at your mother-in-law. It's so smooth and phantom in weight it wouldn't hurt her anyway. . . . The price is almost as low as her opinion of you."[55] Similarly an advertisement in *Sports News* overcame the potential embarrassment of promoting housewares to men by emphasizing that polyethylene had been an "indestructible covering for assault wire" during the war. Under the title "New Handy Equipment," the feature spoke mockingly of Tupperware containers as an antidote to the inconvenient effects of "civilizing" feminine intervention: "Along came Tupper Plastics with the answer for hungry husbands who have been domesticated to the point where they feel uncomfortable eating from the pot with their bare hands."[56]

The Depression had focused attention on self-sufficiency and thrift, and it also had made domestic entertainment popular, forming the context of numerous new items of consumption, each of which belonged to its own specific "system of provision."[57] Changes in modern manners and habits, and accompanying material culture, challenged assumptions regarding popular behavior and social identities; for example, bridge parties (once the preserve of the upper middle classes) and cigarettes and alcohol (once the preserve of men's social life) opened up through the popularization and "democratization" of related products. Such changes, as Michael Schudson points out in his historical study of the integral relation between American culture and the rise of advertising, were not merely the result of producers' and mass marketers' manipulation techniques but were the consumers' own culturally initiated appropriations of socially useful commodities. Cigarettes evolved as a new form of social currency among women, as a "cheap visible . . . identifying mark, both easily flaunted and easily hidden, a topic of talk, a token of comradeship, and to boot a comfort in anxious moments."[58] The cigarette defined a new sense of modernity that challenged divisions of public and private worlds. Between 1918 and 1940 American cigarette tobacco consumption increased from 1.7 to 5.16 pounds (77 grams to 2.3 kilograms) per adult. Consumed individually or offered as a gesture of hospitality to friends or strangers, the cigarette and its accoutrements were used to forge modern identities.[59]

The Tupper Plastic Company's promotion of its earliest commercial products as gifts, affiliated with new manners such as smoking, reveals the significance of the gift economy as a means of introducing socially salient but alien commodities to consumers. Historical shifts in gender relations also proved key to the design and marketing of such products.[60] With no direct precursors, Tupperware intermittently benefited and faltered through its lack of affiliation with a discernible commodity type.

Department stores and hardware stores, ca. 1947, used static displays of the product range to sell Tupperware (referred to, at this stage, as "Tupper Poly-T Products" and marketed as "smooth, odorless, tasteless, non-toxic"). Tupper Papers, series 3, box 10, negative 94-13714, Archives Center, National Museum of American History, Smithsonian Institution, Washington, D.C.

Although Tupper used a distribution method that circulated novelties, gadgets, and inexpensive gifts as mass-produced premiums, he recognized the potentially detrimental aspects of commodities and their associated meanings. Corporate memos reveal how Tupper summoned up the specter of the "dog dish," a cheap plastic item used extensively during this period as a premium, as the antithesis of the Tupperware product. Consumers, he advised, must be protected from the unfortunate and arbitrary associations between the two products. For Tupper the plastic dog dish exemplified all the negative connotations of unbridled mass production and consumption, whereby a truly transformative technology was reduced to a debased and degraded form fit only for animal use. For ideological reasons, as much as long-term marketing aims, the Tupper Corporation thwarted numerous demeaning manufacturing contracts and overcame the temptation of "greed for quick dollar returns" at great immediate loss to corporate finances. "We turned down several offers to manufacture special[s] or sell products for dog feeding dishes," wrote Tupper, "because we did not want Mrs. Jones to say 'Oh yes. I've seen those flexible dishes X Dog Food is giving one as a pet's feeding dish.'"[61] In their introduction of a new commodity to the consumer market, the Tupper Corporation was highly conscious of the specificity of values operating around commodity forms and their acquisition.

A thriving postwar gift economy formed an essential market for new consumer goods, particularly alienable plastic items that suffered from their ambiguous reputation. Tupperware was eased into the home both as a useful household aid and as an ideal gift. Its relationship to social activities, such as gift giving, imbued the houseware with social significance beyond that of a purely utilitarian commodity. Similarly, the postwar woman's shift from "housewife" to "hostess" gave housewares a newfound significance in terms of style and function. The Tupperware party, a direct sales scheme that exalted gifts and premiums, sociality and domesticity in a conspicuous display of consumption, ultimately provided the ideal means of product distribution. Most importantly the Tupperware party, like the marketing devices of product catalogs and booklets, generated consensus about new household practices and goods.

In 1948, however, the Tupper Corporation continued to pursue several modes of distribution in an attempt to domesticate the Tupperware brand. Despite positive editorial reports, the support of the plastics industry, and the use of premium campaigns, stacks of unsold Tupperware collected dust on the shelves of hardware stores across the United States.

f   o   u   r

•   •   •

# "The  Hostess  with  the  Mostest"
## The Origins of the Home Party Plan

B y the late 1940s, despite retailing efforts that included mail-
order distribution and premium and packaging contracts, Tupperware had failed to penetrate the domestic market in any substantial
quantities.[1] Although *Time* magazine reported that a hospital for the mentally ill in Massachusetts found the product "an almost ideal replacement
for its noisy, easily battered aluminum cups and plates" (as patients could
only damage the polyethylene by persistent chewing), Earl Tupper's vision
of the nationwide "Tupperization" of American homes had yet to be
realized.

A concerted public relations campaign between 1946 and 1948
secured manufacturing agreements with companies such as Thermos
Vacuum Bottle and Red Rooster cheese products (to provide incidental
parts and packaging). Consequently the Tupper Corporation's working
capital increased several fold (following a substantial deficit in 1946),
prompting the lending bank manager to suggest sharing a "banana royal"
with Earl Tupper at the local Howard Johnson hotel in celebration of the
company's "big jump in the right direction" and its "more encouraging
picture" of financial growth.[2] Although this trade in containers, parts, and
premiums turned the Tupper Corporation to profit, it failed to make
Tupperware a household name. And Tupper craved recognition of his
product as an outstanding, branded commodity in its own right.

In 1947, the Millionaire Line, a collection of Tupperware consciously targeted at the discerning upscale consumer, was launched in reputable East Coast department stores. Building on intensive public relations campaigns in both the trade and consumer press, the Tupper Corporation strove to expand domestic consumption in the top-end market. Advance publicity aimed to soften consumer resistance in preparation for the expanding national department store promotion that placed Tupperware in almost two hundred cities across the United States. A tie-in feature in *Look* magazine on "alfresco dining" (which included glamorous photographic shots of Helena Rubenstein's New York apartment terrace) showed Tupperware as the ideal container for sophisticated cold soups. A Boston-based advertising company, Chambers and Wiswell, debuted the Millionaire Line (which included pitchers, novel tumblers, cocktail mixers, poker chips, and refrigerator dishes) at New England's largest department store, Jordan Marsh. Within a month Gimbel's and Bloomingdale's of New York City ran advertising campaigns that utilized contemporary graphic design and presentation techniques in the form of complete introductory pamphlets, four-color booklets, and descriptive leaflets.[3] Complementary window displays featured apron-clad mannequin "housewives" gleefully incorporating the product into their mock-kitchen settings.

Ironically the most significant outcome of this department store retailing campaign, which drew on associations with "artful living" and "alfresco dining," was its reliance on the amateur direct selling techniques of traditional street traders. On-site promotional teams (which even included Chambers and Wiswell's vice president and account executive) physically demonstrated Tupperware products to passing shoppers within the department stores. They entreated passing customers to grab a Tupperware container and "yank it, bang it, jump on it."[4] Consumer resistance and antipathy toward plastics necessitated a scheme that would instill the palpability of Tupperware's revolutionary characteristics in a wary consumer public. In-store demonstrations not only increased the product's visual and physical presence, they also assisted the advertising agency in gauging customer reaction. Hands-on demonstrations placed the Tupperware products quite literally in the hands of the consumer in a way that editorial features, glowing as they were, failed to do.

Despite the intensity of the short-term "yank it, bang it, jump on it" campaign, this interactive form of advertising and sales demonstration proved prohibitively costly, labor intensive, and time consuming; demonstration teams could not be considered a long-term solution to raising the profile of the Millionaire Line. But without physical demonstration, consumers remained uninspired by the product's minimal visual impact, comparatively high price tag, and noninteractive shelf displays. In recognition of this problem Earl Tupper devised an elaborate self-service contraption to combat indifference toward his product. The Tupper Self-Merchandising Sales Display Stand arranged products in a cascade of polyethylene, cleverly designed to ensure "one item help[ed] to sell the other." The stand, aimed at selected chain stores and independent dealers, maintained uniformity and exclusivity of display. "Thus the prices and merchandising methods," read an accompanying document, "will be maintained on the highest possible level, protecting the investment of the top grade merchants who handle the Tupper Corporation line." Countering the "careless merchandising" and "cut-throat price tactics" of unscrupulous retailers, the merchandising system aimed to secure an exclusive market for Tupperware. Other concerns such as "Expensive gift shops," "top ranking Department stores (they add prestige)," and "Hotel and Restaurant and Club suppliers" were identified as "outlets which are not in direct competition with our display merchandise."[5] Extensive newspaper advertising, department store promotions, and elaborate self-serve shelving systems made little impact on securing mass consumer interest.

The competitive market in home products during this period spanned a range of retailing and distributive areas. Catalogs such as Sears and Roebuck's offered staple kitchenware including enamel storage containers and tin colanders as well as an abundance of more obscure or novelty items. Individual manufacturers, typified by the Tupper Corporation and Corning Glass Works, offered their own specialized product catalogs aimed at both retail and domestic customers. Independent hardware stores, the homeware sections of department stores, and specialized gift shops offered classic homeware, such as ceramic mixing bowls and aluminum sieves, and an expanding array of modern gadgets. Traditional hardware stores peppered their stock with the occasional state-of-the-art gadget, whereas department stores used sophisticated product displays and sales promotions in the local newspapers to boost their sales. In general terms, the array of new consumer products available in the immediate postwar period led to their increasingly diverse and frequently obscure uses.[6]

In 1948 the National Housewares Manufacturers Association (NHMA) held its annual trade show in Atlantic City and hosted approximately 10,000 buyers, manufacturers, and product representatives from across the country. The increasingly cut-throat nature of the home goods market, with unscrupulous manufacturers using showcases such as Atlantic City as a means of sourcing copy-cat designs, caused the NHMA to introduce urgent security measures to ensure that only bonafide buyers could enter the exhibit.[7] The awards made by a panel of judges presiding over the Atlantic City exhibit, which included the president of the National Safety Council, the director of the Good Housekeeping Institute, and the editor of *House and Garden* magazine, highlighted the direction of the contemporary housewares market. The top-ranking nominees included the Hotlifter (a mechanical holder for hot potatoes), the Smoker's Robot (a device for smoking in bed), and Tupperware tumblers ("cannot break, chip, or crack"), all of which received Honorable Mentions. The properties of these artifacts, which epitomized popular expressions of modernity, were couched by the organizers in terms of health and safety measures. The NHMA, in addition to publicly promoting technical innovation and improved standards, was responding to the increasingly vociferous criticism from the American Consumer's Union regarding the inanity of contemporary household appliances.[8] In 1948 retail home products traversed definitions of utility, novelty, gadgetry, and fashion, and outlets responded accordingly in their attempts to capture the growing consumer market and placate potential critics.

The Tupper Corporation's initial forays into formal department store retailing succeeded in fairly localized terms. Individual stores sold the occasional item through in-store demonstration and display, but as a branded product Tupperware remained ineffective. While intensive advertising campaigns were giving exposure to the polyethylene containers in prestigious department stores and fashionable home journals with only limited success, a largely unacknowledged force of merchandisers was quietly but surely introducing Tupperware directly to the homes of everyday Americans. Door-to-door salespeople appropriated Tupperware, lightweight and stackable, as an ideal article for direct sales demonstration. By the late 1940s several established direct sales companies and individuals selling household products (ranging from cleaning fluid to baby bottles) used innovative products, such as Tupperware, to brighten up a fading stock and maintain consumer interest. Because individual door-to-door dealers acquired their goods independently, ordering from the Tupperware catalog, sales statistics did not recognize them as a specific retailing force. Although the Tupper Corporation acknowledged "Home Demonstration Companies" as useful channels of distribution (one memo noted that "they arouse interest in the products"), on the whole they were viewed as peripheral and inconsequential outlets.[9]

Plastic goods, in general, proved particularly popular as direct sales merchandise. Highly portable, multifarious in their uses and decorative appeal, new plastic items were fashionable, affordable, and considerably more enticing, through demonstration, than traditional household goods. Stanley Home Products Incorporated, the leading home demonstration company of this period, encouraged direct sales recruits to view the demonstration process as "a moving picture that makes the customer see what you see." This highly visual and tactile form of retailing, which amounted to a performance transforming inanimate artifacts into desirable commodities, provided the key to domestic success. Demonstration within the home, the center of consumption and social relations, magnified the immediacy and value of the product considerably.

## "The Modern Way to Shop"
### Courting the Modern Hostess

"Hostess parties," which evolved from ordinary door-to-door sales, proved the ideal vehicle for introducing unfamiliar products to the cautious homemaker. Formally devised in the 1920s by Wearever Aluminum Cooking Products, the sales scheme served as a practical means of showing wares to a gathered audience within the home. It proved a particularly popular method of distribution in areas where occupants had limited access to formal retail outlets, such as rural neighborhoods. Earl Tupper, himself a rural dweller, was familiar with the practice, noting in his journal in 1933 that Marie had "just returned from her mother's where someone gave an aluminum ware demonstration."[10] Indeed, during the Depression direct selling schemes boomed because of mass unemployment. Unlike mainstream market activity, direct selling peaked during times of economic recession by harnessing a displaced work force and offering a form of casual labor that required minimal capital outlay, formal skills, or professional qualifications.

Although derived in the 1920s from a traditional peddling tradition, the hostess party was hailed as the "Modern Way to Shop," as a typical promotional plea read; it combined a unique appeal to modernity, domesticity, and consumption and consequently evolved as the quintessential postwar direct sales method.[11] The scheme involved women meeting under the auspices of sociality in the home of a volunteered "hostess." The hostess lent the hospitality of her home and gathered a range of friends and neighbors as an audience for the product salesperson or dealer. After light refreshments and a demonstration, the product dealer encouraged the captive audience to take advantage of the ideal opportunity to purchase. The hostess, dependent on the generosity of her friends and neighbors, received a gift product directly related to the amount of sales accrued at her party. The direct sales network expanded with the recruitment by the dealer of further hostesses at each home party. Hostesses were keenly encouraged to become commission-paid dealers themselves. Therefore it proved a particularly viable form of sales in geographical areas and social groupings with strong female networks and kinship structures. The sales technique thrived on the social obligation generated by women's networks and the impetus toward reciprocity, which the hostess's hospitality would spark and which the dealer could then transform into a successful sale.

The rise of the hostess party signaled a profound and gendered change in direct sales practice. Stanley Home Products, founded in 1932 by Frank S. ("Stanley") Beveridge, evolved as the leading proponent of the hostess plan. Evidence suggests that Beveridge refined the method used by Norman Squires, a top manager for Wearever aluminum cookware from 1937 to 1938 and self-proclaimed proponent of the "private hostess plan." Squires had reputedly used the technique since the late 1920s but depended on an exclusively male sales team. "The great POWER of this program," he wrote to a manufacturer in 1938, "is in the fact that every lady present usually buys, and still greater is the fact that from each party given a man will generally book two or three more dems [demonstrations] for the immediate future."[12] Squires approached Beveridge (who apparently considered the scheme to be the perfect boost for Stanley sales) with a version of the private hostess plan. Purportedly, Squires proposed the employment of housewives (because they knew more about household cleaning) as an adaptation to the plan, and Beveridge balked at this suggestion until persuaded otherwise by his secretary, Catherine O'Brien.[13]

Certainly, Beveridge recognized the stigma attached to unscrupulous, masculine door-to-door sales practices and viewed the "home party" or "hostess party" as an antidote to this problem. The dubious reputation of direct salesmen during this period had triggered sales legislation prohibiting uninvited soliciting in an attempt to protect householders from overbearing hawkers.[14] The blossoming of the home party sales system in the 1930s can be explained in part as a response to this legislation, for it required the goodwill of the housewife and an invitation-led sales demonstration, thus undermining the principles of the domineering salesman. Product catalogs promoting a full range of wares were used as buffers to prevent accusations of uninvited soliciting; the salesperson could deliver them for perusal and return later to offer a bonus item if invited into the home to make a sales demonstration. Home party dealers, such as those organized by Beveridge, frequently conducted business through pamphlets and catalogs because, as well as overcoming the prohibition of uninvited soliciting, it heightened a sense of customer obligation.

The party plan proved highly adaptable to contemporary circumstances and, by the 1940s, housing shortages, gasoline rationing, and the isolation of servicemen's wives purportedly led to the blossoming of the hostess, or home, party plan, bringing together, as it did, the dual concerns of sociability and household provisioning in a period when both were seemingly under threat. In 1947 the hostess party captured press attention as an apparently newly discovered, quaint, subcultural activity of the contemporary suburban housewife. A male journalist from *Fortune* magazine attended a Stanley Home Products event where, he commented, Mrs. Wyczalek, the hostess, "had done herself proud." "Her parlor fairly shone," he continued, "and she had iced cherry drink, potato chips, peanuts and candy" ready for her guests.[15] The celebration of the home entertainment and domestic sphere, embodied in the contemporary currency of the term "hostess," clearly formed the locus of the proceedings. The dealer began the party by reading aloud horoscopes to a gathering of twelve friends and neighbors, in this case of predominantly Polish ethnic origin. During a demonstration of furniture cream the women swapped opinions regarding the product's performance. After courtesy gift giving (each guest receiving a dish mop, a comb, and a bottle cap), order forms were completed and the women adjourned to the dining room for coffee and cake. "Such a nice sociable way to shop," the dealer, Mrs. Simpson, commented. Her party netted $47.12, giving her a $12.00 profit. A choice of gifts such as Lucite mirrors, nylon hairbrushes, and plated silverware were offered to the party hostess, commensurate with sales accrued, for the lending of her home and friends. The party acted as an intimate sales space and an active forum for the recruitment of future party hostesses.

The amicable social gatherings of the party plan totally overturned the notion of direct selling as the practice of an overzealous salesman, one foot in the door, armed with numerous hard-sell techniques designed to deceive the gullible housewife. Indeed the hostess party effectively inverted conventional sales wisdom, which posited the woman as a passive receptor of newly marketed merchandise. Instead it acknowledged housewives as capable sales recruits and discerning, powerful consumers, keen to explore an expanding array of modern consumer goods. As it operated through distinct social networks it also addressed social and ethnic groups precluded from the images and copy of an increasingly sophisticated and stereotyped mainstream advertising industry. Indeed, the African-American cosmetic business entrepreneurs Madam C. J. Walker and Annie Turbo Malone, who used "agent-operator" distribution systems, were the true precursors to the interwar party plan technique. From the second decade of the twentieth century onward, Walker and Malone trained women to demonstrate and sell hair and beauty products through regional social networks, circumventing formal advertising and business methods, through door-to-door operations and the formation of clubs. As historian Kathy Peiss notes, this woman-to-woman mode of distribution generated its own form of sociality: "Beauty entrepreneurs concentrated on women's aesthetic and cultural practices, weaving their trade into the fabric of women's everyday life. Addressing a heterogeneous public split along racial, class, and regional lines, they devised new forms of female interaction to create a sociable commerce in beautifying."[16] Although the Walker system utilized women's social networks for commercial gain, they valorized traditional feminine skills, such as styling hair and applying beauty preparations, for the mutual benefit of African-American women. In 1912 Walker made a passionate address to the annual meeting of the National Negro Business League, describing her rise from "the cotton fields of the South" and overtly acknowledging the politics of her commercial endeavor, viewing it as a means of self-determination for poor African-American women.[17]

The sociality of purchase and the pleasures of product perusal had not escaped the attention of mail-order firms in the late nineteenth century, who "encouraged women to form purchasing clubs for discounts and premiums." Like the houseware manufacturers of the twentieth century, who used the party plan as a means of reducing consumer resistance, their forerunners, the mail-order companies, recognized that friends who shared catalogs, "discussed products, and wrote up orders together made cosmetics acceptable to one another."[18]

## Sales Personality and Brand Loyalty
### The Legacy of the Fuller Brush Man

It is difficult to understand the full extent of the home party plan's impact without considering the legacy of the contemporary patriarchal cultural icon, the Fuller Brush man. "Most urban housewives had a firm rule never to open their doors to a salesman. To purchase from one was an invitation to be defrauded," commented Alfred Fuller, founder of the Fuller Brush Company.[19] Active since 1913, the Fuller Brush Company stood as the vital precursor to many successful postwar sales operations. Stanley Beveridge had trained as a Fuller Brush man, acquiring his insight into household products and their consumption through the first company, which consciously sought to combat the negativity pitted against the direct salesman. Unlike the fly-by-night traveling salesman of popular imagination, who moved from community to community off-loading second-rate goods, the Fuller Brush man fostered a reassuring and steadfast identity selling quality brushes and associated household products. By association with a recognizable brand name and reputable products, his communally sanctioned reputation distinguished him from the rabble of itinerant salesmen and commercial travelers. This reputation proved highly profitable, as amiable salesmen provoked "sympathy purchases" from women willing to support the livelihood of otherwise unemployed men, especially during times of high unemployment.

The Fuller Brush man thrived on the impact of 1920s domestic economy and scientific management theories. Acting almost as a herald of modernity, a "benefactor to housewives," and "a crusader against insanitary [sic] kitchens," he promoted a range of labor-saving devices unavailable on the general retail market. Home demonstration techniques offered personalized and charismatic service, combined with artful observation of everyday household management and social relations. In this context, contemporaneous concerns could be efficiently embodied and communicated in the material culture of the door-to-door salesman and turned to profit. The Fuller "long-hair invigorator" brush, for example, whose sales had flagged, was successfully reinvented as the fashionable "bobbed-hair trainer" with the onset of the modern working woman's "bachelor girl hairstyle." Fortunately the same bachelor girl earned a disposable income, did her own housekeeping, and could be "sold [to] in apartment buildings at night."[20]

In the 1920s and 1930s, direct sales concerns such as the Realsilk Hosiery Company also targeted men as their sales recruits in the form of college students seeking supplemental income. Recruitment was tied to the networks of all-male colleges despite the intimate nature of some of the female merchandise: "In 1927 I was working for my meals at college. The captain of the basket ball team signed me up for Realsilk's training program. . . . We learned how to approach a customer, how to gain his attention, how to create interest, how to make a presentation, and how to close a sale. . . . During the depression, hosiery was selling for $1.50 a pair. My offering then consisted of, in addition to hosiery and socks, lingerie and a complete line of men's and women's apparel."[21]

Direct sales practice proved expedient at introducing new and modern products, along with a mainstay of traditional items, to a wary consumer public.[22] The close link forged between consumption and production (many Fuller brushes were devised in direct response to customer suggestions) reinforced the door-to-door salesmen's appeal to modern living and consumer culture. To quote Fuller himself, "Speciality salesmen [were] the infantry of merchandising, storming the citadel of public habit with new ideas, new products and new techniques."[23] Although mainstream retailing utilized increasingly sophisticated advertising campaigns and display techniques, it lacked the expediency of direct sales' grass roots response to consumer demand.

Stanley Home Products, and the home party plan system, benefited enormously from the legacy of the Fuller Brush Company. Customers viewed corporate-sanctioned direct salespeople as potentially trustworthy community members, who introduced useful and varied products to consumers in the convenience of their own homes.

Fuller Brush salesmen were encouraged to view themselves as idealistic pioneers in an increasingly competitive consumer culture that threatened to reduce commerce to a newly debased level. Notions of service were tied to an ardent belief in a positive-thinking ethos. Walter Coutu, a dealer in Madison, Wisconsin, epitomized the pioneer salesman promoted by the Fuller Brush Company: "I chose Fuller selling merely to make money. . . . I steadily received literature and personal training from the company which sought to inspire men with courage, faith in themselves and faith in the company's product; literature which contained quotations from the sayings of great men, bristling with ideas, permeated with thoughts of honor and high ideals. After a while I forgot about the money. I began to see the vision . . . the finest spirit of cooperation I had ever known."[24]

As familiar social characters these salesmen offered a potent combination of commerce and community endeavor, indicative of the ideal of American democratic capitalism: "Fuller Brush Men pulled teeth, massaged headaches, delivered babies, gave emetics for poison, prevented suicides, discovered murders, helped to arrange funerals, and drove patients to hospitals. All this was in the day's work."[25]

## Avon Ladies and Fullerette Girls
### The Feminization of Direct Sales

"Stanley People," like their precursors, the Fuller Brush men, evolved as recognizable social figures. But unlike their counterparts the dealers of Stanley Home Products were imbued with status, not as patriarchal heroes, but as activists of a socially responsible female-based group activity. A typical Fuller adage describes the antagonism between salesman and consuming woman:

> Though the women have the vote,
> Do not let them get your goat,
> For tomorrow may bring better luck to you, . . .
> There is just one way to win,
> Tip your hat and grin,
> When the lady you're canvassing says NO![26]

In stark contrast to this aggressive "doorstep" power struggle, hostess parties thrived on cooperative and familial relations. Party events were frequently organized to raise funds for charitable causes and community events. Using the home and female kin as the focal point of commercial activity, "Stanley People" (as corporate associates were called) took on an essentially social role, as company handbooks revealed: "For Stanley is more than a mere business. It is a distinctive service dedicated to making life easier, happier, for the modern housewife by saving her time and work in the better care of her family and her home."[27]

Ultimately the scheme feminized direct sales practices by positively and routinely employing women. Stanley salespeople highlighted the crucial economic and social role of women and the domestic sphere. The company, and the influential Catherine O'Brien, Beveridge's secretary who by the late 1940s had become executive vice president, nurtured the social activities of women and by 1949 boasted a revenue of $35 million, exceeding the profits of the all-male Fuller Brush Company by several million dollars.[28]

During this period Avon Products Incorporated also sustained an active female sales team but relied exclusively on catalog sales and individual door-to-door trading. Originating as the California Perfume Company, Avon employed "Lady Travellers" as early as 1886 to sell directly to consumers, merchants, and small retailers. Like Fuller Brush men and Stanley salespeople, their hard-earned community status distinguished them from the problematic reputation of the itinerant commercial traveler. Their feminine social skills gained them access to societal networks outside the reach of the nineteenth-century salesman.[29] Unlike the male commercial traveler who, according to historian Timothy Spears in *Hundred Years on the Road,* "by his dislocation from the most sacred of all American institutions—the home—. . . inevitably triggered distrust," women were considered safely domesticated.[30] They were keenly encouraged to capitalize on social relations by associating with, according to corporate guidelines, the "*Best* people in town . . . who stand high in the community."[31] By 1939, Avon had established a uniquely female direct sales concern, with more than 26,000 saleswomen. Its postwar success relied, like the party plan system, on the specificity of its products and the integral community status of its saleswomen.[32]

So conspicuous was the advent of dynamic female direct sales forces during the late 1930s and into the postwar period, that the Fuller Brush Company, falling behind in sales figures, created their own small-scale feminized sales team. The "Fullerettes," an exclusively female operation, was devised to promote a newly designed range of cosmetics for the modern woman; it was deemed beneath the Fuller Brush man to sell face creams and lipsticks. The Fullerettes, however, proved equally unsuccessful—exasperated field managers reported that the sales team ended up whiling away their afternoons idly "playing bridge or baby-tending" instead of selling door-to-door. The patriarchal framework of the Fuller Brush Company proved ill equipped to nurture the domesticated social skills praised by rival concerns. The Fullerettes were hastily disbanded.[33]

Avon and other minor ventures such as Spirella Corsetiers used predominantly female sales teams with varying degrees of success during this period. But it was Stanley Home Products that made the home party plan a highly successful method of selling, by fusing quasireligious and positive-thinking sales doctrines to make a unique corporate culture—a culture that would prove integral to the success of Tupperware Home Parties in the 1950s.

## The Power of the "Stanley Prayer"
### Selling as a Moral Crusade

Positive thinking and popular religiosity are common themes in twentieth-century North American salesmanship. The patriarchal Protestantism embraced by the Fuller Brush Company preached self-help and character-building doctrines. The house organ, the *Bristler,* framed sales achievement in terms of ethics and self-improvement. The company spoke of "equal opportunity to all, and due consideration for each person involved in every transaction" and prided itself on being "the host of inadequately educated persons who had risen above their potential."[34] Values of cleanliness, self-reliance, and missionary zeal challenged the wanton, commercial opportunism of the peddling salesman. Even Fuller brushes themselves were imbued with moralistic, as well as practical, meaning; in his autobiography Alfred Fuller describes how the grimy children of "immigrant neighborhoods" might be scrubbed healthy and clean in the course of demonstrating his brushes.[35]

Stanley Home Products, whose founding members were almost all former Fuller Brush salespeople, continued to fuse popular religiosity and positive-thinking rhetoric in the dissemination of the home party plan. The company attracted a population defined by class, however, rather than by ethnicity or religious identity. Predominantly blue collar and lower middle class, they represented a segment of society otherwise precluded from entrepreneurial ventures and public recognition. By the late 1940s thousands of dealers made the "Stanley Pilgrimage" to the newly founded company headquarters, a "home" for the disparate dealers scattered across the nation. Corporate culture included prayers, pep talks, and sentimental rituals. Sales units from around the nation journeyed to attend emotive meetings in Stanley Park in Westfield, Massachusetts. As the inspirational home for Stanley salespeople, the headquarters formed the backdrop for a series of sales study programs and prize-giving ceremonies, framed in patriotic fervor and pseudoreligious sentiment. A typical event involved women gathered around a granite boulder that was emblazoned with a bronze plaque featuring the "Stanley Prayer." Accompanied by "the soft, bell-like tones of [a] Vibraphone" they recited the prayer and admired the awe-inspiring setting of blue spruces and a magnificently colorful flower garden planted in their honor. Stanley dealers unable to make the pilgrimage could be anointed at a later date with blessed water taken from the Stanley Park Fountain.[36]

Popular self-development psychology was crucial to the success of Stanley Home Products; in 1948 Stanley salespeople were encouraged to embrace personal development fourfold—"mentally, physically, spiritually and volitionally"—and to "sow before [they] could reap."[37] The same year, company estimates suggested that Stanley dealers had demonstrated products to 18 million women per year and that more than 15,000 copies of the "Stanley Prayer" had been sent out in answer to requests.[38] Everyone working for Stanley products belonged to the BCH (an abbreviation for "bright, cheerful, and happy") Club.

As a top-selling dealer of Stanley Home Products in the 1940s, Mary Kay Ash (whose cosmetics company, founded in the 1960s, is famous for its pink Cadillac sales incentives) recalled the importance of recognition and reward:

> The third day [of the convention] they [Stanley Home Products] had this award thing, and they had a girl who was crowned Queen of Sales. And Mr. Frank Stanley Beveridge crowned her queen. They gave her, as a top prize, an alligator bag. Well, to me that was a pink Cadillac. I wanted that bag with everything that was in me. I wanted the bag, and I wanted to be where she was. I decided I was going to be queen next year. And so I marched up to Mr. Beveridge, and I said, "Next year I'm going to be queen." He took my hand and looked me in the eye and said, "You know, somehow I think you will." And those words propelled me to queen the next year. And would you believe, they forgot to give me the alligator bag.[39]

By the late 1940s then, the "hostess" or "home" party evolved from its 1920s purpose—a practical means of demonstrating unfamiliar new aluminum utensils—into a unique corporate sales culture set to boom with the rise of postwar North American consumption. Incorporating centuries-old sales techniques that recognized the intrinsically social nature of selling, it changed from a male-dominated practice to a form of feminized sales and consumption. The party demonstration and sales process assimilated new products into a social setting and acknowledged the significance of household consumption. Through positive-thinking and self-help doctrines it appealed both to disenfranchised workers and to peripheral consumers, excluded from the formal workplace or the formal retail environment. Most significantly it acknowledged the potent role of women as skilled provisioners.

## "Patio Dates" and "Poly Parties"
### The Inception of Tupperware Home Parties

In 1949 Earl Tupper was introduced to the significance of the hostess party and, in particular, its immense success for Stanley Home Products. Such a large proportion of mail orders for the Tupper Corporation derived from this practice that the corporation initiated impromptu market research. Questionnaires distributed to more than a dozen direct sales dealers (with indicative names such as "Plastic" and "Poly Parties") who were actively ordering products from the Tupper Corporation focused on the specifics of their operations. The responses, which ranged from suggestions on the best-selling party products to improved distribution policy, formed the basis of Tupper's sustained interest in this method of direct sales. In a few isolated cases distributors fascinated and impressed by the innovative product had already made the decision to deal solely with Tupperware.[40] Successful managers, such as Anne Brittain from San Diego, encouraged her dealers to demonstrate the difference between "bad" polyethylene, available in dime stores, and the quality polyethylene of Tupperware: "I tell them . . . that the Tupper Corporation won the house wares award for 1949. That is quite an achievement I tell them. 'It's like winning an Oscar if you were a movie star.' That seems to make an impression here, being so close to Hollywood."[41] Using the home party plan, she differentiated Tupperware from rival products by advising her dealers to avoid "Stanley methods" such as pushing a sale or insisting on bookings and instead to befriend hostesses and their guests. "We train our girls" she continued, "to be genteel, not too aggressive."

From the onset Tupperware dealers differentiated themselves from other direct salespeople, introducing a special pride and gentility to the sale of their unique products. As well as protecting the exclusivity of Tupperware, dealers and distributors (responding to the Tupper Corporation's initial questionnaire) expressed concerns about marketing the product on the home party plan. They requested strict delineation of distributorship territories and standardization of discounts, retail prices, gift incentives, and demonstration procedure. They also highlighted the need for more efficient distribution and an increased product range to respond to the immediacy of consumer preference. Finally, they suggested the introduction of a regular corporate bulletin, sales training, and party plan apprenticeships. In other words, dealers wanted a formalized approach to their business operations.

In 1950 Earl Tupper identified the six most profitable distributors among his own account holders and invited them to an exploratory conference. He was particularly struck by the activities of Norman W. Squires, who led a Long Island company known as Hostess Home Accessories, whose products resembled, except for subtle differences in packaging, those of Stanley Home Products. Tupper approached Squires to negotiate the creation of a similar, standardized scheme for the Tupper Corporation.[42] By August 1950 the Tupper Corporation had purchased the assets of Hostess Home Accessories and employed Squires as the general sales manager of the new Hostess Division of the Tupper Corporation based in New York.[43] The scheme relied ostensibly on the sale of chemical products, brooms, and brushes, and Tupperware products were incorporated as a sideline.

According to Earl Tupper's account, the Hostess Division disbanded when Norman Squires absconded with $200,000 of invested monies and the legitimacy of his former copy-cat company was brought into question. Squires strongly contested this interpretation of events, suggesting instead that Tupper, once equipped with Squires's knowledge and expertise of home parties, unlawfully dismissed him.[44] By this point, though, Tupper had established a network of highly motivated and inventive top-achieving party plan distributors. Drawn up before Squires's unseemly departure, the company guidelines were written exclusively in the masculine third person, although in reality the majority of Tupperware dealers were women or husband-and-wife teams.

Two such outstanding dealers and managers, Thomas Damigella (part of a husband-and-wife team from Massachusetts) and Brownie Wise (a single mother from Detroit), had worked with Stanley Home Products and had independently recognized Tupperware as a potentially successful home demonstration product. They maintained impressively high sales volumes in their regions, and Tupper was impressed and intrigued by their methods. The profiles of Thomas Damigella and Brownie Wise, although exceptional in terms of their sales successes, were typical of the majority of dealers involved in direct selling in the postwar period. Entrepreneurial in spirit but economically marginalized, they viewed direct sales as a means of bolstering their limited social and economic positions.[45] Damigella worked primarily as a mechanical engineer but needed to earn extra money to support his family. As an established Stanley Home Products dealer, he discovered Tupperware in a hardware store and, recognizing its potential as a product for demonstration, incorporated samples into his Stanley line of merchandise. For his party plan customers, the sheer novelty of Tupperware outshone the familiarity and commonness of Stanley household cleaning and kitchen products. Damigella breathed life into plastic containers that, he commented, would have otherwise "died on the shelf." Through demonstration they blossomed into extraordinary commodities. Successful home demonstrations required an ample product range. The first Tupperware dealers, constrained by a limited product selection, were allowed by their distributors to augment their merchandise with a 40 percent selection of other "kitchen, housewife oriented" goods; these typically included aprons, tablecloths, shower curtains, and baby bibs. By 1948 Damigella's sales of Tupperware so substantially outweighed other product lines that he resigned his Stanley franchise and confined his party plan sales to Tupperware.[46]

Like Damigella, Brownie Wise, a middle-aged, divorced mother from Detroit, urgently needed to supplement the meager secretarial wage she earned working for the Bendix Aviation Corporation. Originally operating as a Stanley Home Products dealer, by 1948 Wise established "Patio Parties" to deal with Tupperware-based stock. She incorporated other branded product lines, like Imperiale Russe personal products and Meadowbrook silverware, to provide party gift incentives including "lipsticks, slicers and bath salt decanters."[47] By 1949 Wise managed an established team of illustrious saleswomen and referred to home demonstrations specifically as "Poly-T Parties"; in a typical week one dealer sold more than fifty-six Wonder Bowls and was promptly requested to share the secret of her dynamic demonstration technique with colleagues. Several other dealers in her team held parties grossing more than $100 at each event. These endeavors were applauded in the pages of an informal weekly bulletin, the *Go-Getter,* initiated, written, and circulated by Wise to her dealers.[48] Such literature united, informed, and inspired the Patio Parties sales team.

## The Housewife's Choice
### The Recruitment of Brownie Wise

In 1951 Tupper made an ambitious and daring appointment: Wise, a woman with no formal business qualifications or capital investment, was chosen to lead the distribution network and establish guidelines and policies for the development of a national organization to "sell all products on Hostess Plan."[49] Tupper's decision to invest wholeheartedly in amateur businesspeople and an informal, peripheral sales activity was either an act of inspired entrepreneurial vision or a reflection of his desperation.[50] After considerable and intense personal research, Tupper surmised that in order to introduce Tupperware to the nation's kitchens in any sizable amount, the domestic focus of the home party plan would prove invaluable.[51] Until then, his promotional ventures had centered on a series of national advertising campaigns and formal retail ventures, and the majority of product sales were confined to corporate accounts (where Poly-T was used as packaging or incidental promotional gifts). Advertisements featured in publications such as *Everybody's Poultry Magazine*, *Kentucky Farmer*, *New England Homestead*, *Barber's Journal*, and *American Hairdresser* appealed to consumers Tupper considered would benefit most from the fruits of modern design and innovation. While promoting to a lower-end rural and small-trade market, the Tupper Corporation maintained its showroom on New York City's prestigious Fifth Avenue in an attempt to promote Poly-T and its numerous product ranges to a more upscale market. Despite this frantic, multiple approach to product pitching, Tupperware had yet to establish a stable domestic market.[52]

With their wily grasp of domestic economy and an assured skepticism of elaborate new product campaigns, housewives seemed to be the most reluctant Tupperware consumers. Despite the Millionaire Line's appeal to function, status, quality, and economy, women homemakers remained firmly unconvinced; the claims of modern advertising and elaborate display techniques failed to win over the female postwar consumer.

Tupper's choice of Wise to organize the new distribution scheme proved fundamental to the success of Tupperware. Dynamic and capable, she convinced Tupper that the key to success of the product lay in her imaginative and tenacious approach to party plan sales and her understanding of women's needs as housewives, consumers, and part-time workers. The success of her own company, Patio Parties, which as the name suggests appealed to leisurely, suburban notions of modern living, certainly substantiated her claims. Wise and her mother, Rose Humphrey, organized hostess parties to sell goods as diverse as the "ketchup pump," "the ash tray with a brain," and "Atomite: the cleaner with ATOMIC like action." As an ideal gift and novelty with contemporary design appeal, Tupperware perfectly suited Wise's clever buying policy. Like the hostess party gatherings themselves, the products that she chose appealed to a new found modernity. Items such as the hand-size "Sunny" featherweight hair dryer (available in "colors as pretty as your cosmetic box: capri, coral, bermuda blue, sahara sand") invoked a provocative allure to a home shampoo; easily mountable on the wall "for those last minute dashes, 'Sunny' will dry your hair as you polish your nails—and then dry your nails too!"[53] Wise's immense business acumen and intuitive understanding of feminine popular culture, gift giving, and attainable glamour would carry the hostess party, and Tupperware, to new dimensions.

Her first appearance as the designated figurehead of THP took place at the newly formed sister company's debut conference in Worcester, Massachusetts, in September 1951. Tupper handed over the entire distribution and promotion plan to Wise and designated her vice president of THP. In a strictly gendered division, Wise dealt with the people, public relations, and promotion while Tupper ran the production plants and continued to engineer and design products for the Tupper Corporation.

The logistics of THP revolved around the delineation of sales territories, associated network configurations, and proportional commission arrangements. At first glance the venture resembled a highly rationalized and intensively hierarchical management structure. The sales manager selected and supervised regional managers responsible for directing area managers and their smaller branch management concerns. Branch managers, assisted by district managers, appointed unit organizers as intermediaries in recruiting, training, and supervising dealers. Wholesale dealers made profit through selling at retail prices on the party plan. Although working independently on a commission basis, the dealer had the full sanction of the company in the form of fully guaranteed merchandise. Finally, at the end of a long chain of managerial and commission-based distributive units, the Tupperware party hostess offered her home and social networks to the dealer in return for a nonmonetary gift.

The entire system relied upon the self-employed, nonsalaried status of its operatives. Managers and dealers covered their own costs in attending weekly assemblies and sales and board meetings and dealt with their own

Brownie Wise, vice president and general manager of THP, demonstrates the power of charismatic dealership as she throws a liquid-filled Wonder Bowl provocatively across the room at a crowded Tupperware party, ca. 1952. Wise Papers, series 3, box 29, negative 94-9987, Archives Center, National Museum of American History, Smithsonian Institution, Washington, D.C.

accounting, credit, and tax requirements.[54] The onus was on each unit to consider itself as a self-reliant entrepreneurial venture supported by a dependable central distribution system and a quality brand-name product.

The divisions within THP appear rigid and overly prescriptive. In effect, however, mobility and flexibility between ranks proved essential to the success of the entire party plan operation. Although management levels dealt with different degrees of responsibility, they all shared the arduous task of recruiting, training, and supervising an ever-expanding sales team. Rapid and effective expansion of the Tupperware sales system, via the growth of managerial and dealership positions and unrestricted promotion, maximized collective profits. Opportunities for promotion through proven and measured commitment, visible in sales and recruitment figures, meant that dealers could rise swiftly to managerial positions. In this sense, the Tupperware system challenged fixed hierarchical management structures. Gary McDonald, ex-sales director of THP, high-lighted the ways in which direct selling defies conventional, formal business procedure:

> Business people . . . are trained — both in school and on the job — to look at business in terms of market share, new products, advertising, and creating demand. As a result, they see these attributes as keys on a piano — when they are played in the right order things work well. . . . Of course, those who have been in direct selling know that our business doesn't work that way. It is not a product business. It is a people business. And if you're not doing the right things in terms of motivating people, creating loyalty, or explaining how it is going to impact the sales organization first, the business simply isn't going to work. . . . To succeed, management must think in terms of how these people feel.[55]

Although direct sales companies experienced a rapid turnover of casual sales recruits (and the demotion of agents if their targeted sales diminished), every managerial level had a vested interest to upgrade and advance the commitment of other dealers and distributors. For Tupperware, market saturation, far from presenting a problem, stood as a goal yet to be attained in the early 1950s. Competition through regional and branch sales contests motivated teams and individuals alike in their endeavor to "spread the Tupperware gospel." Crucially, the Tupperware system developed by encouraging a nurturing and supportive rivalry rather than enforcing the brutal individualism and self-interest of corporate competition. The party plan network built upon flexible, organic, and horizontal managerial development, a feature that became the linchpin of its success and the basis of its compelling employment appeal for women.

In November 1951, *Opportunity* magazine ran an advertisement showing an illustration of several women gathered around a kitchen table, gleefully handling Tupperware items. "Quick money," the copy read, could be made "simply by attending parties!" Church groups, sororities, clubs, organizations, friends, neighbors, and relatives were identified as the social groups ideally suited to the Tupperware party concept. A new Tupperware dealer, "just by having good times," could expect "a whole shower of . . . crisp bills and jingling silver," the advertisement promised.

Potential dealers, offered a "free approval sampler" of products with which to hold a trial party, were assured that "once you see Tupperware you will understand why women are crazy about it." The ad continued, "Tupperware is the herald of a new era in the life of the American

In 1951 Tupperware was withdrawn from formal retail outlets and distribution was confined to the "party plan system." Also that year, *Opportunity* magazine advertised the Tupperware home party as a convivial way for women to generate income in the domestic sphere. Tupper Papers, series 3, box 7, Archives Center, National Museum of American History, Smithsonian Institution, Washington, D.C.

housewife! . . . you need no special selling ability or experience to make money with Tupperware. It sells itself on sight."

Though claims that the product sold itself on sight had been proven patently untrue, the party plan spread in popularity. Tupperware was withdrawn from stores and sold exclusively through direct sales. The adoption of the home party plan fortuitously coincided with the rapid expansion of suburban living. The soaring increase in household expenditure, women doing their own housework, and child-centered consumption led THP to describe suburbia as "a picnic ground for direct selling." Homebound mothers eager to earn extra income and thwart social isolation became enthusiastic organizers and attendees of the contemporary phenomenon, the Tupperware party. This postwar boom in network direct sales, according to Nicole Biggart in *Charismatic Capitalism,* happened almost entirely because of the availability of a "newly regulated environment and a new supply of workers—suburban women."[56] Although Tupperware parties were not confined to suburbia (indeed advocates of the party plan boasted of its adaptability to rural and urban environments alike), they were ideally suited to its newly acquired social structures and increased standards and styles of consumption.

# five

• • •

# "Parties Are the Answer"
## The Ascent of the Tupperware Party

By 1954 the American press described Tupperware parties as "the newest selling idea to take the country by storm."[1] *Tupperware Sparks,* the corporate in-house magazine, announced, "We're 20,000 strong!" as a network of dealers, distributors, and managers (consisting predominantly of housewives between the ages of twenty-five and forty) took the Tupperware "gospel" to the nation.[2]

In response to a surge in domestic sales, the Tupper Corporation expanded to a huge, refurbished plant in Blackstone, Massachusetts, more than doubling the factory capacity. The plant became a beacon of the company's investment in modern technology and increased mass production. "A million dollars worth of molding machines and other equipment are now in production there," read a company brochure, "pouring out more than three times as much Tupperware as formerly available."[3] The Blackstone Mill covered 400,000 square feet (122,000 square meters) and included 223 acres (91 hectares) of land stretching across the Rhode Island–Massachusetts state line. A seven-story building for processing materials was situated by a water and steam generating plant that supplied machinery and equipment. Factory operations resembled a classic Ford assembly line, with highly dedicated machinery and three basic divisions of labor: machine supervision, product finishing (using a power-cutter for trimming) and assembly, and finally packaging.[4]

The Tupperware party, an event that merged sociality and commerce in the space of the postwar home, became a cultural hallmark of 1950s American suburbia. Tupperware Home Parties, Inc., Orlando, Florida, ca. 1958.

Yet despite Tupperware's plant expansion, promotional literature perpetuated the nostalgic and craft dimensions of the development, suggesting it was merely taking up its historically rightful place in relation to the community. The caption accompanying a picturesque aerial view of the new development read, "A neat, old New England village makes a 'picture postcard' now centered around Tupperware, instead of around stone mills as in the days gone by."[5] The description of a later factory in Vassalboro, Maine, was similarly scenic: "A story book setting in a clean, fresh New England countryside, another large Tupper Corporation manufacturing plant produces new and useful products to come to you."[6]

With the construction of a lavish national headquarters for the sister distribution company, Tupperware Home Parties, located in Orlando, Florida, the company was consolidated as a leading direct sales force operating throughout the United States, Alaska, Hawaii, Puerto Rico, and Canada. Sales incentive schemes such as "Operation Doorbell"—a campaign whereby distributorships saturated their localities with party "dates"—introduced direct selling to curious consumers and potential recruits alike.

THP orchestrated the distribution of the Tupper Corporation's goods through the collation and dispatch of party orders received from regional unit managers. A state-of-the-art IBM computer system and sophisticated telephone set-up ensured that dealers across America could communicate sales orders with ease and have them shipped efficiently. Wise managed a team of more than a dozen executives and managerial staff (including only two prominent women—Elsie Mortland, headquarters' hostess, and Mary Starr, sales counselor) working in sales and advertising management, public relations, sales counseling, premium purchase, and accounting.[7] As THP and the phenomenon of the Tupperware party attracted increasing media attention, in 1954 the Ruder and Finn public relations company was chosen to work alongside the in-house team in establishing a coherent corporate profile. Despite their entirely separate geographical locations and managerial styles, THP and the Tupper Corporation operated in tandem. Product and promotional ideas were bandied back and forth between the sister companies. The constant correspondence between Wise and Tupper stemmed from a shared motivation to establish Tupperware as the foremost contemporary household product.

## "A Picnic Ground for Direct Selling"
### The Consumption Space of Suburbia

In 1953 *Fortune* featured one of numerous editorials identifying suburbia as a key new consumer market: "Anybody who wants to sell anything to Americans, from appliances to zithers, must look closely at Suburbia."[8] This "big and lush and uniform" environment offered astute marketers an abundant supply of easily targeted consumers. A contemporary survey of suburban shopping habits, conducted by Boston University's Bureau of Business Research, showed that the "suburban market" remained largely unrealized. Although established city department stores opened branches in outlying suburban areas, they merely transposed the merchandise and marketing techniques of high-end city retailing to a suburban environment.[9] Suburbia, espoused numerous articles, required a specific and radically new approach to consumer taste and marketing. The Boston University report showed that suburbanites preferred simpler and more casual items in keeping with a trend toward informal living. Hard-wearing and robust furnishings, designed to withstand years of wear and tear from child rearing, also appealed to an increasingly child-centered population. Journalists keenly observed that such requirements heightened rather than precluded a taste for fashion and stylistic innovation: "Suburbia has a good eye for color, and it keeps abreast of the latest developments in the art of living, at least as that art is set forth in the women's and home magazines."[10] Although most suburban inhabitants still relied on downtown shopping for their purchases, many women expressed a preference for home shopping; according to one survey, 43 percent of suburbanites shopped by telephone and 25 percent by mail.[11]

Since 1947 suburbia's population had grown by approximately 1.2 million per year, reaching an estimated 30 million by 1953. During the same period the U.S. population increased by 11 percent; that of suburbia, 43 percent.[12] A major factor facilitating this steep national increase in suburban migration was the advancement, by the Federal Housing Authority, of low-interest loans to returning veterans, meant to ease the shortage of housing for newly formed couples and families. Easily accessible credit facilities boosted sales of homes and household goods.[13] "In the five years after World War II," comments one historian, "consumer spending increased 60 percent, but the amount spent on household furnishings and appliances rose 240 percent."[14]

Some contemporary commentators and sociologists recognized "suburbanization" as a complex and multilayered phenomenon; *Fortune,* for example, divided its analysis of suburban migration into interdependent categories: "Semi-Suburbia" (outlying countryside, hamlets, integrated towns, garden apartments) and "Suburbia" proper (a metropolitan area tract whose inhabitants had higher-than-average income, home ownership, and number of children). Commentators even recognized that, despite a superficial homogeneity, suburban migration and its ideals crossed many class, ethnic, and religious boundaries. Aided by increased credit, suburbanites' discretionary income was steered toward the domestic sphere in the creation of new, child-centered homes. According to contemporary discourse, then, suburban dwellers were considered a vital new consumer population; Old World values and diverse social backgrounds might divide them in the realm of production, but through consumption they were redefined as a culturally bound, aspiring middle-class group. Although postwar suburban dwellings varied enormously in location, status, size, and design, the defining feature of suburbia was that it boasted "a much larger proportion of family units in the middle-income groups than the rest of the country."[15]

Despite acknowledgment by popular commentators and contemporary academics alike that suburbia encompassed complexity and difference, consensus formed regarding this homogenizing impact of affluence and consumer culture. The accoutrements of the new suburban lifestyle hinged on the outward and social nature of domestic consumption rather than traditional American conventions. "Instead of the old-time porch and terrace and hedged-in lawn, the suburbanite now takes pride in his picture window, open patio, his barbecue equipment," noted a typical observer.[16] Consumption became the crucial underpinning of this postwar social change, and direct sales companies were poised to reap the benefits of dislocated communities ready to open their doors to any element that offered some form of social cohesion.

In 1953, Avon Products, distributing exclusively through door-to-door saleswomen, achieved more than three times the profits of its major retail outlet competitor, Helena Rubinstein.[17] Stanley Home Products, Fuller Brush Company, and the Electrolux Corporation continued to increase their profits as suburban developments provided a keen consumer market. Direct sales boomed as an antidote to the increasing depersonalization of sales exchanges exemplified by the new shopping centers, large department stores, and self-service supermarkets. Just as nineteenth-century peddlers provided rural areas with an invaluable combination of service, goods, and information, the postwar door-to-door salesperson offered "neighborly" contact by association with new products and customs. By 1953 an estimated "26,000 Stanley sales demonstrators arranged and staged some 3 million demonstrations in the living rooms of housewives whose friends and neighbors were invited to buy more than $98 million worth, retail, of brushes, mops, toiletries, household chemicals, personal aids, and vitamins."[18] Out of the leading eight direct sales companies of this period, 75 percent relied on a predominantly female salesforce.[19] By the late 1950s more than three-quarters of a million women were involved in direct selling, a phenomenon attributable at least in part to suburban development and the ensuing rise in household consumption.[20] Home parties accentuated this sociality of consumption and keyed into newly formulating suburban manners, rituals, and social groupings. As historian Veronica Strong-Boag points out in her account of women's lives in the postwar suburbs of Ontario, "Women . . . remembered visits from Avon 'ladies' meaning much more than an opportunity to purchase cosmetics. On their rounds, often of their own neighborhoods, such saleswomen made their own contribution to sociability and information exchange. To be sure, relationships incorporated clients into patterns of consumption, but their success also occurred because they meant much more than sales."[21] The sheer newness of "mass-produced" suburbs, as described by a contemporary report in *Harper's* in 1953, created radical modifications in social behavior. "Socially, these communities have neither history, tradition, customs, institutions, 'socially important' families, or 'big houses,'" wrote one investigative reporter.[22] As such, suburbia became "a picnic ground for direct sales" due to the increase in consumption and a concomitant desire for new forms of knowledge and sociality.

Throughout the 1950s the suburban home became the focus for critiques and celebrations of postwar change and national identity. This culminated in 1959 with the renowned "Kitchen Debate" between Vice President Richard Nixon and Soviet Premier Nikita Sergeyevich Khrushchev at the American National Exhibition in Moscow. A showcase for American consumer goods and technology, the exhibit featured a fully equipped model of a ranch-style suburban home, representative of the supremacy of the U.S. average standard of living. "Thirty-one million families own their own homes," asserted Nixon in his depiction of a postwar consumer republic. "America's 44 million families own a total of 56 million cars, 50 million television sets and 143 million radio sets. And they buy an average of nine dresses and suits and 14 pairs of shoes per family per year."[23] Whereas Khrushchev argued that such excessive consumption was a testament to the inferior quality of American "gadgetry," Nixon flaunted free enterprise, home ownership, and the abundance of goods as a means of diffusing class conflict and creating social cohesion.[24]

In this context Tupperware dealers were, the corporate culture stressed, "privileged to have their voices heard in the world's largest auditorium — the American living room."[25] "Direct selling," they were told by the mid-

1950s, "is as American as corn on the cob. We must conduct ourselves . . . in such a way that we can make our own individual communities and our country proud of the direct selling industry."[26] As archetypal postwar developments (epitomized by Levittown, Long Island, and Park Forest, south of Chicago) differed radically from older residential and urban communities, showing none of the reassuring signs of established and immutable communities, they created their own institutions and rituals, which were embodied in the Tupperware party—the ideal home-based networking opportunity for a newly displaced population.

## The "Tupperware Party"
### Sociality, Modernity, and Mass Consumption

By 1951 the Tupperware party had captured the direct sales market by offering its overtly fashionable, fun-filled events. Regional distributorships with titles such as Patio Parties and Vogue Plastics spread the party plan network nationwide, upgrading this established sales scheme by reconstituting it as a radically modern, leisurely, and convivial event. The Tupperware party promoted home shopping as a time-saving, sociable, and integral part of the modern homemaker's life: "Tupperware Parties are fun! You 'feel at home,' because they're informal and you shop relaxed."[27]

As a women's event, the Tupperware version of the hostess party acted as a celebratory and consciously feminine activity. With the "Modern Way to Shop," a woman could combine "a neighborly visit with armchair shopping" and improve her knowledge of household economy, by benefiting from novel recipes and homemaking tips.[28] A Get-Acquainted Set of basic Tupperware pieces initiated novices to the social relations and commodities of the Tupperware system. For more experienced party guests the introduction of new product types ensured a sustained consumer (and dealer) interest. For example, as "the latest in modern design," a set of slim-line TV Tumblers, which made their debut in 1955 under the slogan "Christian Dior isn't the only one coming out with a 'new look' these days," drew on popular references to women's fashion. Devised as "the perfect answer to beverage serving when watching your favorite TV program," the "soft-glowing" modern tumblers, which brought together the dual concerns of fashion and television culture, came equipped with Tumblemates (12-inch [30.5-centimeter] drink stirrers) and matching wagon-wheel coasters.[29]

Tupperware parties animated the product range using detailed description and highly tactile, even sensual, displays. Women were encouraged to touch and handle products. Party game sessions, in which miniature Tupperware trinkets were awarded for performance, broke down inhibitions and countered the passivity of the captured audience. With titles such as "Clothes Pin," "Waist Measurement" (best avoided if "expecting mothers are present," warned a corporate booklet), "Game of Gossip," and "Chatter," the games celebrated overtly feminine issues. Games such as "Elastic Relay," "Partner Balloon Burst," and "Grab Bag" required physical contact between party guests. Other games played at these sessions were vaguely subversive (and according to oral histories, immensely memorable), such as "Hubby," in which guests were asked to write hypothetical newspaper advertisements to sell their unwanted partners, and then they were told to swap ads and read them aloud to the group. One, for example, read: "One husband for sale. Balding, often cranky, stomach requiring considerable attention!"[30]

In addition to serving as a highly rarefied sales forum, the party acted as a ritual ceremony that, while focusing on Tupperware products, was filled with social significance among maker, buyer, and user. The structure of the party plan system blurred the theoretical boundaries of several identifying categories such as domesticity and commerce, work and leisure, friend and colleague, consumer and employee. "It was developed," according to the trade journal *Speciality Salesman,* "to appeal to women who wanted to earn extra money but were too timid to use pressure or endure rebuffs in conventional selling. In party selling you never have to ring the doorbell of a dark house . . . guests will be coming where the party is scheduled. Every time you have a party, you earn money."[31]

Gifts and commodities abounded as the hostess offered the intimacy of her home and the range of her social relations with other women (relatives, friends, and neighbors) to the Tupperware dealer in exchange for a nonmonetary reward. The dealer, overseen by an area distributor, used the space to set up a display of products and recruit further hostesses from among the guests, benefiting from commission accrued on sales and the potential for further party reservations.

*Dorothy Dealer's Dating Diary,* a full-color cartoon booklet issued to potential dealers, outlined strategies of informal salesmanship, networking, and "friend finding." Women were dissuaded from adopting a corporate image and encouraged to use their own social skills to "create incentive or change excuses into a positive party date." A typical scenario read:

*Potential hostess:* Oh, but Janice I just can't have a party . . . I'm right in the middle of redecorating.

*Dealer:* But wouldn't that be a wonderful chance for your friends to see your newly decorated home?[32]

Other scenarios included reluctant husbands less than keen on "allowing" their wives to act as hostesses to an event that would fill their home with neighborhood women and plastic pots. The *Dorothy Dealer* remedy to this problem revolved around a woman's rational appeal to her husband, reassuring him that the gifts accrued by hosting a party and the savings made through Tupperware food storage far outweighed the inconvenience.

The booklet described the benefits of "prospecting" among a wide range of people and situations (for example, the single working woman, the widow, the urban apartment dweller), and suburbia formed the focus of its attentions. The "Check List for Party Dating," asking dealers "Whom do you know?" proceeded to map out the social relations of suburbia with suggestions ranging from "Your Real Estate Agent" to "Your Neighbors, Church Members and Club Members."[33] Suburban communities were offered the Club Plan and Round Robin schemes, whereby Tupperware parties could be used to supplement the treasury funds of charitable organizations.[34] Dealers were advised, "[W]atch the society page in *your* paper and contact an officer in every club in *your* community!" and they were encouraged with proclamations such as "[I]n every block of homes, in every city and every town, in this wonderful United States of America, there are parties waiting for you."[35]

Although increased community activity provided the Tupperware home party plan with the ultimate arena, the social gathering of women had a historical precedent in the traditional American sewing circle and quilting bee, which appear inextricably bound to the concept of the Tupperware party. Middle-class leisured women gathered to sew together for charity, even if they had seamstresses and servants, within the afternoon sewing circles. It provided a legitimated focal point for a social activity and female companionship. Working-class women had less opportunity to sew on a casual basis but regularly joined the formalized gathering of the quilting bee, which according to historian Susan Strasser was well established in the 1820s as an important women's social activity.[36] Here women across the generations could exchange ideas, hints, and methods in sewing and broader aspects of life, while their small children could be attended communally by the quilting party. A nineteenth-century contemporary

By 1954 Tupperware parties were described as "the newest selling idea to take the country by storm." Tupperware dealers visiting the THP headquarters for their annual sales gathering, which was referred to as the Homecoming Jubilee, spelled out the ascendancy of the Tupperware party—"Parties Are the Answer." Wise Papers, series 3, box 30, negative 94-10899, Archives Center, National Museum of American History, Smithsonian Institution, Washington, D.C.

account provided by Frances Trollope describes these affairs as "quilting frolics," noting that "they are always solemnised with much good cheer and festivity."[37]

Similarly, Tupperware parties were incorporated into the time and labor of everyday domestic economy. Morning events demanded an informal approach indicative of the kaffeeklatsch culture of suburban society, during which light refreshments, "just coffee and doughnuts or sweet rolls," were served. Tupperware parties preempted the daily habits of women as mothers and homemakers. The "second cup of coffee," for example, taken "when the younger set is finally off to school," made a splendid opportunity, Tupperware brochures reiterated, "to enjoy the company of your neighbors by inviting them over for a Tupperware Party." A Tupperware party at "a bake sale, a white elephant sale, a rummage sale or bazaar" contributed to a broader aspect of community life

and informal economy.[38] Evening parties—more formal occasions requiring make-up and stylish attire—sanctioned all-female gatherings under the auspices of homemaking duties and offered a welcome escape from
homebound activities. The Tupperware bridal shower party solved the potentially hazardous prospect of gift giving; "each guest contribut[ing] toward the Tupperware gift set," instead of debating "what to buy? or making costly mistakes."[39] Similarly, the Tupperware housewarming party,
organized by the local dealer and aimed in particular at newlyweds, offered "every new homeowner" the opportunity to enhance the household with the pastel, jewel-tone colors and modern designs of Tupperware. The significance of Tupperware, "so new in design and principle,"
as an appropriate, contemporary, feminine gift pervaded corporate literature: "When it comes to gift giving, . . . you may be . . . sure that it is
something she will cherish."[40]

In 1954 top-achieving party dealers working under distributorships
such as Par-T-Wise Sales in Chicago, Partying Around in Connecticut,
Party Progress in Detroit, and Poly Sales in Los Angeles made weekly
turnovers of between $533 and $629, with an average party attendance of
twelve guests. *Tupperware Sparks* told of women grossing $200 with their
first party event and achieving multiple party profits of $431 during one
week.[41] Sustaining such sales figures proved more difficult as neighborhoods became saturated with the party plan. Ideally the Tupperware party
operated as a serial rather than singular occasion; as gestures of reciprocity,
party guests honored their hostess's hospitality by agreeing to host their
own future event, thus extending the sales network. Corporate literature
revealed how women might use a round of parties to amass their collection of Tupperware: "Many people attend six or seven parties without
getting all the Tupperware they need and want . . . for after a while, almost everyone feels that they need a great deal more!"[42]

Tupperware items, from Jell-O molds to flour sifters, expanded as well
as consolidated established forms of kitchen culture. Items such as Ice-
Tups—do-it-yourself Popsicle molds—proved highly successful, circumventing the need for the commercial equivalents. Although aimed at
mothers catering to their children's needs and desires, these products elicit
highly personal and intimate memories for many women: "I'd make up
the strongest daiquiri mix, you know, and freeze them up in my Tupperware and get through the whole lot of them doing my chores; oh yes, I
used to stand there pressing a shirt, happily sucking on one of my Tupperware ices!"[43]

The dealer's practical demonstrations, some of which amounted to performances fusing entertainment and information, introduced unfamiliar products and reiterated the value of tried and tested favorites. Charismatic demonstration was an imperative. "We can turn a casual desire," advised the corporate literature, "into actual need by making a sale on an active visual demonstration. By demonstrating effectively we actually CREATE the need."[44]

The "Tupperware burp" (the technique of pushing the center of the seal to fully engage the lip with the edge of the bowl, creating an airtight seal) formed the focal point of all demonstrations. "I put my finger here—we call this Tupperware's magic button—press down and just 'wink' the edge of the seal. Hear that?" the dealer would ask rhetorically.[45] Elaborations included bouncing a sealed Wonder Bowl full of liquid across a nervous hostess's living room or standing one-legged on an upturned canister to reveal its outstanding durability. As well as emphasizing the airtight qualities of the product, features such as the Tupperware burp justified the mode of sales. "We have chosen to sell Tupperware on the popular Home Party Plan," read a party brochure, "because we know that you will derive greater benefits from its use after you have seen its varied and distinctive features demonstrated and explained."[46] Tupperware required a currency of vocabulary to maintain its consumer vogue; party initiates showed their familiarity with the product range by deciphering an often obscure product language: Scrub-E-Z, Serve-n-Save, Hang-It-All, Fly-Bye-Swat, Square Round.

Although demonstrations and brochures suggested conventional product use, internal corporate literature aimed at dealers also acknowledged consumer appropriations and re-interpretations of the Tupperware design. Dealers used anecdotes gathered from women at parties to espouse the product's tried and tested versatility. A typical testament read, "This canister is one of the most useful storage items ever designed . . . my next door neighbor uses it for her crochet thread . . . and pulls the end of the thread out through the small opening[;] then her thread never gets soiled . . . and it doesn't get tangled up."[47]

## "Turning Left-Overs into Plan Overs"
### The Dichotomy of Thrift and Excess

Suburban living, as well as providing a practical justification for the party plan (as the "modern way to shop for your houseware needs; con-

"The Nicest Thing That Could Happen to Your Kitchen": A doting mother appreciatively regards her collection of Tupperware as she provisions her thriving nuclear family. *Tupperware Catalogue,* Tupperware Home Parties, Inc., Orlando, Florida, ca. 1958.

veniently, leisurely, economically"), underscored the broader ideology of THP's advertising images and corporate ethos.[48] Backdrops for product promotional shots showed white picket fences and comfortable split-level interiors. A typical full-page spread promoting the community role of the Tupperware dealer delineated an idealized suburban lifestyle with illustrations of a ranch-style home, state-of-the-art household appliances, contemporary furnishings, fishing boat, limousine, and for the children, college graduation. The depiction of affluence and material abundance happily coexisted, however, with earnest appeals to economy and frugality.

Thus Tupperware embraced the contradictions of thrift and prodigality manifest in the transition from the 1930s Depression to postwar affluence. "The answer to the Housewife's demand for efficiency [and] economy . . . [and] the woman's demand for beauty," as the product catalog claimed, Tupperware appealed to the rational concerns of home economists and the frivolities of contemporary homemakers alike. It was the tension between thrift and excess that, as some cultural historians have suggested, formed the impetus behind modern consumerism and even the foundation of national American identity; the material culture of Tupperware perfectly embodied this contradiction. Likewise, salespeople working on the party plan were praised for their services to the American economy, for enabling the shift from wartime manufacture to increased postwar consumer spending: "If it were not for sales people . . . throughout the country, like ourselves, chances are 100 to 1 that we would, right now, be faced with a serious recession. During the war, productive schedules, production facilities were stepped up to such a point that they were manufacturing far more merchandise than had ever been sold before the war. If it had not been for you . . . to create the demand for this increased production, what would have happened? . . . recession or depression."[49]

Despite increased postwar consumer spending, the hardships of the Depression and wartime rationing heightened Tupperware's appeal to economy. "Tupperware doesn't cost . . . it PAYS!" declared a cartoon advertisement featuring several Econo-Canisters with women's faces and limbs, their hands gripping fistfuls of dollars, egg timers, piggy banks, and stop watches.[50] Typical of Tupperware's appeal to frugality, such depictions were followed by mottoes coined to describe the virtues of the thrifty product: "Save Waste, Taste and Space"; "Reach for a Treasure of Flavor and Freshness"; and "Waste Not Want Not: Tupperware Doesn't Cost a Lot."[51] Cleanliness and saving were vital Tupperware virtues; useful products such as the Tupperware Pastry Set ($4.67) were "sanitary, easy to clean," and the Cake-Taker ($4.67) protected pies and cakes "against insects and dust" and vermin.[52] The booklet *How to Guard Food Values* warned housewives how precious nutrients, essential to a family's well-being, might be lost through incompetent storage methods. With Tupperware containers and associated tricks of the trade, "We hope," read the pamphlet, "to put more nourishment into your family and less into thin air . . . and more value into your food budget."[53]

The threat of contamination, which ironically had been a danger associated with plastic during the 1940s, added another facet to the virtuosity of Tupperware. As a former 1950s dealer commented, "When you talked to people about what the product would do for them, they could in their mind's eye visualize, they could visualize food that became tasteless, visualize onion flavors in their refrigerators and their ice boxes . . . transfer of odors and tastes and things of this nature."[54] This notion of containment and hygiene is paralleled with a protectionism that grew, according to historians such as Tyler May, with the paranoia of the cold war and shifting class and gender roles: "Within the protective walls of the modern home, worrisome developments like sexual liberalism, women's emancipation, and affluence would lead not to decadence but to a wholesome family life. . . . Suburbia would serve as a bulwark against communism and class conflict."[55]

The Tupperware ethos circumscribed the contradictions of thrift and excess, decorum and caprice. Items such as the Econo-Canister and Wonder Bowl enabled bulk storage, the protection of clean, crisp lettuce leaves, and the ability to turn "Left-Overs into Plan Overs." But more frivolous articles, such as the spindly legged condiment holder described as a "salt and pepper caddy," provided the perfect centerpiece for impromptu buffet parties. Similarly intricate plastic doilies, "lacy, frosted" table mats, and flower-arranging centerpiece ornaments such as the Floralier denoted a domestic culture geared toward conviviality rather than stark rationalism. The Party Susan, a segmented hors d'oeuvre dish with a snap-on plastic handle and a center recess for cocktail picks, proved ideal for informal and leisurely home entertainment. "Your 'special' occasion will sparkle, when appetizers are served in this attractively designed Party Susan," read the catalog description.[56] The barbecue, a fashionable and gendered expression of suburban living, thrived with Tupperware's "Patio Partners for easy outdoor meals."[57]

Recipes suggested in corporate brochures, party demonstrations, and laminated recipe cards incorporated Tupperware into every conceivable culinary concoction. The modern homemaker could combine thrift and excess by serving leftovers in the form of "Chuck Wagon Casserole" for the family and "Deluxe Cream Cones" (with a strawberry dip) for the afternoon guests. Officially "kitchen tested" Tupperware recipes, such as "Tropicana Salad" (cottage cheese and canned pineapple), "Hearty Bean Salad" (two cans of kidney beans and garnish), "Spring Glow Angel Cake" (made from cake mix and a can of peach pie filling), and "Spring

Vegetable Salad" (vegetables set in lime Jell-O), required specific Tupperware items and techniques. Social historians have suggested that 1950s food disguised ethnic diversity in a bland and homogenized culinary "melting pot."[58] Processing techniques eliminated the food's natural taste, texture, and color and replaced them with artificial coloring, preservatives, and flavors, creating the era's taste for frequently bizarre juxtaposition of food types. The transgression of traditional food boundaries such as sweet and savory (as in "Spring Vegetable Salad") derived in part from experimentation with processed and packaged foods and their associated modernity. The preservation and bulk storage techniques of the 1930s were born of necessity, but those of the postwar period celebrated novelty, convenience, and lavishness. The widespread and elaborate use of packaged, easy-to-prepare foods did not automatically pay testament to the hegemony of the supermarket or signal a decline in homemaking skills during this period. Although women still looked to the back of packages for handy serving tips, in so doing they now inculcated a conscious reinterpretation of the values of homemade goods in relation to the commodities of modern living. Poppy Cannon's *Can Opener Cookbook,* published in 1953, demonstrated how the truly accomplished homemaker required a keen knowledge of new consumer skills, exemplified by recipes that blatantly defied traditional ingredients, preparation, and cooking procedures. In 1956, a direct relation between convenience food and Tupperware was formed under the auspices of Betty Crocker, the fictitious doyenne of cake mixes. Officials at General Mills, impressed by a Tupperware demonstration, incorporated the product into a special promotional offer. Consumers were assured that "Betty Crocker cakes mixed in Tupperware rise just as high as those [mixed] in ordinary mixing bowls."[59]

The Tupperware party acted as a forum that melded modern manners, new consumer products, and contemporary recipes. Women were encouraged to offer their interpretations of particular items, swapping homemaking advice and ultimately contributing to the formal design process (as dealers reported back to the Tupper Corporation with product suggestions or adaptations). Elsie Mortland, an "ordinary housewife" turned "expert hostess," led consumers and dealers alike through the quandaries of Tupperware use, compiling tips on food preservation and recipes for entertainment. Throughout the 1950s THP employed Mortland as a reassuring figurehead responsible for disseminating her accumulated knowledge at national "Sales Clinics" and annual events. Mortland

Brownie Wise, seated in her famous peacock chair, ca. 1954, discusses the merits of the Wonder Bowl with Elsie Mortland, the official THP hostess responsible for disseminating *Know-How* among Tupperware dealers. Wise Papers, series 3, box 29, negative 94-10895, Archives Center, National Museum of American History, Smithsonian Institution, Washington, D.C.

bridged the gap between production and consumption with her adept understanding of household provisioning and associated skills: "I knew how far a housewife expected her budget to stretch, what her storage priorities were, and what kind of cookies she might like to make for her children."[60] As Earl Tupper developed his designs in the Woonsocket research laboratory and sent them directly to Mortland for approval, she contributed to a unique design process, dependent as much on consumers' suggestions and women's domestic experience as on the formal drawing-board designs of an engineer. Notably, as an executive of THP and celebrated hostess, Mortland raised the status of homemaking skills from invisible labor to marketable skill.

Stationed at the headquarters' kitchens, she combined the tacit knowledge of homemaking with hands-on product testing. With her intimate understanding of Tupperware products, their uses and possibilities, Mortland acted as the ideal corporate hostess devising demonstrations and product identities. She created themes and seasonal demonstrations—an Easter Hostess trolley, for example, featuring a napping bunny surrounded by fluffy chicks breaking out of Tupperware bowls. In the Market Basket demonstration, a photographic backdrop featuring an ensemble of familiar supermarket commodities encouraged dealers to explain "how Tupperware tucks away groceries," prompting guests to think of the many ways that "Tupperware, *and only Tupperware* will fit into the kitchen."[61] Women were encouraged to throw away commercial packaging and decant the products into their trusty Tupperware, ensuring that "cupboard shelves are never littered with a lot of open boxes spilling their contents out." Certain Tupperware items, such as a canister "made to order for the larger package of Ritz crackers," were designed with direct reference to specific branded goods.[62] Images of "before" and "after" cupboards illustrated how Tupperware could transform a chaotic kitchen into a modern homemaker's dream, and meticulous calculations showed moneys saved through enhanced storage (for example, "20 to 25 cents on each pound of coffee, because Tupperware seals the flavor in so that it can't be lost"). And with the all-important word-of-mouth recommendation generated by the Tupperware party, by 1957 the product was firmly entrenched in the kitchen culture of America with an institutional "seal of approval" proffered by *Good Housekeeping* and *Parents* magazines.[63]

## Keeping the Lid on Liberation?
### Tupperware and the Ideology of Domesticity

The ambiguity of the Tupperware party, the intrusion of the "market" and its commodities into the sanctity of the home, has led some academics to berate it as the ultimate antifeminist, exploitative capitalist device: "This form of organizational parasitism [the party plan], while it has unique features, is analogous to that form of colonialism which extracted taxation by utilizing the existing tribal structure rather than developing its own grass roots system of administration and collection."[64]

Furthermore its appeal to an idealistic domesticity seems to substantiate the familiar historical tenet of postwar American culture as a period of depoliticization and repressive domestication for women. "Survival in the Doldrums" and the "Dark Ages" are indicative of titles used to describe a waning radicalism and the postwar decline in overtly political feminist activity.[65] Within this context, suburbia, mass consumption, and a newly domesticated feminine identity are frequently blamed as symptoms of an increasingly bourgeois and alienated society. "Suburbanisation broke up old urban, ethnic neighborhoods . . . middle-class images on television became ubiquitous, the social reality of all women was increasingly dictated by the consumer culture . . . it created an illusion of change and freedom while encouraging passivity and 'private' solutions."[66]

Popular historical narrative casts women of the 1950s as hapless victims lost in a chaotic wilderness of products "available in a lurid rainbow of colors and a steadily changing array of styles."[67] The upward economic mobility of suburbia, so the narrative runs, with its abundant supply of desirable household appliances, supplanted the authentic social relations of the extended family. With the rise of corporate power and manipulative advertising, the sanctity of the "private sphere" diminished as commerce followed "women into their own kitchens and laundries."[68] The housewife-hostess combined her duties as a moral educator and socializer through consumption. Many critics have attributed this newfound role, in which the woman becomes subsumed in the consumer culture and becomes a commodity herself, to the manipulative practices of sophisticated postwar advertisers: "Her personality and looks were integrated into her multifarious commodified skills of survival and were posed as the way to vie in a world where concrete productive capacities had nearly evaporated, and where "keen and critical" glances constantly threatened her. As her homemaking skills had been reconstituted into a process of accumulating mass-produced possession, her sexu-economic capacities were reinforced on a commercial plane."[69]

This insidious state of alienation, similarly delineated in Betty Friedan's book *The Feminine Mystique,* was the direct result, historians have argued, "of post-war suburban migration . . . and the demise of any feminist or socialist sentiment."[70]

Academic consensus and popular history alike frame this era as a low point, a shameful regression in women's history.[71] Although domestic subordination is commonly aligned to the ideology of the moral home as defined by cold war politics, Friedan's account of "The Problem That Has No Name" popularized the notion of women in the postwar period as incomplete human beings, "domestic and quiescent."[72] As one historian recounts, "Friedan concluded that the loss of female identity engendered in the suburban image was equivalent of those in Nazi death camps who had 'surrendered their human identity and gone almost indifferently to their deaths.'"[73]

More recently, this overly simplistic account of women and consumer culture in the 1950s has been subject to an increasing amount of critical scrutiny. For example, Friedan's classic work, widely understood as one of the first best-selling feminist critiques to reach a popular audience, is confined to the experiences of comparatively wealthy, middle-class white women. Similarly, the consistent emphasis on domesticity during this period precludes the radicalism of politicized and working women as a counterpoise to the pervasive suburban stereotype.[74] Women's lives as union activists or accomplished professionals are rendered invisible. Revisionist histories have sought to rectify this bias but in so doing have created another form of hierarchy, in which the "middle-brow"—the apolitical and the nonradical—remain largely unacknowledged. For example, historian Joanne Meyerowitz, in *Not June Cleaver,* an edited volume challenging stereotypes of postwar women, admits that although she undermines the pervasive image of women as domestic and quiescent, she fails to address "women on the right" and "consumerism, and glamour."[75]

Certainly the lives and achievements of pioneering female activists provide an essential component of postwar history. But unless the lives of nonradical women involved in a feminine popular culture that embraced consumerism and glamour are acknowledged, the mendacious elitism previously ascribed to white patriarchal history prevails here as well. For, as one feminist historian points out, the representation of 1950s suburban women leaves much to be desired: "Rich or poor, Catholic or Protestant, British in origin or not, female suburbanites emerged . . . as a homogeneously sorry lot, deserving little serious attention from scholars or others."[76]

Tupperware, a product that developed contemporaneously with postwar suburbia, wholeheartedly embraced both domesticity and conspicuous consumption. Its fashionable pastel designs and amiable hostesses embodied the burgeoning aspirations of white, middle-class America. Tupperware products like the Party Susan and the TV Tumbler filled what has been called the "perfect consumption space of suburbia," and the Tupperware party became an emblem of the niceties of a suburban life. "Tupperware is polite," read a sales slogan, "won't scratch shelves or counter tops, and won't leave rust marks. Tupperware colors are soft, and blend with any home. Their appealing design goes well in any style

# TUPPERWARE

## ...what dreams are made of!

Every woman dreams of spending less time on housework and more time enjoying fun with her family. At Tupperware parties held throughout the nation each day, thousands of women discover that this dream can become a reality. They see a demonstration of unique work-saving, time-saving ideas made possible only by advanced Tupperware plastic household products. They learn about the patented Tupper Seal—how it seals food flavors and values *in* while it locks air and moisture *out*—keeps stored foods fresher, longer! To make your dreams come true, plan to have a Tupperware party in your home soon. Your friends will enjoy this relaxed, informative way to shop and you'll receive a lovely gift, just for being hostess! Check your phone book for your nearest Tupperware distributor or write Dept. C-4, Tupperware Home Parties Inc., Orlando, Florida.

TUPPERWARE HOME PARTIES INC. Orlando, Florida
SOLD ONLY ON THE POPULAR HOME PARTY PLAN BY YOUR LOCAL TUPPERWARE DEALER

Corporate advertising may have depicted Tupperware women as immaculately groomed, white, middle-class, suburban housewives, but many dealers were divorcées and single mothers from a variety of social and ethnic backgrounds and geographic locations. Tupperware Home Parties, Inc., Orlando, Florida, ca. 1956.

kitchen."[77] Maligned by social commentators as a metaphor for the shallowness and socially "unnatural" matriarchy of suburban living, Tupperware embodied all the academically vilified constructs of postwar feminine identity.

Depictions of conscientious mothers abounded in corporate literature, which promised Tupperware's time- and labor-saving features as a boon to women attending PTA meetings and thinking up imaginative packed lunches for their offspring. Awards from *Parents* magazine praised the safety aspects of the nonbreakable products, and pastel tumblers, cereal bowls, and Ice-Tup molds became staple features of 1950s postwar childhood. "Momism," a term used to describe contemporary critiques of mothering (particularly the mother–son relationship) in the post–World War II period, made an uncomfortable link between women's increasingly overbearing maternal roles and the emasculation of American men. As historian Wini Breines states, "Social scientists pointed to the situation of women isolated in the suburbs which supposedly created the conditions for mothers' extreme attachment to and involvement in their children's lives. The suburbs in the 1950s were repeatedly . . . referred to as a 'suburban matriarchy', suggesting the image of an all-female society, one in which women control everything."[78] In a period defined by contradictions and inconsistencies, women were called to domesticity as a meaningful pursuit and simultaneously scapegoated for their "over-accomplishments" in this arena. The gender politics of the postwar period revolved around a paranoiac fear of suburbanization and the creation of an avaricious, domineering breed of women. "Homogenized homes," so contemporary commentators thought, "produced homogenized people. Since women were the primary inhabitants of the suburban home, they suffered the brunt of its failings. Perpetually bored by conformity, women used their consumer power to reduce the monotony in their lives."[79]

Certainly THP exploited the homebound situation of many women as well as their sociality. As a dealer, it was suggested, the housewife was simply extending her concerns as a caring homemaker to provide a service for other housewives. Care was taken to construe work at any level with THP as an enhancement rather than threat to family life, as one 1950s distributor recollects: "She [the housewife] didn't want to leave her children and the husband and the home, so we pointed out to them that being a Tupperware dealer just would take a couple of hours a day. There were a lot of daytime parties back in those days because women were home . . . so that in a couple of hours she could earn twenty-five or thirty dollars.

We went on the idea of providing education for her little children, putting that money away for education."[80]

Many women may have opted or been obligated to dedicate themselves to husband and children, but the overriding attraction of the Tupperware party to women, as dealer, hostess, or guest, was the escape from the domestic sphere: "Some of them [women] couldn't afford to play bridge. . . . Tupperware gave them the opportunity to get out into the public, to make some money in addition to that."[81]

According to oral histories and corporate documents, the consumption and distribution (for the two were intertwined throughout the party plan) of Tupperware was a heterogeneous and pro-active rather than passive process. Top-selling Tupperware dealers often turned their pursuits into full-blown family businesses. These "Tupperized" families (as corporate literature referred to them) were promoted as ideal domestic units brought together in the pursuit of a shared economic goal. Although these business ventures frequently followed conventional gender divisions of labor, the company firmly acknowledged the primacy of the woman: "She would usually be into being the party demonstrator and he was the person to pack out the product and do a lot of the bookkeeping . . . she was kinda the front man — sorry, front woman . . . ladies, I think, tend to be much warmer and better communicators, and that is certainly part of the Tupperware story."[82]

The Tupperware party, like suburbia itself, is commonly criticized as an empty, parochial, and divisive institution. To quote Scott Donaldson in *The Suburban Myth,* "most social commentators regard . . . suburbs [as] homogenous, conformist . . . conservative, dull, child centered, [and] female dominated." Suburban living is viewed as a form of moral and social bankruptcy, the ultimate relinquishment of political responsibility. "People in the suburbs, it is charged, regard each other as tools, or commodities."[83]

In a famous in-depth study of a North American suburb published in 1956 under the title *Crestwood Heights,* the suburban home was described as "little more than a repository of an exceedingly wide range of artifacts." The purpose of the picture window, the Crestwood Heights study concluded, "seems less to give the occupants a view of the outside . . . and more to extend an invitation to the outsider to look in . . . [at] a grand piano, valuable crystal chandelier, or a striking red brocade chair."[84] The accumulation of material culture, then, was automatically associated with pecuniary emulation and the normalization of bourgeois taste.[85]

It is perhaps not difficult to understand why the Tupperware party, with its blend of goods and social relations, slotted so neatly into place with the critics' version of an alienated and consumer-oriented suburban expansion. Even the mass-produced, injection-molded plastic items equated with the critics' descriptions of standardized postwar living and the vacuity of the commodity form, such as Lewis Mumford's: "a multitude of uniform, unidentifiable houses, lined up inflexibly at uniform distances, on uniform roads, . . . inhabited by people of the same class, the same income, the same age group, witnessing the same television performances, eating the same tasteless pre-fabricated foods, from the same freezers, conforming in every outward and inward respect to a common mold."[86]

These frequently patronizing critiques, which romanticized the authenticity of the city in contrast to the superficiality of the suburb, nullified any apparently constructive endeavors the suburbanite might make. "The suburbanite clearly can't win, if he leaves his home as he found it, he is accused of standardization and conformity; if he attempts to alter his home, he is accused of a shallow competition for status."[87] Similarly, ethnic groups moving to the suburbs were described as "selling their souls" to the American dream rather than reaping benefits and opportunities that were rightfully theirs.

In 1958 Robert C. Wood's contemporary analysis, *Suburbia: Its People and Their Problems,* highlighted historical notions of American community and the tendency to condemn modern forms as less "meaningful."[88] The Tupperware party was deemed an inauthentic charade, which sought to disguise the meaninglessness of contemporary commodity culture with the mock authenticity of applied sociality: "Rather than adding decoration to products, Tupperware added a ritual, the party, which helped new suburbanites deal with the insecurity and loneliness that was part of their pioneering lives. The company added the ritual for the same reason that most manufacturers added the decoration."[89]

But as one commentator pointed out, suburbia demanded new manners and rituals that constituted genuine and authentic meanings within themselves, despite their variation on traditional forms. "In the suburbs, modern interdependence among neighbors is not expressed in fighting Indians or gathering crops, but in sharing children's clothes and alternating trips to the supermarket."[90]

Consumption and consumer products, according to numerous historians and social scientists, have acted as a homogenizing force in the naturalization of middle-class values. It has even been suggested that advertisers of the 1950s consciously manipulated the television viewer, using product design placements in sitcoms to eradicate social tensions. "The class and gender related tensions inherent in consumer decisions could be identified through market research and alleviated through design," thus eradicating class and feminist consciousness. Female consumers, depicted as leisurely homemakers liberated by labor-saving devices, merely contributed to the invisibility of their housework by glamorizing it. The domestic space of suburbia, strictly delineated in terms of white, gender-divided, middle-class America, was constructed as the "corner stone of the American social economy of the 1950s."[91] Suburban social relations, design, and material culture formed part of an ideological system pervading everything from popular television sitcoms *(Father Knows Best, Leave It to Beaver, I Love Lucy)* to advertising images. Indeed at the peak of Tupperware's popularity the producers of *I Love Lucy* approached THP asking if they might base a plot around a Tupperware party; despite the publicity opportunities the management declined, fearing, as Brownie Wise later stated, that the show might make a farce of the Tupperware party.[92]

In an equally reductionist way, consumption is commonly represented as the cause of diminished self-determination among women in the postwar period. "Women's family role was glorified by advertisers to sell commodities, and the suburban home was the perfect consumption space — new, bare, needing to be filled with furniture, appliances and cleaning aids."[93]

In her study of the American suburban home, and its association with postwar middle-class identity, historian Lizabeth Cohen considers the crucial role of domestic consumption in a world of open-plan kitchens and neighborly leisure. Unlike many historians, though, Cohen queries whether homogenization was a phenomenon automatically linked to suburbanization and its material culture and consumption. Although the move to a suburban lifestyle signaled a newly formulating (predominantly white) middle-class identity, it was an identity of increasing complexity, differentiation, and segmentation. "Suburbanites of the 1950s were not converted overnight from culturally and socially diverse urbanites to more conformist, Americanized and middle-class suburbanites," argues Cohen. Instead, "They sought to express their individuality as much as their conformity in the homes they created."[94] Far from losing themselves in an orgy of mass consumption, many suburban dwellers relied on activities of informal economy (using second-hand goods, growing their own produce, borrowing kitchen equipment) and "sustained strong ties with ethnic and working-class family and friends in their old urban neighborhoods."[95]

In the context of critiques of homogenization, the Tupperware party stands as an iconic metaphor of white, parochial suburban culture. Corporate images featured well-groomed, affluent, white American housewives embracing consumption and conservative feminine roles. But it is essential to understand the disjuncture between representation of the Tupperware corporate culture, whose images obviously belonged to a broader hegemony, and its practice.

The very nature of the party plan system meant that Tupperware infiltrated sections of American society otherwise precluded from the trappings of the American Dream. Dealers tapped into their specific and localized networks of women. Consequently, black and Hispanic women, single mothers, and divorcées formed the less visible force behind Tupperware's expansion.[96] Many women appropriated Tupperware as an accessible symbol of modernity and a viable means of employment. Transcripts of Tupperware sales seminars make consistent reference to "the Negro market" as a significant arena of consumption. Vice President Brownie Wise made several guest appearances at black colleges, promoting the role of business and positive self-growth philosophy.

It is true that employment with THP was organized on an informal basis, therefore offering little security and no formal insurance benefits. But in a pragmatic sense this flexibility allowed women to be casually employed and maintain their traditionally circumscribed roles as mothers and homemakers. Tupperware women enhanced their self-respect and utilized their skills in service to their neighborhoods as valued members of the community. To quote one oral history, "When I had been with Tupperware [for] just two weeks, folks said I was no longer the shrinking violet they had once known!"[97] Joe Hara, former president of Tupperware US, remembers the effect of the Tupperware party on new hostesses: "When [women] put on that first Tupperware Party, when they were given the opportunity to stand before a group of people in the quiet of someone's home with maybe eight or ten women listening to them, and heard their voice above the quiet of the room, it gave them a sense of self-esteem; they thought they had passed away and gone to heaven. It was just an image building experience."[98]

For all women, employment with Tupperware and THP raised the status of feminine and homemaking skills. Tacit homemaking and management skills were paramount in the party plan sales system, as was sociability and sharing in the process of establishing successful sales networks. Though it exploited sociability and economic disadvantage, Tupperware offered nonradical solutions to domestic isolation and boosted support networks and confidence: "Before I attended a Tupperware party I thought the last thing I'd like to do was sit with a whole load of other homemakers and talk recipes. But I had a sociable time and it helped me with my first boy, because you know I wasn't so confident about childcare in those days."[99]

Tupperware did not act merely as an empty vessel, a neutral commodity upon which social relations were brought to bear. Tupperware was appropriated in systems of informal economy to expand existing fissures and enable social and material alternatives. Dealers with children might barter Tupperware to enable themselves to accrue income selling Tupperware: "I remember as a Tupperware dealer, with my babies, I exchanged time for Tupperware with my neighbors. In other words, let's say you would watch my children for three hours, well, rather than paying you fifty cents an hour . . . I would give you a dollar and a half worth of retail Tupperware. Now please remember, that was a set of cereal bowls back in those days."[100]

Tupperware parties provided sanctioned, all-female gatherings outside the family. Loyalty to neighbors and friends was the linchpin for attendance at many parties (some informants even recalled budgeting within the monthly housekeeping for attendance at Tupperware parties), but for many women it was an opportunity to socialize outside the home at little expense. Although the pretext of the gatherings was domestic, this did not preclude women from directing the conversation and interaction toward other concerns. A sociological study by Elayne Rapping, for example, suggests that Tupperware parties have offered a viable forum for the politicization of working-class women.[101]

Tupperware, then, embodied the contradictions of a growing postwar consumer culture. While substantiating predominantly conservative and traditional feminine roles, it also provided a pragmatic, if compromised, alternative to domestic subordination. As the "Tupperware Lady" evolved as a common feature of neighborhoods across the United States, Brownie Wise, vice president of THP, led the company with an increasingly public and cultlike profile.

s   i   x

• • •

# "Faith Made Them Champions"
## The Feminization of Positive Thinking

I n April 1954, Brownie Wise, vice president and general manager of
Tupperware Home Parties, became the first woman to appear on the
cover of *Business Week*. "If we build the people, they'll build the business," she announced assertively. The inside pages explained the miracu-
lous ascent of Wise, an ordinary housewife, to the position of chief in
a top grossing corporation. Her merchandising principles were described
by *Business Week* as "off-beat tactics" that would make any conventional
merchandiser shudder. These included deployment of elaborate incentive
schemes, recruitment of inexperienced salespeople, and elimination of
high-pressure sales techniques. Faith, respect, and sorority, Wise asserted,
created the overarching principle that had led to a triple increase in
profits since 1953, leaving the estimated turnover figure for 1954 at $25
million.

Women's magazines lauded Wise as a popularist heroine—a woman
who had turned her life around and survived abandonment by her husband, lone parenthood, ill health, and insolvency to become a "sunny and
successful" role model for ordinary women across the nation. Self-
determination and the opportunities offered by the party plan had rewarded her with "a palatial Florida lakeside home" and a "salary offer of
$125,000 a year from a rival concern."[1] Like many Tupperware women
she had begun as a nervous hostess, so "flustered she tripped over her sample case and left [her first party] with a nose bleed," commented *Woman's*

*Home Companion* in its lead article, "Help Yourself to Happiness."[2] After bursting into tears and vowing never to make another call, Wise persevered, picked up her 50-pound (22.6-kilogram) sample case, and several years later, at the age of forty, became the head of one of America's largest and most dynamic home-demonstration sales companies.

Although Tupperware celebrated domesticity and "feminine" skills, Brownie Wise also preached a potent doctrine of positive thinking, sisterly concern, and self-empowerment.[3] As a divorcée and single mother she plainly understood the economic and social hardship of women precluded from secure and affluent lifestyles. Contrary to the ideals of contemporary corporate culture, she deemed caring and nurturing to be intrinsic elements of a successful business operation. Promoting shared experience, rather than individual competition, she held feminine reciprocity and loyalty as the mainstays of increased productivity. "Success," she declared "is reciprocal."

In her reassessment of *The Feminine Mystique* (in which the author, Betty Friedan, condemns the cult of domesticity and passivity promoted by postwar feminine popular culture), Joanne Meyerowitz highlights the significance of popularist trends such as positive thinking in her plea that "historians need to explore further the influence of human potential psychology on contemporary feminism."[4] Meyerowitz also asserts that both mainstream and African-American women's magazines in the postwar period, contrary to Friedan's interpretation, actually celebrated the biographical profiles of accomplished and career-oriented women, often reducing domesticity to little more than "a sideshow." It was in this context that numerous press articles represented Brownie Wise, who openly praised the pursuit of full-time careers for women and glorified "frenetic activity" rather than passive domesticity. As a darling of the women's press she consistently united the apparently disparate concepts of glamour and pragmatism. Under the auspices of the party plan she advocated self-advancement and human potential psychology. "The only proper way to help people in trouble is to help them help themselves," she told an inquiring journalist.[5]

Domestic ideology and self-help platitudes, though intrinsically conservative in origin, took on a potentially subversive role as orchestrated by Wise. Inspired by Norman Vincent Peale's maxim, "Faith Made Them Champions," she equipped women with a cohesive and sympathetic corporate structure that offered a pragmatic alternative to assigned feminine roles. By 1958, as reported in *Salesman's Opportunity,* the Tupperware

# BUSINESS WEEK

WHY BUSINESS
KEEPS SPENDING FOR
**Capital Goods**
PAGE 104

INDEX
YEAR
AGO

Brownie Wise of Tupperware: "If we build the people, they'll build the business" (page 54)

A McGRAW-HILL PUBLICATION

**APR. 17, 1954**

In 1954, Brownie Wise became the first woman to appear on the cover of *Business Week* as the leader of a multimillion-dollar corporation. Reprinted from the 17 April 1954 issue of *Business Week* by special permission. © 1954 by McGraw-Hill Companies.

party plan offered "everyday" women a source of income and the possibility of a meteoric rise in public status. "Doris Stewart's rise in selling has been . . . electrifying. An active member of the Tupperware organization for a little over two years, she has quickly moved from the rank of dealer and manager to distributor . . . and has, through her own efforts, made many of her dreams come true."[6] Acknowledging the appeal of direct sales work to women, the magazine ran a dedicated column, "Woman's Opportunity," which addressed the problems of scarce and inflexible labor possibilities and proffered the party plan as an ideal remedy. Similarly the January 1952 edition of *Charm,* "the magazine for women who work," listed Tupperware as a miracle product with an especially attractive sales method. Although there were various levels of involvement with direct sales schemes (from one-time hostess to full-time distributor), many women actually relied solely on this type of work for their income as a vital contribution to dwindling household resources. A typical feature, "An Angel with a Sales Kit"—the true story of a single mother brought to ruin and desperately seeking ways to provide for her three children—illustrated the appeal of the party plan. "First of all, I couldn't leave the children to take an office job," commented the single mother, "and besides, I figured that even if I could work daytimes, I simply couldn't make enough money to give the little ones all the things they should have."[7] Needless to say, her problems were solved by the flexible employment opportunities of direct selling.

## "Sunshine Cinderella"
### Tupperware's Fairy Godmother

"Brownie," noted a women's magazine article in the mid-1950s, "is convinced that people, especially women, never get enough recognition in their own lives." In the same interview, when asked if she had ever considered remarrying, Wise replied assuredly, "Why should I? My work provides me with all the fun, excitement and emotional outlets I could ever want . . . it enables me to give other women in financial trouble the same chance I had to help themselves to happiness."[8]

Despite the domestic ideology of the 1950s, Tupperware women were openly encouraged to consider their jobs as potentially serious career prospects; the image and activities of the company far exceeded the mundane experience of part-time work for "pin-money." As an ordinary middle-aged housewife and single mother, Wise herself could be seen to have turned from rags to riches with the "Cinderella Company" (as it became known).[9] With Tupperware, the classic fairytale (in which romantic love conquers poverty and social injustice and recognizes true worthiness) held particular resonance. Tupperware could transport women to a world beyond the confines of thrifty homemaking and "making do." Brownie Wise evolved as a cult figure, transforming the party plan system into a spectacle of magnificent conspicuous consumption, in which the Tupperware object formed merely the tip of a commodity iceberg. With her penchant for high fashion, glamorous living, and the color pink (she sponsored the hybridization of a pink "Tupperware Rose," drove a rose-pink convertible with green leather upholstery, and adored her pink canary, named "Mr. Crosby," which complemented her office decor), Wise utilized an aesthetic recognizable to women across class and ethnic boundaries. "'She shall have music wherever she goes' at least in the office. . . . Brownie wanted a canary, and her favorite color of everything—from flowers to cars—is, of course, Tupperware Rose pink. So the obvious answer was a pink canary," declared the in-house magazine in celebration of Wise's unique style.[10]

Pink, and its association with femininity, was a familiar commercial device used in the 1930s by businesswomen such as Elizabeth Arden, who promoted a distinctly "woman friendly" cosmetics company. "Arden Pink," the color chosen for her salons, packaging, and apparel, formed part of a broader intimate appeal to the female consumer and obscured a distinctly wily business acumen: "Pink femininity concealed Arden's acts as an exacting and tough manager who broke a threatened strike, fended off complaints from the Food and Drug Administration, and remained the sole stockholder of her company despite several marriages and buyout offers."[11] Notably this confluence of feminine business and the color pink anticipated the "pink Cadillac" incentive schemes of the Mary Kay Cosmetics direct sales company, founded in 1963, by several decades.

As well as following the Arden business precedent, Wise shared her pink fetish with First Lady Mamie Eisenhower, who used pink to decorate and accessorize the more intimate rooms of the White House and the presidential vacation home, from pink-tufted headboards to pink tiles and soap dishes. To quote art historian Karal Ann Marling, "She favored pink evening gowns and pink hats. She kept two brandy snifters full of pink rosebuds at her elbow." So crucial to Mrs. Eisenhower's identity had the color become by 1955 that "First Lady Pink" was a recognized hue for "dresses, linoleum flooring, dishware, plastic buckets, nylon curtains, bathroom fixtures, and hardware-store paint chips."[12] By 1956, the contemporary mania for pink provoked parody in the Audrey Hepburn film *Funny Face,* in the scene in which the editor of America's leading fashion magazine exhorts her staff and the entire nation to "Think pink!" if they "want to get ahead."

Just as the contemporary propensity for vivid color, used in and on everything from breakfast cereal to kitchen appliances, signaled "a culture in love with novelty, change, and visual stimulation," specific objects of material culture signified a quintessential 1950s notion of romantic love and affluence. Mink stoles, diamond rings, couture dresses and limousines, icons of popular feminine fantasy as depicted in films such as *How to Marry a Millionaire* and *Gentlemen Prefer Blondes* (both in 1953), became the staple diet for top Tupperware dealers and managers. Competitions, incentive schemes, and hostess premiums encompassed a carefully chosen array of material culture to bolster a corporate culture of self-worth.[13] Wise was frequently featured on the front cover of *Tupperware Sparks,* the monthly in-house magazine, in charismatic and glamorous poses: flanked by the kneeling male executive proffering gifts; standing resplendent in a strapless satin and lace gown; embracing high-achieving Tupperware women while showering them with treats. The pages were filled with her anecdotes, household tips, and descriptions of her lace couture dresses, pastel pink convertible, luxury lakeside home, dyed pink canary, and pet palomino pony. Foibles such as her compulsive eating habits were discussed at length for a popular female audience: "Brownie fixes herself a favorite snack of pickles, cheese and walnuts before going to bed. Her other eating habits are equally odd. She packs away enormous breakfasts frequently topped off by ice-cream, eats dessert before her hamburger at lunch and munches ice-cream sticks whenever she feels hungry during the day."[14]

Although acknowledged as a top corporate executive, Wise purportedly attended work wearing "feminine dresses and frilly hats looking like a young matron on her way to a bridge party."[15] From the onset Wise, a woman enabled through her "ordinariness" to tentatively transgress the limitations experienced by the majority of her female contemporaries, acted as a shrewd corporate figurehead by consciously constructing her unique image. Many direct sales concerns, such as the Stanley Home Products and Fuller Brush companies, used presidents as easily recognizable and revered spokespeople to motivate a disparate sales force. Earl

Tupper, reclusive to the point of being physically sickened by large gatherings of people, was reluctant to play the public role of leader himself. According to oral history Tupper made it quite clear that he was "more interested in things than people." Therefore Wise's agency in transforming and directing the THP business can hardly be overstated; strongheaded and exceptionally charismatic, she often encountered disagreements with Tupper concerning proposed moves within the company. Far from acting as a malleable puppet of the male executive, she led her 95 percent female sales team with a calculated, but genuine, devotion.[16] General sales manager Jack Marshall, initially reluctant to work for a woman, admitted, "She never gets cute or coy. During a crisis she's the calmest, least emotional person in the place."[17]

Despite her cool business acumen Wise built up the Tupperware company through immense interpersonal and emotional investment. As one business journalist commented, "It is the first time that a woman has taken a business by the heart instead of the purse strings."[18] Love and inspiration created a sense of reciprocity and a thriving support system within the Tupperware sales force. Gifts and letters of appreciation arrived daily at the THP headquarters, and Wise responded personally to the inquiries, comments, and achievements of her Tupperware women. Her high-profile position led to numerous coast-to-coast visits. At many of the destinations she partook in lavish spending sprees, buying earrings, ornaments, scarves, and outfits, which she would later convert into gifts for incentives schemes.[19] She frequently advised women in times of emotional or financial hardship, writing to them in person, and remembering the details of their family circumstances.[20]

The dynamic of this "special" relationship between Brownie and her sales team is exemplified by the prose of a Tupperware dealer who, taking notes at a company sales session promoting confidence in feminine intuition ("Know-How"), was compelled to leave her leader a testament of her affection. The note read: "Brownie—just sitting here looking at you and listening to you talk I wonder if you can ever realize the tenderness in our affection for you, and the really deep and abiding gratitude that most of us (me in particular) feel for this wonderful opportunity in business we now enjoy. Thank you Brownie for being a constant shining example of never tiring energy and a moving force that keeps us all in constant motion—love Helda Degraves."[21]

The "Cinderella story" of rags-to-riches women was typified by the testament of Corliss Levitt in 1953. A single mother of three children,

Brownie Wise demonstrates stackable Tupperware containers to attentive male executives, ca. 1956. Despite the conservatism of postwar American gender politics, corporate images promoted rather than avoided displays of Wise's power in relation to the predominantly male executives. Wise Papers, series 3, box 29, negative 94-10886, Archives Center, National Museum of American History, Smithsonian Institution, Washington, D.C.

with "inimitable charm and unbounded enthusiasm," she became the first National Merit Award winner to enter the Tupperware Hall of Fame. Promoted to managerial level within a year of dealership, she wrote to the corporation expressing endless thanks for her achievement. "This is really a wonderful business with a wonderful product, isn't it, Brownie? . . . Now I'm so happy, my children are happy, and I know for sure that my future with precious Tupperware is, as you said at the very beginning, exactly what I want to make it."[22]

The treatises of prominent positive thinkers such as Dale Carnegie and Norman Vincent Peale pervaded THP culture. Throughout her career Wise collected and collated the prose of inspirational writers, educators, and preachers and recycled their sentiments in her numerous sales speeches and addresses. This contemporary taste for self-help ideology similarly pervaded entrepreneurial and amateur business publications including *Success Unlimited* and *Salesman's Opportunity*. These magazines regularly featured "The Tupperware Success Story" as a model entrepreneurial venture and "the result of the positive thinking, vision and enthusiasm of two people—an industrial designer and a housewife."[23] Unlike the Museum of Modern Art's twentieth-century exhibit, which accounted for Tupperware's success in terms of the logic of "good design," such articles identified the savvy of women in direct sales as the driving force behind the product's success. Despite the nice pastel colors of Tupperware displayed in the stores, they wrote, "something was missing." "It was the woman's touch," they insisted, "a touch [that] had to be given in the home—at a demonstration for other women to see, before the powers of this new product could be realized."[24]

Self-realization, according to Wise, was an eternal obligation, "the obligation to make the most of what we have—to make the most of our lives."[25] And in this context, the party plan could contribute to women's self-determination, human growth, and increased financial security. Although personal reward, emotional and material, served as a legitimate motive, true self-actualization came through giving and sharing, particularly in the form of knowledge. "Your knowledge becomes a reality only when you give it away. . . . You must keep the stream running."[26] In this sense women were encouraged to share their Tupperware know-how, from demonstration techniques to accounting advice, with fellow dealers and so perpetuate and consolidate a range of tacitly acquired knowledge.

"Hitch your wagon to a star," suggested Wise, and see "your dreams come true with Tupperware."[27] After visiting the company in 1954, positive-thinking author Napoleon Hill commented that the atmosphere of "democracy of thought" and the "encouragement of initiative" put into play "the most perfect practical application of my Master Mind Principle."[28] This air of harmony, dedication, and inspiration became known as "Tupper Magic," a concept celebrated in corporate songs and rituals, even today. "Seeing every day the results of their work in other people's happiness," observed one journalist reporting on Tupperware dealers, "they find in their activity a kind of religion."[29] The THP corporate creed (1953) epitomized this theme: "In the unity of our ideas and our ambitions lies our greatest strength. . . . A drop of water contains but an infinitesimal molecule of strength . . . powerless in itself. But the merging of billions of drops of water produces the tremendous power of Niagara Falls.[30]

## "The Garden That Loyalty Built"
### Envisaging a Tupperware Mecca

By 1954 a classically inspired, gleaming-white colonnaded building, situated among 1,000 acres (400 hectares) of lush, lagoon-filled gardens replete with Italianate statuettes, meditative pathways, and dedication plaques, stood as a monument to the "Tupperware Gospel."[31] The million-dollar "Startling New Look" building on the Orange Blossom Trail in Orlando, Florida, was devised as a mecca for Tupperware women nationwide. This "beautiful, streamlined building" housed three spacious auditoriums—the Pacific Hall, Midwest, and Gulf rooms—each fully equipped with lighting and sound systems in preparation for the "gatherings of the ever-expanding Tupperware family."[32] Tupper Lake was designed to reflect the shining white beauty of the "new Tupperware home." Rose Lake and the Lagoon of Cypress were landscaped to connect through a verdant woodland crisscrossed by the occasional rustic bridge. A tropical garden, containing rare native Floridian plants and flowers and interlaced with tiny winding paths, formed the centerpiece of the executive wing. The Garden Pavilion provided seating for up to a thousand Tupperware "Homecomers," and a swimming pool equipped with brightly painted changing rooms allowed a refreshing dip for employees. During the final stages of the headquarters completion, top distributors and managers were requested to send a pair of their old shoes to THP in order that imprints could be made, Hollywood style, in the Tupperware Walk of Fame. Poly Pond, which Brownie blessed by casting a handful of raw polyethylene pellets to its depths, made a focal point at which women could be baptized with "Tupper Magic" at the water's edge. "Surely you realize now that you are *home,*" announced Wise to a gathering of sales managers in 1955. "Everything here is dedicated to you . . . the flagstaff, the garden court, our beautiful administration building, this pavilion . . . the very ground here is consecrated to a program of furthering the interests of you in the Tupperware family."[33]

The Loyalty Garden, based on a plant collection cultivated by M. J. Daetwyler (one of Florida's leading horticulturists) featured a shrine and a statue, *Growing Things.* Across the grassy lawn of the Loyalty Garden stretched a shining chain, each of the 10,000 links bearing the name of a Tupperware person responsible for building the company's success. The reflective beauty of Lantern Lake reminded visitors of the individuals who had dared to carry the lantern of knowledge and so helped light the trail for others.

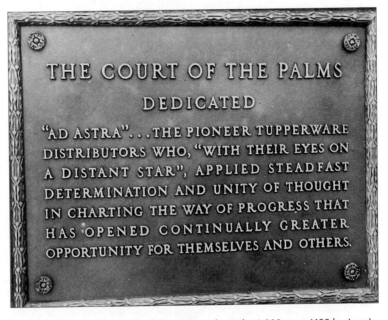

Dedication plaques, strategically placed throughout the 1,000 acres (400 hectares) of dramatically landscaped and lagoon-filled grounds of the THP headquarters, ca. 1954, paid homage to the women who built the Tupperware empire. Wise Papers, series 3, box 29, negative 94-13616, Archives Center, National Museum of American History, Smithsonian Institution, Washington, D.C.

The air-conditioned distribution offices, covering 60,000 square feet (5,580 square meters) and equipped with state-of-the-art technology provided by IBM, ensured the efficient processing of the rapidly expanding volume of Tupperware party plan orders. Presiding over the newly constructed empire with requisite style, Brownie Wise chose the furnishings for her lavish, personally designed corporate suite ("half the size of Grand Central Station," according to one journalist) with the help of contemporary architect Frank Masiello.

The headquarters foyer featured a 42-foot-long (12.8-meter) mural, *Evolution of Dishes,* painted by beatnik artists in the "contemporary style" and depicting the history of dishes, prehistoric to the present day. The final panel showed a typical Tupperware mold and the "hands of Mr. Earl Tupper."[34] In a similarly didactic fashion, the Museum of Dishes (or "housewives' museum," as it was defined by one publication) featured kitchen vessels ranging from "caveman's utensils" to the modern home-

Women line up to receive "Tupper Magic" by dipping their hands in the sacred Poly Pond at the Tupperware headquarters in Orlando, Florida, ca. 1952. Wise Papers, series 3, box 30, negative 94-13609, Archives Center, National Museum of American History, Smithsonian Institution, Washington, D.C.

maker's designs, with Tupperware positioned as the culmination of technological evolution and the sole representation of late-twentieth-century material culture. The exhibit showed wooden Shaker boxes, ancient Persian ceramics, Native American ceremonial vessels, and decorative Tiffany glassware and, omitting ritual, religious, social, and cultural context of the objects, used a dramatic display of Tupperware as the pinnacle of progress in domestic design.

Adjacent to the foyer, the Consumer Lounge featured a display of archetypal Tupperware forms floating against a black velvet background and a lollipop tree for the pleasure of visiting children. The THP national headquarters quickly gained popularity as a regular sight-seeing destination for tourists on Florida's Greyhound bus route. By September 1954 the Greyhound Bus Florida sight-seeing itinerary included a visit to the million-dollar headquarters.[35] Open to the public, the Magic Kitchen, designed to include modern conveniences, offered daily demonstrations and experimental product testing. "As new products are introduced, new and

Wise stands proudly before the mural *Evolution of Dishes,* ca. 1952. Wise Papers, series 3, box 29, negative 94-13610, Archives Center, National Museum of American History, Smithsonian Institution, Washington, D.C.

diversified uses will be developed in this kitchen," dealers and managers were informed.[36] An exhibit home placed Tupperware in situ, from tea beside the traditional inglenook to vacations in a recreational vehicle. "Before" and "after" cupboards, supervised by home economists, showed the benefits of Tupperware organization to the modern homemaker.

The Tupperware Art Fund, which Wise devised to promote "an appreciation of beauty in daily living," distributed three annual $2,400 scholarships to artists across the country.[37] It reflected a broader national craze for art, particularly the amateur art epitomized by the boom in paint-by-numbers sets, and drew on a contemporary romantic image of the artist encapsulated by films such as *An American in Paris* (1951).[38] The first award, for a painting titled *Mother and Child,* was presented to "a housewife artist" who, a local paper commented, "admits she knows more about Picasso than about meat balls."[39] Contestants had been asked to submit paintings that "typified the theme of home, family life, community living," the winning works to be added to the permanent collection of the Tupperware Art Fund Museum. Directed by Ernest Fiene, president of the Artists' Equity Association, the competitive scholarship scheme formed part of a broader vision regarding the public role of art. Alongside the Museum of Dishes, the *Evolution of Dishes* mural, and the extensive collection of imported statuary in the courts and gardens of Tupperware grounds, the art fund consolidated Wise's "beautification program." Fountains, carved marble benches, and figurines, including Brownie's sentimental favorite, *Turtle Baby,* added "loveliness and grandeur" to the THP headquarters.[40]

## All-Girl Gatherings
### The Extravaganza of the Tupperware Homecoming Jubilee

The magnificent setting of the THP headquarters created a fitting backdrop for the annual Tupperware Homecoming Jubilees. Themed events of corporate sociability and spectacle, these lavish celebratory gatherings, which took place over a period of five days, brought together as many as 2,000 Tupperware managers and distributors from across America. The schedules included intensive sales know-how sessions, speeches by prominent retailing experts and positive thinkers, and elaborate award ceremonies. Sales seminar titles included "People Want to Be Sold," "You Never Recruit Alone," "A Profitable Triangle," and "Forceful Gentility."

In 1954 the "Big Dig" Homecoming Jubilee, which celebrated the third birthday of THP, featured the theme of gold prospecting as a metaphor for pioneering American spirit. The corporate memo system, with messages referred to as "Sparko-Grams," prepared visitors for the fervor of the forthcoming venture. "Be sure to tell all of your dealers who are planning to attend the April Home Coming, that the 'Gold Digging' calls for 'blue jeans' or other clothes just as casual. . . . it would be rather difficult in high heels."[41]

The "Sparko-Gram" went on to assure "homecomers" that there would be opportunity to change into "something more dressy" for the evening events. Jack Marshall, head of general sales, used the same means of communication to remind distributors that their dealers would be attending the event with serious intentions and so should be supplied with a minimum of four stenographer's notebooks and a mechanical pencil.[42] Regional units were encouraged to display outfits significant to their locality: "The Kansas City dealers, are coming . . . dressed as Indians and the

Houston dealers will be fully attired in cowboy regalia."[43] A promotional campaign preceding the Jubilee used the history of the 1849 gold rush to draw analogies between gold mine labor shortages and the need for consistent dealer recruitment. The metaphor was extended, in keeping with a notion of American pragmatism, to equipping Tupperware recruits with effective sales techniques: "Workers must be shown how to use [the best tools] in order to unearth the most gold in the shortest period of time."[44] Similarly, the word-of-mouth sales promotions and public relations of the company were compared to the "contagious joy" expounded during the gold rush.[45]

A pre-Jubilee sales campaign, the "Gold Digger Drive," had been announced in August 1953, and distributorships competing in sales and recruitment pledges were designated "sites" on a "Big Dig" map in accordance with their success. A "Tupperware Trail," which featured landmarks such as "Prospectors Peak" and "Datebook Mountain," designated areas for digging in accordance with sales ranks. The greater the achievement, the further along the trail the Tupperware woman was allowed and the greater the worth of the "buried treasure."[46]

Within a "golden acre" of roped-off land in the company grounds was buried an approximated $48,500 worth of commodities, secured before the opening of the "show-down" by a team of armed police and guard dogs. Mock Western props, such as a Tupper general store, perpetuated the theatricality of the scene in which women were instructed to "Strike It Rich." Six hundred erect shovels, set in the sacred Tupperware grounds, awaited the eager gold diggers decked out in cowboy hats and denims and ready to "Dig for Gold." Brownie Wise, dressed in cowgirl ranching garb, supervised the event on horseback, while women dug frantically to retrieve items including mink stoles, diamond rings, radios, gold watches, toasters, and attaché cases. After five hours of intensive digging few women left the scene disappointed. A toy car was dragged from the soil by Fay Maccalupo and later traded for the full-size 1954 Ford model. Mrs. Elsie Mortland dug herself a giant diamond cluster ring, and Betty Long paraded her newly claimed $500 mink stole around the digging area.[47]

The event received national press coverage. Reporting the "All-Girl Gathering," *Life* ran a major photo-essay of the bizarre proceedings, using three pages of action shots and the subheading "Sales Bonus Winners Are Paid off in Buried Loot."[48] *Business Week* ran an in-depth article regarding the company's unprecedented success and unusual business approach, and the CBS network televised the occasion. Local papers provided extensive

At the 1954 "Big Dig" Homecoming Jubilee, Tupperware women pulled their prizes—everything from attaché cases to mink stoles and diamond rings—from the ground. Wise Papers, series 3, box 30, negative 94-11126, Archives Center, National Museum of American History, Smithsonian Institution, Washington, D.C.

photo coverage of Tupperware's "Big-Dig," and even the United Kingdom's BBC carried a telecast of the strange American gold-digging bonanza.

The "Big Dig" event served as a hybrid charade of American cultural mythology, incorporating the pioneer spirit of the Wild West cowboy and American Indian adventure and gold rush fervor. Within this analogy the spoils of a new industrial America replaced raw gold and were plentiful for those truly dedicated to the democracy of the American Dream. The resonance of this display was further pursued in an array of addresses and ceremonies, particularly those of the key speakers. Dr. Ralph W. Sockman, pastor of Christ Methodist Church in New York and presenter of a popular Sunday program, *National Radio Pulpit*, "heard weekly by an estimated 6 million listeners," was invited to give the initiation speech of the Homecoming.[49] A "Sparko-Gram" had been released to announce the excitement and honor associated with the proposed visit from Dr. Sockman, who was also president of the Protestant Council of New York City and director of the American Hall of Fame.[50] He delivered a combination of sales talk and sermon in a speech, "How to Live," which "stressed the value of the home, as the magic circle to transform society, and spirit of the community as defensive bulwarks against communism."[51] In the cold war climate of incrimination, it was not extraordinary that Tupperware should accentuate its all-American virtue.

Indeed the legacy of Tupperware's glowing business history, one of entrepreneurial risk justly rewarded, was presented in an appropriately patriotic light. H. K. Inteman, vice president and general sales manager of the Bakelite Company, commemorated the eleven-year connection between his company and Tupperware and emphasized their association in developing the first commercial production of polyethylene in America. In outlining the history of the plastics industry, from "the days of the celluloid collar some seventy-five years ago," he positioned Tupperware at the end of an evolutionary process matched by better consumer understanding of plastics. He concluded by praising "the house and ground that Direct Selling built" as more than a spectacular headquarters: "It is also a monument to ingenuity and resourcefulness, which is the basis of the free enterprise system."[52]

The Tupperware College of Knowledge, which provided a curriculum of sales advice, offered a form of certificated qualification to a social class otherwise precluded. At the close of the Jubilee celebrations a graduation ceremony, incorporating soft, stirring choral music and candlelight, ac-

Women receive certificates and commemorative gifts of a best-selling, positive-thinking book after successful graduation from the Tupper College of Knowledge, 1954. Wise Papers, series 3, box 30, negative 94-13623, Archives Center, National Museum of American History, Smithsonian Institution, Washington, D.C.

knowledged women of all ages in a formal commemoration of their achievements. The Tupperware Choraliers set the mood as women met Wise, their inspirational leader, who pinned a fresh orchid corsage to their breast and handed them a certificate, commemorative medal, and a copy of her positive-thinking autobiography, *Best Wishes, Brownie Wise*. The playing of the national anthem signaled the close of the emotional ceremony. Decorated with purple sashes and silver stars and congratulated by every member of the faculty, the women proudly descended the steps of the Garden Pavilion. Several weeks later the company magazine featured an honor roll of "all those who had triumphed."

The Homecoming Jubilee solidified corporate identity. Although many managers and distributors were unable to attend the annual events, as attendees were mostly self-financing with the exception of a handful of scholarship awards, tales of the proceedings bolstered morale and recruitment. Promotional film reels, purchased by distributors as a recruitment tool, recorded the proceedings for the delectation of absent "Tupperites" and would-be dealers. Oral histories and personal correspondence received by THP reveal how this event consolidated women's feelings of belonging to the "Tupperware Family" as a major enhancement to their self-esteem. The anthems that pervaded sales gatherings celebrated these sentiments:

There's only one place for me
One place I want to be
A part of the Tupperware Family
With my head held high singing praises to the sky
As a part of the Tupperware Family
Gone are the lonesome days
These are the golden days
Glad to be up with the sun
There are Oh! so many sensations
To enjoy with all your relations
In the Tupperware Family.[53]

## "Ours Is a Woman's World" — So "Help Yourself to Happiness"

Throughout her career in direct sales, which spanned three decades, Brownie Wise keenly followed contemporary debates regarding women and their changing social and economic roles. Similarly she documented the highlights of her own career, including foreign visits, attendance at prestigious sales events, and her accolades as a premier businesswoman. At the 1958 convention of the National Association of Direct Selling Companies, Wise made plain her advocacy of women in commerce when she delivered a keynote speech, "Ours Is a Woman's World."[54]

In 1956 a *Newsweek* article, "American Women at Work," featured America's top achieving women and paralleled Wise's success with that of Dorothy Shaver, president of New York's retailing venture Lord and Taylor, and Genevieve Decker, vice president of First Federal Savings and Loan Association. The report proclaimed "that women have moved out of the home and . . . into the factories, offices and board rooms of U.S. business" but, through the words of the top achievers themselves, it acknowledged the prejudice, hostility, and discrepancies in pay that most women experienced doing business in a "man's world."[55]

Throughout the 1950s, men constituted at least 5 percent of Tupperware dealers, usually recruited as part of a husband-and-wife team. The company spoke of Tupperized families who took the lead from the wife and mother and ultimately built up a family distributorship, as one oral history describes: "Phil worked twenty-four hours a day making sure the merchandise was in the warehouse. . . . We raised our children in the business; our girls would staple bulletins they [had] put together."[56] More significant, however, is the indisputable fact that at least 75 percent of the THP executives were male. Although its "feminized" corporate culture ostensibly displaced the inequities of patriarchal structures (women received equal pay and equal opportunities within the ranks), in many ways it perpetuated the classic bureaucratic model of a male-dominated hierarchy. It is important to note, however, that the male executives were consistently depicted, and indeed treated, as subordinate players. Top executives were typically recruited from reputable advertising agencies or retail firms, thus limiting accessibility of such positions to women. The male executive clearly followed Wise's leadership, not just for the benefit of a novel corporate image, but as a reflection of her genuinely powerful position.

Tupperware women relished this inversion of power relations. At the 1957 Homecoming Jubilee the male executives, directed on stage by Wise, performed a fashion show for the amusement and titillation of hundreds of women. With some of the men wearing little more than silk boxer shorts and dressing gowns, Brownie coaxed them into provocative turns and twirls, in response to the delighted screams of the audience; while feigning coy blushes, she fanned herself theatrically with the pages of her program.[57] Images of Brownie and "her" male executives blatantly protracted this power relation — on their knees bearing gifts to her on the front cover of *Tupperware Sparks,* walking ten paces behind her in Jubilee promotional films, seated in deferential poses in magazine features as she administered instructions from her splendid peacock chair at the head of the board room. Under the title "All-Girl Convention," a *McCall's* magazine article described how the "executive staff of eight men delighted the female audience by bowing in exaggerated homage, kidding their lady boss, who refers to them as 'the fellas.'"

The "Woman's World" of Tupperware treated their dealers as "natural sales people" whose communication and social skills, derived from traditional female roles, endowed them with unrivaled talents. In a 1955 newspaper piece, "'Just a Housewife' Builds $30,000 Business on Faith," Wise presented herself as a self-help role model: "I knew that there's nothing a woman can't do if she tries. I believe that with faith in the right thing, you must succeed — and all this [success] proves it."[58] The altruistic nature of many women's lives, as wives and mothers, might be combined with a positive-thinking strategy that allowed them a sense of personalized liberation and self-confidence.

Wise gleaned many of her self-empowerment ideas from contemporary popular psychology publications. Typical of this genre was an article aimed at women, "Accent Your Own True Self," featured in the July 1954 edition of *Your Psychology*. It implored women to "stop hiding behind clichés," "have fun," "dare to be different," and not "be afraid to show anger, where anger is merited."[59] Of particular significance, considering Wise's personal circumstances and the age range of Tupperware dealers, was the appeal to women past the age of forty who should no longer consider themselves "hemmed in the world of [their] mother and grandmother" but instead should pursue interests outside the home.[60]

Stories of nervous shrinking violets transformed through the therapeutic practices of Tupperware abounded in corporate mythology. As illustrated by a typical speech, "Tupperware Is the Way," the unification of sales and self-development formed the cosmological world of Tupperware. "Selling is the way to a lot of things. It is the way to making money. It is the way to earning the respect of people. It is the way to winning recognition for your efforts. It is the way to self-improvement. Yet, above and beyond these things, it is the way to forgetting yourself." The speech went on to explain the apparent contradiction of simultaneously upholding self-worth and self-denial by arguing for a state of enlightenment that enables the "surrendering of the self" to a "greater cause"; "you become worthwhile, not because of *what belongs to you*, but because of what *you belong to*, what you do, what you are able to give other people."[61] Similarly, Wise directly addressed depression and anxiety as resolvable conditions, which should not be indulged through inactivity. "The very best therapeutic thing you can do for yourself is to get away where well-meaning people . . . can't get at you; I don't mean for you to go on a buying spree and bring home three or four new hats . . . get out and do something for someone who needs *you* more than you need *them*."[62]

## "Think Tupperware, Talk Tupperware, and Live Tupperware"

Popular psychology, positive thinking, and therapeutic self-help advice formed the crux of the Tupperware ethos, pervaded literature and sales rallies, and fed directly into the instructions of sales manuals. *Know-How,* an eighty-page dealer's guide to sales procedures, applied and promoted the use of contemporary success techniques. "Be a cheerful person if you would make friends. When you speak during your demonstration re-member that your physical action begins with your eyes. LOOK at the guests! Don't avoid their gaze."[63] Personality, communicated through voice, appearance, body language, and disposition, proved vital to the quality of the Tupperware demonstration: "Your whole body speaks a language descriptive of what you are." Consequently women were dis-couraged from presenting an "ambiguous," lackluster, or slovenly perfor-mance. Instead they should express "sparksmanship," a Tupperware term used to describe the verve of an effective sales transaction. Toying ner-vously with jewelry, interlacing fingers, and playing with hair were irri-tating mannerisms to be avoided at all costs. "Educated hands," read the manual, "don't drag on lapels; they don't keep buttoning and unbuttoning jackets. Educated hands don't lean on furniture."[64]

The manual offered in-depth commentary on the minutiae of the Tupperware party using the addition of a third-person narration (pre-sumably the "voice" of Brownie Wise) to make insightful observations from the sidelines. These prompts (literally transcribed in the margins of the main text) guided the dealer through possible scenarios and responses, but far from prescribing a rehearsed repartee, it gave sophisticated but generalized tips to be interpreted according to circumstances of the social group and personality of the dealer. "You're developing kinship here; make it a personal comment!" read a typical sideline comment. "Keep it conversational. Don't lecture," advised another.[65] Similarly, Dale Carnegie courses for better public speaking were routinely offered to managers, who were advised, "If you LOOK enthusiastic and ACT enthusiastic, you BE enthusiastic."[66]

The growth of popular psychology and success manuals forms part of a broader historical shift toward the use of "personality" and social rela-tions to further commercial profit, as defined by Arlie Hochschild in *The Managed Heart: Commercialization of Human Feeling* (1983).[67] Similarly the idea of "self-management," according to Nicole Biggart in her historical study of twentieth-century American success manuals, shifted from an emphasis on religious and ethical standpoint to, post-1950, a "purely in-strumental," rationalized version advocating "that people view themselves as objects to be manipulated." Although Biggart acknowledges that self-help manuals acted as anchors in a modern world of displaced values and ill-defined beliefs, ultimately she considers them an efficacious means of management "originally applied to machines, material, and workers" that in the latter half of the twentieth century impinges on the everyday thoughts and lives of individuals.[68]

In this context, critics of the party plan and its ensuing ideological culture have viewed "self-help" as a highly manipulative form of corporate control. "The fact that women are spatially independent requires that they be able to use self-discipline which is achieved through the ideology of the company over a period of time," writes one such critic.[69]

The increasingly rational, secular, and bureaucratic nature of modern industrial societies, defined by sociological literature since Durkheim and Weber, has been contrasted with the ideological, emotive ritual of religiosity. A business enterprise that seeks to unite these supposedly contradictory features seems an anomaly to both sociological and economic discourse. For example, in a 1968 paper, "The Use of Religious Revival Techniques to Indoctrinate Personnel: The Home-Party Sales Organizations," Dorothy E. Peven set out to describe the "evangelicalization" of an "unnamed" direct sales concern selling plastic bowls. With products rarefied to the point of iconic status ("dealers are told to arrange the chairs in a living room so that the guests face the product as if on an altar") and demonstrators operating with "religious zeal" ("invest[ing] their bowls with qualities demanding 'reverence', 'awe', and 'respect'"), the "religious-like rituals" and inspirational recruitment techniques of the company aimed to counter the large turnover of personnel. The sales rallies (or jubilees) were considered particularly coercive events, similar to Billy Graham crusades, where "the emotions of the audience are deliberately evoked and manipulated by techniques such as mass singing to create a collective consciousness."[70]

Although by the late 1960s (in keeping with a more general trend toward evangelical-style events) THP may have incorporated more religiosity into its proceedings, the assumptions of critics regarding the gullibility of the audience fail to fully explain the continued success of the Tupperware phenomenon and its self-help appeal to women.

Certainly this formed part of a broader cultural phenomenon. Postwar consumerism coincided with a massive turn to religious organization; toward the end of the decade an estimated 63 percent of the American population was officially enrolled in churches.[71] Figures such as Norman Vincent Peale and Charles B. Roth, both regular speakers at Tupperware

Homecoming Jubilees, led the way with their combinations of religious and positivist philosophizing. By 1955 Peale's book, *The Power of Positive Thinking,* had sold more than 2 million copies, and he had been included in a tribute to the best salesman of the year. This spiritual fervor apparently cut through religious, class, and social divisions, emphasizing the quest for individual salvation as opposed to social activism. But though actual religiosity of the experience might easily be exaggerated as a symptom of conformity, in fact, as Herbert Gans later argued in his ethnographic study, *The Levittowners,* it harbored genuine social intent.[72] Will Herberg, in *Protestant, Catholic, Jew: An Essay in American Religious Sociology,* characterized this American condition as a "religiousness without religion," which provided dislocated individuals with a sense of belonging and sociability.[73]

## "If You Believe in a Thing, You Work for It"

Incentive schemes, positive thinking, and self-help doctrines maximized the resources of women's personal interrelations and increased corporate profitability. Moreover, the affirmation and personalization of the Tupperware corporate culture indisputably offered opportunities, social and economic, to a section of society neglected in the formal workplace and devalued in their domestic positions.[74] Self-help manuals published in the post–World War II period, according to Biggart, became increasingly preoccupied with "self-preservation and wealth" rather than "ethical pursuits such as devotion or the development of character." Tupperware corporate ideology, in keeping with the more nineteenth-century notion of self-improvement, consistently appealed to self-improvement as an act of altruism and an expression of Protestant ethic. "We must pay for a room on earth," urged Wise repeatedly. Though formal self-help literature, as defined by Biggart, appealed to a predominantly middle-class male population, that espoused by THP was differentiated as a positively "feminized" interpretation.

In *Women and Self-Help Culture* sociologist Wendy Simonds identifies Betty Friedan's *Feminine Mystique* as the first self-help book to address women explicitly. As an instant best-seller, Friedan's much-debated popularist inquiry into the state of middle-class women's lives provoked a massive response ranging from ecstatic praise to frustrated rage. "I'm mad, I'm

sick, I'm tired of being told by every article in every magazine that because 'I'm just a housewife' my husband finds me a dull companion, my
children are not self-reliant, and my time and talents are being wasted on
'trivial unimportant matters,'" wrote one reader in response to Friedan's
polemic.[75] Notably, the self-help treatises of Tupperware, written and directed by a woman specifically for women, preceded Friedan's work by
more than a decade. Although both dealt with the problem of domesticity and the restraints of being "just a housewife," they clearly addressed
gender from different historical and class perspectives. Friedan's idea of
liberation included the abandonment of housework and overconscien-
tious child care and the condemnation of artificial beautification. Wise,
on the other hand, emancipated women by awarding them new washing
machines, Ford convertibles, and romantic weekends away (while making
the baby-sitting arrangements, in some cases, for up to eleven children).
Whereas Friedan's book addressed a predominantly educated, white,
middle-class readership with a radical call to action, Tupperware offered
pragmatic solutions that appealed to an ostensibly working-class and
lower-middle-class section of the population for whom radical social
change held little promise. "This book," wrote a contemporary "housewife" in response to Friedan's work, "seems only to apply to fairly well off
women. . . . You say one should get an outside job, and in some cases
hired help to do the housework. Yet somebody still has to do this work,
and it's still a woman, so these women are still in bondage."[76] For many
women "still in bondage," experiencing expanded domestic labor and inadequate social and economic opportunities, Tupperware was an alternative and pragmatic solution.

Understood as an opposing force to homogeneous, patriarchal corporate culture, Tupperware's self-help ethos countered alienation and fostered self-determination. The trappings of romantic heterosexual relations
(mink coats and diamond rings, affection and recognition) "borrowed" by
the corporation effectively circumvented the role of men as the sole
providers. Conventionally defined feminine characteristics such as caring
and nurturing, rather than being problematized (as is the case in much
self-help literature today) or confined to strictly domestic contexts, were
facets of identity that women were encouraged to expand. Of course the
coalescing of selling and caring is integral to the American free-market
economy, as Simonds notes: "People involved in direct selling organizations are taught (by those who sell them on becoming salespeople) *not* to
see what they do as selling."[77] And although the popular psychology of

selling might be seen to disguise the reality of capitalist consumer culture, it also reveals the social embeddedness of economic activity.

So crucial to direct selling was the self-help ethos that Tupperware confidently extended its "call to service" beyond white, lower-middle-class and working-class women as its most accessible segment of the workforce. In 1955, the year of the Montgomery bus boycott, Brownie Wise addressed the Jackson College for Negro Teachers in Jackson, Mississippi, as a "representative of the business world," with a speech titled "Write Your Own Ticket." She advised the audience to make the most of their "small opportunities" and told them that the greatest success could begin in "your own backyard." Set within the historical context of African-American migration to the North, ironically, Wise's speech sought to reassure young African Americans of a secure and prosperous future in the South. "Perhaps some of you are wishing at this moment that you had been born in another section of the country. Perhaps you think that the South is not one of the best places to live." But, she pleaded, "the South today is the land of *real* opportunity."[78] Wise acknowledged this social group as one of the most vulnerable, disempowered, and underprivileged. Consequently she addressed them as a potentially vital workforce, inverting the plight of social injustice and poverty, making it instead a challenge, a disadvantage to overcome courageously. As the new pioneers of an uncharted America, African-American women, like all other women, might begin to "write their own tickets." This speech provides one of the few examples of Wise's direct reference to gender inequalities, whereby she controversially parallels the past discrimination against women with the present position of African Americans: "Twenty years ago, the position of women was a difficult one . . . a woman was a housewife, secretary, teacher, maid or scrubwoman and that was all. . . . They were regarded as emotional, impractical creatures with no mind for business."[79] Acknowledging African Americans and teachers as potentially disenfranchised and disenchanted social groups, Wise saw them as a fecund source of salespeople. In terms of gender discrimination, "The rise of the home party plan . . . has made the world see the rightful place of *women* in our sales economy," she remarked, inferring that African Americans might also better themselves through direct sales and thus raise the status of their overall societal profile.[80] The ability of direct sales to open up largely untapped localized markets, through its word-of-mouth recommendations and social relations, made what transcripts of Tupperware sales seminars referred to as "the Negro Market" an entirely feasible marketing opportunity.[81] By 1953, Artie Watts, an African-

American unit manager operating in the Boston area, appeared in a small, inset photograph on the front cover of *Tupperware Sparks,* receiving an award for sales merit.[82]

The introduction of such entrepreneurial schemes to an African-American population was far from new. Indeed there were striking parallels between the success of Madam C. J. Walker, the renowned African-American woman entrepreneur established in the first half of the twentieth century, and Brownie Wise in the latter. Walker began her cosmetics business in an attempt to prosper as a single mother and was motivated by a larger "struggle . . . to build up Negro womanhood." Using allocated sales agents, the "Walker System" not only introduced modern products to African-American women, in the form of beauty culture, but also provided a form of social and economic emancipation. As historian Kathy Peiss describes it, "Beauty culture, Walker argued, offered economic emancipation for black women subjected to a rigidly sex- and race-segregated labor market. Indeed, thousands of women, rural and urban, made a living or supplemented their income selling the Walker System."[83] Like Tupperware and the home party plan, the Walker System offered a unique product, related forms of acquisition, and social and economic opportunities.

Although Tupperware formed part of a direct sales legacy that included the vital precedents of the Fuller Brush Company, Stanley Home Products, and Madam C. J. Walker, in 1953 Brownie Wise boasted of the company's unsurpassed reputation: "We have built a business and an organization unique in Modern enterprise. This is a co-operative organization the success of which has confounded many of the best thinkers in direct selling today."[84]

Corporate culture of the postwar period was heavily scrutinized by social scientists and commentators who sought to expose the alienating and dehumanizing aspects of increasingly rationalized organizations. *White Collar* by C. Wright Mills (1951) and *The Organization Man* by William Whyte (1956) typified a genre of literature that equated societal malaise with the expansion of corporate power and the strictures of a Weberian "iron cage" bureaucracy. The daunting, gray, and antisocial visions of Whyte's *Organization Man* contrasted dramatically with the flexible, pink, and supportive image of THP. "Why," asks Nicole Biggart rhetorically in her study of direct sales organizations, "should a 'less rational' form of organization, one that creates and manipulates social bonds, grow precisely when a market mentality seems to be spreading inexorably throughout the developed world?"[85] Indeed, the growth of American corporate capitalism and an ensuing sense of alienation underpinned THP's success in the 1950s. Women, and other social groups ostensibly precluded from corporate career life or offered little in the way of "quality" work opportunities elsewhere, embraced the working conditions of direct sales concerns as a viable option and a highly attractive alternative to overtly patriarchal forms of capitalism. Furthermore, as the following chapter explores, the blurring of social and economic activity, of fantasy and pragmatism, created a dynamic corporate culture that continues to thrive into the twenty-first century.

seven

• • •

# "A Wealth of Wishes and a Galaxy of Gifts"

## The Politics of Consumption

The notion of "pure capitalism," whereby a free market economy is driven by rational consumer choice, lies at the root of formal economic theory. The United States in the 1950s is popularly understood as the archetypal expression of this construct: "In the mid-twentieth century, it became . . . axiomatic that access to consumer goods was a fundamental right of all people, that this was best fulfilled by free enterprise, and that free enterprise operated optimally if guided by profit motive unimpeded by state or other interference."[1] Freed from the constraints of Old World customs and ensuing relations, according to many historians, North America ensured the ascendancy of a capitalist democracy premised on increased access to consumer goods and a "culture of consumption."[2] Many contemporary advertisers and social critics depicted America as a commodious tabula rasa, ideally suited to furthering a lucrative and conveniently homogenized consumer culture. However, as more recent historical studies suggest, the processes of consumption are far more complex than such approaches have traditionally recognized.[3] As sociologist Vivianna Zelizer notes of the twentieth-century rise in mass production, "Americans were not reduced to a nation of interchangeable consumers. Instead, people turned their new material possessions — such as cars, radios, washing machines, clothes, or cosmetics — into socially meaningful objects, integrating mass-marketed products into personalized networks."[4] Historians such as Andrew Heinze, in his study of European Jewish immigrants to America, argue that consumption, rather than providing a merely escapist or compensatory diversion, plays a historically vital role in allowing for both cultural differentiation and assimilation.[5] Similarly, Lizabeth Cohen, in her consideration of class identity and the growth of post–World War II suburbia, argues that identities were pursued and negotiated, rather than erased or diminished, through consumption, material culture, and newly formulating concepts of taste.[6]

Although Tupperware undoubtedly offered practical solutions for women in terms of efficient food storage and an accessible means of labor through party plan dealership, explanation of its tremendous postwar appeal cannot be explained by rational debates about labor-saving housework and economic theory alone.[7] Tupperware is better understood as a cultural marker with a multitude of meanings, generated through historically specific processes of consumption. For as Zelizer states, "Far from standardizing tastes and practices, consumerism created novel ways to endow social and personal life with multiple modern meanings."[8] Material culture, economic transactions, and monetary relations were remade through elaborate processes that stood as an antithesis to the rationale of economic theory. Elaborate gift giving and the other seemingly anachronistic practices of the Tupperware sales system and corporate culture, which bolstered concepts of religiosity, ritual, love, kinship, and informal economy, embraced rather than negated the complexities of social relations and defied the logic of conventional business practice.

The Tupperware artifacts and the party plan both relied on a historically specific rendering of "glamour" and domestic consumption — cultural manifestations treated by academics until relatively recently as trivialized aspects of popular feminine identity.[9] In a period that abounded with contentious debates regarding consumption, abundance, and the potentially detrimental effects of unchecked affluence, Tupperware's seemingly contradictory appeal to excess (manifest in lavish displays of gift giving) and thrift (embodied in the function of the Tupperware container) held particular resonance. The shift from a prewar economic depression to postwar affluence constituted itself in what Elaine Tyler May has described as the "Commodity Gap," a race toward material accumulation that overtook the arms race in cold war America in terms of political significance: "In appliance-laden houses across the country, working-class as well as business-class breadwinners could fulfill the new American work-to-consume ethic."[10] Undeniably, the postwar period witnessed a surge in consumption, as the acquisition of material goods became feasible for a wide cross section of people. But the appropriation of goods was by no means an arbitrary or homogeneous process that automatically allayed social conflict or class consciousness. Consumption, its objects and modes of acquisition, operated according to definitions of class, gender, ethnicity, and age, categories that intersected under the auspices of domestic economy.

## In Defense of Glamour
### Meanings of Domestic Consumption

In 1953 Brownie Wise sent a memo to Earl Tupper, regarding a New York press party, which in effect read as a statement in defense of glamour.[11] It began: "The setting for the party was the most beautiful, undoubtedly, that I have ever seen. . . . tables were set on blue-grey linen and . . . centered with huge vases of the new Tupperware Beauty Rose," and the cocktails and luncheon served could "only be described in superlatives."[12] Wise defended the occasion by reiterating that "at least 40%" of the editors present were male. She continued, "I had to shed a little personal glamour for the benefit of the editors . . . who were primarily engrossed in determining just how any appreciable amount of honest-to-goodness business was conducted by 'a mere woman.'"

Also that year, Wise issued Tupper an in-depth business plan, including comprehensive sales projections, and implored him to maintain the exclusivity of the Tupperware party distribution method. Tupper had insinuated that the immense success of the party plan system, though it boosted Tupperware's public profile and turned the company into a multimillion-dollar concern, had somehow undermined the objects' propriety. Expenditure on extravagant celebrations, gifts, and glamorous press parties obscured the inherent value of the Tupperware product and potentially diminished profits. Wise defended these "extravagances" as essential assets of the Tupperware business. She also strongly advised Tupper that redistributing the product through formal retail outlets (as he had suggested in response to the now-established and successful market position of the product) undermined the immense effort of her dealers and jeopardized the entire party plan network.

Although Tupperware appealed to increased refrigeration facilities, domestic rationalization and hygiene standards, and technological innovation, clearly it was modernity, in the form of "glamour," rather than rationalism that had made the product into a contemporary icon. "Cadillacs and new homes are the hallmarks of Tupperware distributors," boasted the corporation.[13] These material signs were not merely the trappings of an emulative materialism; rather, they were the rightfully gained outcome of women's affirmative self-help. Although the notion of material riches as a sign of God's favor pervaded American culture through the Protestant ethic, Tupperware corporate culture was far from advocating self-denial and deferred gratification. Instead it positively celebrated pleasure and desire and provided a unique space for female fantasy and wish fulfillment. Women's wishes were viewed as a recognizable force: "Without *your* wishes where would we be? Everything begins with a wish."[14] Tupperware served as a functional object, but its success relied upon a potent articulation of modernity and gender, embodied in the activities and discourse of consumption and manifest in the notion of "glamour."

Whereas Earl Tupper's vision of social progress involved finding "the true purpose and intent of everything" without "jarring harmony," Brownie Wise viewed modernity as a liberating celebration of human potential through "use"—or consumption. In this context Tupper's family home in Rhode Island was a bastion of New England Protestant aesthetic values. Ironically, considering his dedication to the furtherance of Poly-T, the house negated any reference to technological advancement or "contemporary style." It contained antiques, a traditional open fireplace, wood-paneled walls, decorative china, and a spinning wheel—settings used in the earliest Tupperware promotional photographs to reassure consumers of the steadfast and trustworthy "pedigree" of Tupper's designs.[15]

In stark contrast, Brownie's lakeside home was filled with modern rattan furniture, flamingo pink upholstery, and contemporary artworks. The living room, wrote one journalist, was reminiscent of "the lobby of a swank beach hotel" with "sections to fit your mood."[16] The open-plan kitchen featured an automatic dishwasher and a trendy breakfast bar complete with swiveling bamboo barstools. Fashionable patterned fabrics adorned the windows, and colorful rugs the floors, and a "terrazzo tile" walk led toward a luxurious indoor swimming pool.

The image of a single, middle-aged woman presiding over an expansive lakeside estate, complete with island, cabin cruiser, and livestock, all attained without the support or intervention of a man, certainly ran counter to the notion of postwar domestic acquiescence and female passivity. Earl Tupper was, for the benefit of public relations, occasionally featured in corporate publications proffering gifts to Brownie Wise—the pet Palomino pony and pink convertible. But on the whole, she was represented as an economically independent woman whose domestic life was as ordinary as any housewife's, with the addition of a more lavish living environment.

Women's magazines often featured Wise enjoying her fabulous home, accompanied by her teenage son, Jerry, as a sharp contrast to the bitter reality of her earlier life story. Born in 1913 to a tradesman's family in Buford, Georgia, Brownie Humphrey recognized the limited employment opportunities for women in the South. After meeting Robert Wise at the Texas Centennial in 1936, where a Ford Motors exhibit promised new livelihoods in their manufacturing plants, she married him and promptly moved to the Detroit area. Three years after the birth of their only child, the couple divorced in 1941. Most significantly, according to oral history, Brownie suffered dreadful injuries during her pregnancy in a drunk-driving accident, caused by her husband, which left her hospitalized and largely unable to care for her newborn child. During this period of her life she began writing for a woman's column in the *Detroit News,* in an attempt to establish a career and eventually secure a meager income.

Through Wise's prose, we can see that her picturesque Florida residence, Water's Edge, was not the first dream home Brownie shared with an empathetic female audience. By 1939 she had adopted the pen name "Hibiscus" and, contributing to a literary space devoted to women's discussion of the trials and tribulations of domestic life (the "Experience Column"), she created her own imaginary family and home. Discussing her doting husband, "Yankee," and baby son, "Tiny Hands," in this particular extract she surveys their new dream home, the soon-to-be-occupied and aptly named "Lovehaven":

> I let the door swing back, and I stood in the kitchen . . . so efficient looking, so sleek so shining. "That," I thought, "would look like an ordinary kitchen sink to anyone else, but to me it's a magic carpet." I shall stand before it and watching Tiny Hands busy in the sandpile outside the window, dream wonderful dreams. . . . I went into the nursery . . . my mind's eye ran ahead again, and I saw the pink and blue nursery paper which tells the story of Peter Rabbit coming down from its wall, to be replaced with a saga of trains and airplanes and boats, and still later . . . a striped wall plastered with . . . football schedules and athletes' pictures.[17]

Home furnishings and decoration, as Wise's female readers recognized, constituted far more than bricks and mortar or spaces of conspicuous consumption. Although deliberately exaggerated here for sentimental impact, minute choices, such as the style or pattern of wallpaper, were invested with all the significance of social relations, exemplified in the house's nomenclature, Lovehaven. Wise's alter ego, Hibiscus, regaled readers with romantic tales of domestic bliss and economic security (expressed in details of consumption and material culture), but in reality Wise suffered abandonment by her husband and was in dire financial straits. Her fictional roles as newlywed homemaker, mother, and demure southern belle provided numerous opportunities for wishful and fanciful storytelling. Hibiscus received endless gestures of recognition and affection. Glamorous flower arrangements arrived, such as "an avalanche of yellow roses" from her ever-attentive husband and a box of "scarlet hibiscus in a damp nest of Spanish moss" flown directly from New Orleans to Detroit, courtesy of the southern hospitality of her caring relatives.

In 1939, *Home Edition,* an anthology of *Detroit News* column contributions, featured a story written by Hibiscus that bore an uncanny resemblance to the tragedy of Brownie Wise's real-life experience. A sentimental parable of medical misfortune, it described how, after enduring months of separation from her baby because of a tragic accident, the author eventually left her wheelchair to hug her baby son, only to fall and refracture her broken leg. "Here I am back by peculiar coincidence," she wrote, "in the same room in the hospital where I spent five months when Tiny Hands was born." Suspended in traction, separated once more from her child, Hibiscus could only gaze longingly from her window every afternoon to catch a glimpse of Tiny Hands, who was precluded from the potentially dangerous germ-ridden environment of the hospital. "I can picture that highlight of your day at 3 o'clock, dear 'Hibiscus,'" commented the compassionate editor, Nancy Brown. "Every mother — every woman — in the Column will be seeing that picture of the white-clad figure holding your tiny son up for you to see, from the window four storeys above."[18] The extent to which this dramatic scenario was autobiographical remains unclear, but throughout her life the welfare of her son remained a priority to Wise, whose impetus for getting involved with direct sales, beginning with Stanley Home Products in the 1940s, was to cover his medical bills and provide an improved standard of living.

Through her semi-autobiographical writings, which included letters, prose, and poetry, Wise used fantasy and fiction to reinvent a sad and unsatisfactory life while taking pragmatic steps to redeem her social and economic situation, the same formula of fantasy and pragmatism that later proved vital to the "Tupperware story." Her uplifting tales of domestic consumption and motherhood, in which altruism and hope overcame hardship, popularized and glorified the otherwise mundane experiences of many women's lives.[19]

The prose belongs to a broader genre of popular literary romance, but these early writings reveal an understanding of homemaking and consumption as crucial components of popular feminine identity. Throughout the 1950s, Wise sustained a genuine interest, despite her high salary and glamorous image, in home dressmaking (which she used to supplement her appetite for contemporary fashions) and crafts, skills she frequently used to identify with other women.[20] Ultimately, the pages of *Tupperware Sparks* and the direct sales seminars offered to salespeople across America were founded on this initial foray into an almost subcultural literary genre that directly combined romance, domesticity, and self-help ethos.

Just as Tupper's Rhode Island home celebrated traditional Protestant ethics through his use of plain and sturdy New England aesthetics, the high-style, open-plan glamour of "Water's Edge" presented an idyllic home life where mother and son shared recreational pursuits in a modern, nonpatriarchal setting (typical public relation images showed Brownie loading rifles or riding on horseback side by side with Jerry).[21] Tupper's antiques-filled house, featuring numerous display cases and china collections, stood as a monument to traditional American craftsmanship and resembled a static museum collection. Wise's "swank beach hotel" ranch-style abode, ideal for informal entertainment, revealed an unabashed desire for color and transitory style, and it boasted all the accoutrements of a high-style 1950s home.

## "You Are Your Own Treasure Chest: Don't Hide Away Your Precious Jewels"

In the post–World War II period, as numerous historians have noted, consumption took on a formally politicized role as the American government (coining the term "consumer citizens") promoted it as a patriotic duty.[22] Although this broader, institutionalized concern with consumption directly affected the success of Tupperware (direct sales proponents addressed their salespeople as crucial components of the American economy, fanning the flames of consumer desire), a more culturally

Brownie Wise and her son, Jerry, frequently posed together for features in popular women's magazines, such as *Woman's Home Companion,* which described her exemplary rags-to-riches story. Pictured here in 1953 at their fashionable lakeside mansion furnished with rattan pieces and state-of-the-art phonograph equipment, Wise and her son enjoy the luxuries and conveniences of a modern home realized without the support or salary of a husband or father. Wise Papers, series 3, box 28, negative 94-13622, Archives Center, National Museum of American History, Smithsonian Institution, Washington, D.C.

bound understanding of consumption drove the Tupperware phenomenon. For just as Tupper's ingenious designs drew on an acute understanding of household provisioning, thrift, and moral economy, Wise's philosophies of self-actualization drew on an inspired understanding of social relations and informal economy. Her writings on relationships, happiness, faith, and love, which argued for a broader humanitarian vision, incorporated analogies of "getting" and "spending," "gifting" and "possession"—that is, consumption.

Objects and subjects, their relations and aesthetics, were deemed inseparable. In a rally speech titled "Things We Should Use," Wise condemned stinginess as a morally deplorable state. She implored women to "use it all. Use yourself freely. For you'll never, never, never use yourself up!" This philosophy extended to the tangibility of material culture itself: "We put slip covers over furniture to save the upholstery and never see the beautiful color . . . or the pattern of the material . . . we put away our precious lingerie, save junior's suit for Sunday School wear, until it's too small for him."[23] Inverting the moral rectitude of thrift and saving, Wise similarly scorned what she described as "the waste of hoarding."[24] In troubled times, such as World War II, people selfishly "hoarded sugar and coffee and flour and soap flakes . . . so long that all the flavor and aroma wasted away." Moreover, she argued, people grow sour, rancid, and valueless, just like groceries, if they save themselves up. In a modern civilization preoccupied with material acquisition, Tupperware embraced reciprocity and the social relations encapsulated in the classic notion of the gift. Quoting Emerson's famous prose, in which he considers the inherently personalized nature of the ideal gift, Wise advised her dealers to write in their "mental notebooks," the phrase: "'A portion of thyself.' This is the greatest gift to give."[25]

Most significantly, the pursuit of material comforts did not automatically preclude the pursuit of meaningful human relations; in a speech titled "Thoughts ARE things," Wise depicted material goods as expressions of self-determination made concrete. Everything from "table glass, [the] permanent in your hair, roof on your house, engine in your car," she declared, began with a valuable thought and purposeful choice. This equability of thoughts and things also pertained to people and things. "Some women collect china cups and saucers. I collect people," commented Wise in an interview with *Woman's Home Companion*. "I have the most amazing collection of interesting and heart-warming people tucked away in the pigeon-holes of my mind."[26]

Under the title "You Are Your Own Treasure Chest," women were taught to value their inner resources, the validity of their experiences and opinions; for they, wrote Wise, "are as much a part of the inventory of our mental and spiritual possessions as anything else." Like precious jewels, women should share their pearls of wisdom and reveal their priceless gems, rather than selfishly, warily hide them in the darkness of the attic or the safe deposit box. With the Cinderella Company, the experiences, fantasies, and wishes of women constituted acts of positive self-determination, "for everything" declared Wise, "begins with a wish." In this sense, consumption took on a potentially radical role that challenged the gender power relations of pin money or allocated payment for housekeeping expenses. "Pin money" (money set aside for incidentals) culturally constituted the economically dependent relation of a wife to her husband. It was also used to describe a "trifling" amount of money associated with women as opposed to a formal wage, salary, or payment associated with men's economic power. Indeed, set within the context of women's shifting social and economic roles in the postwar period, pin money became a highly contentious issue, the pursuit of which was aired in popular sitcoms such as *I Love Lucy*. Increasing household consumption, which according to contemporary accounts necessitated women's employment, undermined the middle-class notion of the stay-at-home mom. An ideology of domesticity and social mobility also led to an ever-greater need to disguise women's frequently essential wage earning as pin money, as reflected in the gifting practices of the Tupperware Corporation.

## "Wishes Do Come True with Tupperware!"
### Or Why Wanting Things Is Good

"There is nothing wrong," wrote Brownie Wise in 1952, "with wanting things." Although idle wishing should be condemned, hopes and aspirations if "directed at all times into the proper channels" formed the very foundation of human accomplishment.[27] Just as Tupper's early writings berated the wasteful pursuits of the lottery-playing, bar-hopping masses in favor of the self-reliant and productive individual, Wise viewed consumption and desire as potentially productive forces when harnessed appropriately. The intricate contrivances of the Tupperware ceremonies and schemes managed a delicately balanced moral economy, which surrounded each and every commodity.

Historians of consumer culture suggest that the midtwentieth century United States advanced a "model [that] established the predominance of individual acquisitiveness over collective entitlement and defined the measure of good society as private well-being achieved through consumer spending." But the success of Tupperware — the quintessential manifestation of capitalist free enterprise — totally contradicted the rational models of exchange in which consumers pursue maximum utility for minimum price.[28] As a "flawed" model of neoclassical economics, the Tupperware enterprise relied on systems of barter, reciprocity, and displays of ritual, mysticism, and gift giving.

Wish fulfillment was an enduring corporate theme. In 1956 the THP headquarters acquired a stone wishing well into which dealers were encouraged to throw their wishes, encased in miniature Tupperware containers, "to be concealed forever." *Tupperware Sparks* featured the wishing well, juxtaposed with the iconography of fairy-tale princesses and castles on hills, as a testament to the magical world of Tupperware.[29]

By 1957, with the debut of an event referred to as the "Wish Party," Tupperware followers were assured that "Wishes *Do* Come True." Across the nation a Tupperware wish fairy, complete with tiara, gold tutu, and magic wand, visited sales meetings to grant chosen women their heart's desire. Tender ambitions were translated into the tangibility of consumer goods. At the Masonic Temple auditorium in Spokane, Washington, Mrs. Bernadine Olson, who had wistfully dreamed of "a paradise for children to play in" received "a gym set placed in a landscaped yard, fenced safely away from traffic" courtesy of THP. Elsie Burns, who longed to provide her five-year-old daughter with a musical education, was granted a brand-new electronic organ. Describing the lucky recipients as "modern-day Cinderellas," the THP program for the event encouraged hostesses and dealers to put their wishes to work so that "a new home, a car, children's education, new clothes, new furnishings for the home" might materialize before their very eyes.[30] In Peoria, Illinois, a thirty-year-old mother of seven children received fifty-seven pairs of shoes with matching handbags, cowboy outfits for her sons, dolls for the girls, and a Shetland pony for all seven children to enjoy. Interviewed on radio the next day, Mrs. Rowell admitted, "I tried on shoes until nearly three o'clock in the morning." Meanwhile Norma Stockner became a televised "queen for the night," and the wish fairy ordained TV personality Bob Hill, from Peoria's WTVH television station, as a royal page in her attendance.[31]

The Tupperware wish fairy's antics culminated in the extravaganza of the 1957 "Around the World" Homecoming Jubilee. Having pinned their wishes to an official "wish list," attendees filled the pavilion auditorium to await the fairy's "magical" selection. As Brownie paced the stage, wearing a tight-waisted, floral chiffon dress, hundreds of expectant Tupperware dealers were asked to concentrate on realizing their deepest wishes. With the sudden sound of a whirring siren, the radiant wish fairy tapped the chosen women one by one with a jeweled wand, and mounting the stage, they read aloud their wishes to the delight of the gathered audience. Overwhelmed by emotion, a tearful Mary Cooper, from North Carolina, described her wish for a home fit for offering hospitality; behind her the curtains parted to reveal "a complete living room and bedroom suite, to be duplicated in her favorite color and style on her return home."[32] While

The Tupperware wish fairy awards to the tearful Naomi Lyons *(center)*—Tupperware dealer and mother of eleven children—a new wardrobe for her husband (including silk pajamas and dinner jacket), while Brownie Wise looks on affectionately, 1956. Wise Papers, series 3, box 29, negative 94-11113, Archives Center, National Museum of American History, Smithsonian Institution, Washington, D.C.

Naomi Lyons received a new wardrobe for her husband, from pajamas to formal attire, to everyone's joy and astonishment the wish fairy also produced Mr. Lyons, all the way from Chicago, where Naomi had thought "he was looking after their eleven children!" The wish fairy, of course, had considered all eventualities and arranged for a baby-sitter back home in Chicago.

Less extravagant wishes were "allowed" to be granted without such scrupulous attention to the needs and desires of family members, though they were still invariably directed toward household provisioning and were collectively recognized as useful and desirable products: a Westinghouse roaster, a venetian blind, a Universal cooker-fryer. The wish fairy made her final exit from the Jubilee ceremony on a lighted float, presided over by "a court of dainty dancers," and waved off on her magical journey across Tupper Lake by the assembled THP executives.

Throughout the twentieth century, women's monetary contribution to the household economy, though differing widely according to class, has remained consistently problematic despite the emancipation of women and the practical attempts of home economists as early as the 1920s to "rationalize" the allocation of resources. "Despite the increasing individualization of consumption patterns and the encouragement by home-economics experts to allot personal funds for each family member in the domestic budget, personal spending money for wives still was obtained by subterfuge or spent with guilt," states Zelizer in *The Social Meaning of Money*.[33] The concept of "pin money," though effectively trivializing women's contributions to the household economy, became of paramount importance to the pursuit of increased consumption in post-1945 America. Regardless of the need for women's wages as part of a collective budget, defined as "pin money" it remained a notion of supplementary earnings, earmarked for expenditure on extras such as clothing, jewelry, cosmetics, vacations, or family expenses such as a child's education. As such, pin money has historically been used as an extension of a moral debate regarding the threat of women's labor to the livelihood of the male provider and indeed consumption itself. Tupperware's full-scale use of gifts, including overtly nonessential offerings such as mink coats, diamond rings, and fifty-seven pairs of shoes with matching handbags, compounds the notion of women's labor as operating outside the market economy, thus deflecting the criticism of women subsuming the role of breadwinner. Such lavish gifts and treats, however, provocatively mimicked intimate presentations associated with courtship and sexual union—particularly as played out in an illicit or extramarital affair—and as such were also dangerously disassociated from the safety and altruism of the domestic sphere.[34]

## "Around the World in Eighty Days"
### Glorious Gifts and Tempting Treasures

From the inception of THP through to the late 1950s, the public Tupperware gift-giving schemes gained considerably in sophistication and theatricality. As well as incorporating the magical presence of the wish fairy, the 1957 "Around the World in Eighty Days" Homecoming Jubilee featured the material culture and costumes of more than a dozen countries. Using local Native Americans on horseback to drag commodities, including record players and barbecues, from authentic teepees, the Ju-

The "Tupper-ette" water-ski team, shown here ca. 1956, performed at Homecoming Jubilee sales rallies wearing painted Tupperware containers as helmets. Wise Papers, series 3, box 30, negative 94-10891, Archives Center, National Museum of American History, Smithsonian Institution, Washington, D.C.

bilee celebrations ran close to parody in their pseudo-anthropological depiction of cultural practices, and in particular, the significance of the gift. Polystyrene igloos, human totem poles, cardboard pyramids, and nylon Arabian tents formed the backdrop for the display of a multitude of exotic commodities that were ultimately proffered as gifts at the culmination of the celebrations. Dealers, dressed up as cultural ambassadors ranging from a "Bombay snake charmer" to a "cannibal from Zanzibar," attempted to barter their goods to passing Tupperware people. "Hindu prince Ben Voss bids the treasures of the East be distributed to those who have journeyed from afar," read a Jubilee supplement. "His harem waits upon him," it added, as cavorting Tupperware women dressed in sunglasses and chiffon yashmacs enticed "travelers" to sample the exotic Arabian wares.[35]

Hawaiian music and hula girls (impersonated by the staff of the THP administration offices) set the scene for a fabulous luau on Brownie's personal "Isla Milagra" (Miracle Island) in the middle of Lake Tohopekaliga. A joyous feast of "roast pork, whole chickens, huge lobsters and heaps of fresh fruits" awaited dignitaries including the publishers of *Cosmopolitan* and *American Salesman*. The "Tupper-ette" water-ski team (adorned with painted Tupperware canisters on their heads) performed a special show. Then "as darkness fell on the beach and moonlight rippled on the water," the award ceremony for the "Around the World in Eighty Days" campaign commenced. Among the prizes of Indian brass, Oriental jade, Chinese carvings, and German gilt bronze clocks, Francis Witt of Oklahoma won a complete wardrobe "including a Marmot stole, seven dresses, seven pairs of shoes, five hats and a gown, a negligee and slipper set" of undetermined national origin.[36]

THP continued to court women with glamorous gifts and flamboyant displays of appreciation. The overt emphasis placed on the power of women as self-reliant individuals was manifest in their abilities to secure material, social, and spiritual well-being. As such, the meanings of consumption, and the precariousness of its moral implications, became of paramount importance to the Tupperware endeavor. The appropriate "framing" of lavish ceremonial gift-giving awards and women's business achievements proved crucial to the maintenance of a respectable corporate image. THP avoided promoting unmitigated examples of avarice and materialism by publishing, for example, letters of praise for Tupperware's contribution to family stability. This is not to suggest, however, that the company had an official policy regarding its use of gift incentives, award schemes, or Jubilee "potlatches"; rather it reveals consumption, and the constant negotiation of its meanings, as the cornerstone of the Tupperware enterprise. "We would like to say 'Thank You' for the new car we just got," read a typical letter from an area distributor addressed to Vice President Brownie Wise, "and for the new home we moved into in May and many things that Tupperware money has made possible. But certainly Tupperware has given us much more than money. Working together as closely as you do in this business, has added to our marriage."[37]

Altruism, as expressed through gift giving and officiated presentation, transformed the alienable commodities of numerous corporate schemes, from party premiums to jubilee ceremonies, into artifacts of a profound significance far outweighing their monetary value. Many of these gifts relied on the intimacy of the donor and recipient enacted through the provenance of the specific objects and the ritual of their acquisition. In 1953 distributor Jeanne Lavigne received a diamond-studded gold ring,

Tupperware dealers collect their gifts, given by THP in accordance with sales accrued, in one of the many elaborate gift-giving ceremonies organized by the corporation, ca. 1955. Wise Papers, series 3, box 30, negative 94-10897, Archives Center, National Museum of American History, Smithsonian Institution, Washington, D.C.

originally a gift to Brownie from Earl Tupper himself, in recognition of her "unselfish . . . thoughtfulness." A photograph of the public, spot-lit service, reminiscent of a marriage rite, appeared in *Tupperware Sparks* to commemorate "that breathless moment when Brownie transferred the Number One Service Emblem 'T' signet ring from her hand to the finger of Jeanne."[38] Similarly the Vanguard, a team of elite salespeople who received personal addresses from Wise at sales meetings and the opportunity to win "women-only" weekends with Wise at her lakeside home, had access to the ultimate accolade in gifting rituals. Initiated in response to women's persistent requests, Wise donated her own publicly worn gar-

TUPPERWARE *Sparks*

JULY - AUGUST, 1953 — VOL. X, NOS. 6 AND 7    ORLANDO, FLORIDA

*Both symbolic of enduring perfection —
the exquisite artistry of Tupperware...
and the matchless and delicate
beauty of the regal rose.*

*Tupperware Sparks* shows Wise in a pink batiste and lace couture dress that became the ultimate prize offered to top sales achievers known as the "Vanguard." Wise Papers, series 3, box 8, Archives Center, National Museum of American History, Smithsonian Institution, Washington, D.C.

ments. This highly coveted award was described, as part of the "Sales Spell-Down" awards, in the most tantalizing and indulgent detail:

> The dress I wore at the last jubilee graduation is to be one of the awards . . . (it's an original of imported pink batiste . . . fine pin tucks and lovely Irish lace,

with flaring gores breaking at the knee with a deep permanently pleated flounce, and a matching pink taffeta slip). Two other dresses are included . . . one, my very special pet, almost entirely hand-made, which I bought in Italy . . . a heavy black crepe princess line with yards and yards of fullness, so simple I'll be smart 10 years from now . . . and a two piece suit of maize and black—British imported wool, a Solman original.[39]

The value of such gifts, which one publication described as "high class hand-me downs," resided in their intimate relation to their previous owner. Wise's in-depth descriptions and fastidious attention to fashion detail imbued the outfits with an incommensurable worth—that of her own knowledge. The consumptive discernment of their revered leader, the fact that Brownie herself had chosen, worn, and appropriated these clothes, made them singular and priceless.

If the divestment of intimate apparel proved too risqué, the "Tupperware Family Album," an illustrated publication offering dealers a range of gifts (acquired through accrued sales points) "to thrill" their "entire family," placed commodities firmly in the context of a domesticated moral economy. Simulating a conventional photograph album, each portrait-size picture of the white, suburban, extended family was mounted in juxtaposition with chosen commodities. The gift objects, with consistent and prominent reference to their brand names, were themselves represented as potential "members of the family." Each was photographed, in open and availing presentation boxes, as if poised in anticipation of a family snapshot and identified according to gendered and social relations: "Mother" with the "Crown Jewel Ladies Schick Razor," "Manicure Set by Griffon," and electric knife ("delicate slicing action"); "Father" with a "Garcia Mitchell Fishing Rod Outfit" and a traditional carving-knife set ("Dad will be master of the holiday meals!"); youngest daughter "Judy" with a "Giant Doll Playhouse" ("the dream of every little girl") pictured opposite her brother "Tommy" and his "Deluxe Microscope Set" ("not a toy") and "Electric Racing Car Set."

Gender and material culture overlapped in the promotion of Tupperware as a gift item itself. The "Little Miss Tupperware Party Set," a range of miniature pieces packaged in "an attractive pink box," instilled in young girls an impression of the significance of the product and its associated role. Building on the importance of the mother–daughter kinship and socialization at home, the promotional plea noted that "with each box comes a descriptive leaflet so Mama can show daughter what each piece is." By 1960, the winner of a Miss Teen contest—"Blonde hair . . . Blue eyes . . . Fair skin . . . Meet the prettiest teenager in U.S.A."—was awarded, along with a Hollywood screen test, a complete wardrobe from Bobby Brooks, a beautiful Lane sweetheart chest, and "a set of terrific Tupperware that will last a lifetime."[40] In same year, *Co-ed: The Magazine for Career Girls and Homemakers of Tomorrow,* featured recipes, illustrated with Tupperware, for the "smart hostess" to serve at her swim party, where a "revolving 'Party Susan'" could offer sophisticated snacks by the poolside.[41]

Such examples reveal the interrelation of gender and consumption. The identities of Miss Teen and the "smart hostess" underscore notions of public and private spheres relying upon consumption as the locus for individual and social self-construction. In this sense material culture and mass consumption provided a means through which women formed, mediated, and challenged prescribed racial, class, and gender roles. Mass consumption and commodity forms are used in countering alienation and constructing meaning in contemporary social life. The sociality of the gift, the nuances of household provisioning, and the complexity of social identities are pursued through, as much as jeopardized by, mass consumption. Objects of everyday life are thus meaningfully put to use in developing sociality, kinship, and identity in modern industrial societies.

Tupperware, as its corporate Museum of Dishes suggested, belonged to a hierarchy of "things" made most evident through its juxtaposition with artifacts of historical authenticity or, as in the case in the following example, artifacts of ritual significance.

In 1954 an amateur explorer named Hassoldt Davis wrote to THP, praising Tupperware as "the greatest boon to exploration that I have found in twenty years of traveling through exactly seventy countries." Presenting Wise with a Tupperware canister that had endured the tropical climate of Africa for more than a year, he claimed the product had received "the roughest treatment that the natives could subject it to, including the use of the canister as a container for 'magic' witchcraft powder." *Tupperware Sparks* included a photograph showing the khaki-clad "explorer" surrounded by clearly staged, inquisitive "natives" looking on.[42] Mr. Davis concluded, "Our native boys, when first confronted by it grind their teeth at being unable to break it." Several years later, another amateur explorer forwarded a film of African adventures to the Tupperware headquarters, in which ritual ceremonies, such as palm milking and ox blooding, were altered through physical intervention: traditional ceremo-

In 1954 this photograph of explorer Hassoldt Davis proudly introducing Tupperware to an unnamed African tribe was published in *Tupperware Sparks*. Wise Papers, series 3, box 8, Archives Center, National Museum of American History, Smithsonian Institution, Washington, D.C.

nial vessels replaced, midceremony, with pastel Wonder Bowls and gleaming white Tupperware canisters.[43] These stories boosted the vision of "Tupperization" beyond Earl Tupper's wildest dreams. As an icon of modernity and North American technological prowess, Tupperware seemed set to conquer the world. However, much to Tupper's increasing frustration, the utility and beauty of the Tupperware products still remained a secondary factor in the success of their introduction to a consumer public. Gifts and ceremonies, superstition and mysticism, all the elements of "primitive" societies, continued to form the basis of the Tupperware sales achievement.

## "Be a Princess . . . Not a Peasant"
### The Meaning of Things

"Economic books tell us that the barter system is long outmoded and has been replaced by the monetary system," wrote Brownie Wise in 1955.

"But," she continued, "when you stop and consider, isn't the monetary system just an improved barter system?"[44] Wise maintained that as a commodity, Tupperware was inseparable from economically unmeasurable concepts such as time, taste, novelty, convenience, thrift, and enjoyment. Successful trading depended on recognizing the import of these nonutilitarian motives for consumption, motives better understood in the workings of preindustrial or "primitive" exchange systems.

The sophisticated use of gifts and premiums was not seen as a replacement for proficient commercial conduct or a crutch for bad salespeople. In fact, THP condemned the escalating and arbitrary use of premiums as an epidemic, trivialized commercial device. Questioning the rational, economic effectiveness of incentive premiums as efficient methods for increasing sales, Wise told her dealers, "I wouldn't know how many million Hopalong Cassidy guns or Howdy-Doody thing-um-a-bobs you'd sell in a week if you offered them with a chocolate flavored castor oil." Rather, Wise viewed gifts not as incentives but as awards integral to the overall operation of the Tupperware scheme: "Premiums are not step-children; they receive the same close attention that the members of our Tupper product family receive."[45] As such, the order and meanings of selected gifts, the very specificity of the material culture, determined the outcome of the commercial success. "The acceptance of a hostess gift will vary in some cases according to the geographical location of a sales area (an item extremely popular in New England may be a dud in southern California or Texas)," and, continued Wise, "they vary according to the calendar, of course."[46] This astute understanding of consumption and material culture, the bedrock of Tupperware's postwar success, utterly defies the notion of consumerism and material acquisition as an automatically hegemonic and homogenizing force. Although Tupperware, Wise acknowledged, "fits into homes everywhere — of every financial bracket, in every part of the country," this did not preclude a diversity of meanings and social and cultural contexts.[47] The influx of new, colorful, and modern commodities opened up a realm of possibilities but also required the formulation of new forms of "order" and knowledge. Spatulas, teacloths, and ceramic figurines were deemed respectable "door gifts" for arriving guests at a Tupperware party; measuring spoons, coasters, sewing kits, and perfume were ideal as parlor-game awards; but hostess thank-you gifts might include whistling kettles, lace tablecloths, percolators, jewelry, and cameras. However, the hierarchy of this material culture shifted according to locality, geography, season, and historical setting.

"The Tupperware Galaxy of Heavenly Gifts," announced a 1954 in-house publication, was fully available to those who "zoom into a vast ocean of Sales." Exploiting the popularity of space-travel science fiction, the pamphlet organized a nine-tier gift-giving system under the headings of assigned planetary orbits. Mercury offered an array of mink jackets, an "Atom Runabout" sailing craft, a "treasure chest" of photographic equipment, and an "all-expense paid Air cruise for two" around Mexico. Uranus offered "a beautiful baby grand piano," "the brilliant new Packard Clipper de luxe touring sedan," and a brand-new speedboat.[48] Moon, available for wholesalers grossing more than $500,000 of annual Tupperware sales, offered a "series sixty-two convertible" Cadillac and a personalized light aircraft.

Gifts and privileges varied according to rank of achievement reached by individual dealers and distributors. The Vanguard Charter, established in 1955 to acknowledge "Brownie's exclusive honor guard of managers," mimicked a medieval honorary structure complete with a coat of arms and a specialized publication, the *Banner.* Shaped like a heart, the Vanguard coat of arms celebrated the golden rule of the organization, "Do Unto Others." Stars (symbolizing aspiration), an acorn (symbolizing growth), a lamp (symbolizing knowledge), a bee (denoting industry), and a rose and Wonder Bowl (suggesting beauty and the enduring qualities of the product and party plan) made up the Vanguard shield. In the center "four hands represent[ing] the helping hands of consumer, dealer, manager, distributor and Tupperware Home Parties" reminded managers of the need to "extend a helping hand to help ourselves and others."[49]

Pledged to the Vanguard, the unit managers showing the greatest leadership capabilities could proudly display their specially designed Vanguard pins but never forsake the individuals who had contributed to their success. As one Vanguard awardee put it, "Being co-operative, and being able to get along with people are stepping stones to a Vanguard Unit."[50] Ambition, as the Vanguard charter reveals, was a blatant feature of many Tupperware women's experiences. "With most jobs," wrote Cleo Mohiman, a Vanguard manager in 1957, "you 'Stay-Put' regardless of how hard you work, in Tupperware you go farther and forward . . . it makes me feel so very proud to know that not having an education even—has not kept me from going to the top."[51] Other programs such as the Order of the Rose, Gold Key Hostesses, Lamplighters and Lamp Club, Red Carpet Award, Star Award, Step-by-Step prize, and Operation Grassroots offered a multitude of stratified incentive schemes that bolstered public recognition and private meanings. In the Treasurama prize scheme, "Your Road to Royal Riches," women were implored to "Be a Princess . . . not a Peasant" and increase their recruitment figures in pursuit of glittering prizes. "Winner of the $1,000 diamond ring contest was Mrs. Margaret Pire, Beloit, Wisc. . . . shown here," read a caption in *Tupperware Sparks,* "gazing at the ring minutes after it was presented."[52] In Escambia, Michigan, Joyce Lequia showed off her Red Carpet award of a "high style wrought iron and brass lamp with shade of smartly textured Cocanada" to her four children.[53]

In preparation for the elaborate corporate rituals and ceremonies, Wise accumulated a vast array of supportive formal and informal knowledge regarding gift giving and its associated material culture. In a file marked "Birthdays," for example, she kept research tracing the history of associated customs, astrological definitions, and birthstone descriptions. Referring to volumes such as *Curiosities of Popular Customs* and *Folklore Mythology and Legend,* she noted that "birthdays are the times when good and evil spirits and influences have the opportunity to attack the celebrants who are at these times in peril," but that "the presence of friends and the expressions of good wishes help to protect the celebrant against the unknown pervasive peril."[54] This amateur anthropological and folklorist interpretation gave the schemes and their gifts a more authentic edge; for example, in the "Birthday Month Contest," rings were awarded in keeping with women's specific birthstone charts and astrological trajectories. A "Birthday Festival Tree Planting Marathon," in which "trees of life" were planted in the headquarters grounds, symbolized the nurturing of fruitful lives, each tree dedicated to a particular distributorship or Tupperware individual. The folklore of European peasantry and Native American wisdom transformed the commodities of twentieth-century manufacturers into sacred and resonant artifacts, and Wise similarly used her own household and personal expenditure to transform everyday commodities into highly charged entities.

The delineation between Wise's corporate image, her personal life, and her ensuing spending habits was far from clear. Shopping sprees for Water's Edge (which officially belonged to the THP enterprise) and the Tupperware model home and kitchen reveal how Wise effectively "converted" her consumption from a highly skilled preoccupation into a practice that ultimately constituted the backbone of the THP enterprise. Antiques and artworks, which adorned the Tupperware headquarters and Brownie's lakeside house, were vital elements of a broader public relations profile. As extravagant Tupperware prizes, lavish visits to hotels and restaurants in Rome and Paris, which Wise invariably attended as leader of THP, were reported in corporate publications and national newspapers alike. Hats purchased at expensive local department stores for Wise's personal use were frequently "converted" later into gifts for awestruck women who, upon visiting their leader's abode, might leave the premises with a chosen article of her apparel. Books were purchased for the Tupperware library, vases and figurines for the model home, dresses and jewelry as gifts for achieving women. Wise retained receipts for many articles of clothing purchased during this period; a typical monthly record of clothing labels reads: "Spun jacket and rayon dress: navy and red silk dress $47.95; black and gold print cotton 2 pc $49.95; natural linen costume $134.95; pink linen dress jacket $49.95; mauve lace dress $39.95; brown silk dress $29.95; print cotton $25.95; navy crepe $39.95; Paul Aprenes original $69.95; blk skirt $29.95; navy silk linen $39.95; pure silk and cashmere sweater $110."[55] It is most likely that a large percentage of this expenditure was claimed as justifiable corporate expenses, especially considering the recycling of garments as gifts. Jerry Wise was often featured in public relations articles in women's magazines and similarly incurred corporate costs. For the "Big Dig" Homecoming Jubilee he required a Levi's jacket, several cowboy shirts, Wrangler jeans, and equestrian accessories including "Hot Rod Cowboy" spurs.

## Best Wishes, Brownie Wise
### The Demise of "Sunshine Cinderella"

While Brownie Wise defended glamour, in the form of mink coats, couture frocks, and hybridized pink roses, as a marketing and incentive ploy, Earl Tupper sought to protect his product from being overshadowed by a tasteless and expensive orgy of excess. The glorification of items such as the Wonder Bowl and its Tupper seal had been central to the vision of "Tupperization," yet the home party plan, with its fancy rituals and gimmicky gifts, had shifted Tupperware proper to the sidelines, where it played an increasingly peripheral role beside the vast array of gifts and commodities. Potlatch ceremonies and kitsch Italianate statues such as *Turtle Baby* took aesthetic precedence over the Tupperware product's "enduring beauty and function." By the late 1950s deep rifts had developed between Tupper and Wise in which notions of taste and consumer discernment played a pivotal role.

In 1957, a battle ensued between Earl Tupper and Brownie Wise regarding perceived conflicts of interest between the Tupper Corporation and THP. The increasing expenditure of THP activities, the unprecedented power of Wise as a national businesswoman, and the diminution of the Tupperware designs by the success of the home party sales system contributed to Tupper's concern over the company's future. Tupper and Wise fought initially through correspondence and interoffice memos, and later in the courts, and finally the conflict culminated, in 1958, with the controversial dismissal of Brownie Wise as vice president.

Strangely, for the conflict obviously revolved around much deeper disagreements over corporate procedure, it was a proposal for a Tupperware dog dish that provoked a series of veiled but acrimonious exchanges. Tupper consistently had sought to distinguish his Tupperware products from the cheap polyethylene items found abundantly in dime stores and exemplified by the common dog dish, against which he had frequently railed. It was intriguing, then, that a year before Wise was ousted from the THP top rank, she should provide Tupper with a "Hand Made Sample of a Dog Dish," intended as the basis for a product prototype. Taking into consideration Wise's comments regarding the problem of "sliding" dog bowls, Tupper initially promised the production of "samples before long," apparently deeming the suggestion entirely unproblematic, even useful.[56] Then, after several months of consideration, he abandoned the dog dish prototype altogether and responded instead with a vitriolic memo. In tones of moral superiority, Tupper accused Wise of betraying the corporate ethos and endangering the Tupperware reputation; she had been observed, by an unnamed source, using a Tupperware bowl as a dog dish in her glamorous lakeside home. In addition to intrinsically questioning Wise's taste and judgment, the memo hinted at some deeper form of treachery and reminded Wise that her behavior was subject to the closest corporate scrutiny. "Memory courses are based on association and repetition," wrote Tupper, continuing: "I thought you followed my thinking about the use of Tupperware for a dog-feeding dish. I never saw a dog's or cat's dish at a back door or anywhere that looked appetizing. When it's a dish that is normally associated with human food storage and serving, I think it scars the mind of any user or potential user who sees it." He concluded, in an accusing tone, "It's bad, at your house of all places. Don't you agree?"[57]

In 1957 Brownie Wise published her autobiography, *Best Wishes, Brownie Wise*, which provoked bitter reprisals from Tupper regarding the prima donna–like behavior of the THP vice president.[58] The book, written in the genre of positive-thinking, self-help psychology literature, featured a foreword by Norman Vincent Peale and included Wise's dedication to her mother: for "Rose Stroud Humphrey . . . who took the words of my grandmother and taught me that wishing with a purpose works a magic all its own!"[59] Filled with references to the wisdom of her grandmother, the book built on the notion of feminine knowledge and the conversion of "wishes" into pragmatism. She attended book-signing appointments in local bookstores and used the publication as an integral part of public relations campaigns.

Earl Tupper was infuriated. He viewed the release of the autobiography as the blatant and unsanctioned act of a rampant self-publicist. How much corporate time had Wise spent, he asked, promoting her book? Why had she not seen fit to discuss with him how she might "handle its promotion through THP?" And why, a month after its publication date, had he not even received a copy for review?

Wise responded by asserting that she had not wasted any corporate time on the book, that she had, in fact, turned down numerous requests for personal interviews on TV shows and was donating all her royalties to the Heart Fund charity. In response to Tupper's "feeling that there is some strange and perhaps not-so-good reason" for the absence of his copy, Wise explained that she had commissioned especially for him a spectacular gold-leafed first edition, which had been unexpectedly delayed. Wise maintained a calculated, deferential stance that placed her safely back on the moral high ground: "Mr. Tupper, I think you are entitled to know that you have made a lot of 'working Wishes' come true for a great many people . . . and that thousands of them have the consciousness to be grateful. It was intended that this book would be dedicated to you, though I was a little uncertain about whether you would approve." The change in dedication occurred, wrote Wise, only when she had discovered the seriousness of her mother's illness.[60]

Despite the astounding success of Tupperware sales under the auspices of THP, and the resounding failure of Tupper's early attempts at formal retailing distribution, throughout the 1950s Wise often felt compelled to justify her unorthodox business procedures to her reluctant, and occasionally skeptical, boss.[61] She constantly pleaded with

Tupper to ensure a plentiful supply of merchandise to facilitate the sales efforts of a burgeoning force of Tupperware dealers. Although national material shortages periodically caused a crisis in supply (notably the years 1952–53), Wise pointed out that unlike the majority of retail concerns, the Tupper Corporation had the luxury of having distributors that were "running a closer inventory than 90% of other business people in this country." The very nature of the Tupperware party enabled an incredibly low-risk forecast on sales, which Wise insisted should facilitate an efficient production schedule. "Every piece of Tupperware that goes out of Farnumsville is pre-sold," she advised Tupper. "It is very safe, for instance, for you to estimate at all times that five times the amount of merchandise for which you have orders on hand has already been 'sold' by dealers."[62] The party plan system relied on the assurance of product availability. If ordered items did not materialize within an acceptable time frame, the failure disappointed party hostesses and guests and made dealers despondent, thus jeopardizing the entire operation of the home party by drastically undermining morale. In this context, Homecoming Jubilees provided the forum for the release of new product types, which proved essential in updating the dealers' repertoire of merchandise and maintaining Tupperware's profile as a contemporary design.

The presentation of *Best Wishes, Brownie Wise* as an incentive gift at the 1957 Homecoming Jubilee had been motivated, Wise argued, as a last-minute compensatory measure to stymie the disappointment of a failed Tupperware product release. Wise's frustration with an inadequate production schedule and her resolve regarding the potential of the party plan led her, as early as 1953, to deliver Tupper an ultimatum regarding his commitment to increased distribution: "I think this is time for you to decide whether you want Tupperware to step into the big time . . . I have a feeling you don't know how close you are to rocking this whole direct selling picture back on its heels," she warned. In defense of her extravagant schemes, Wise reiterated that Tupper's reluctance to address his sales force publicly was a major hindrance, which could only be overcome by high-profile sales assemblies and premium drives. "If this Corporation had a President," she wrote forcefully, "who was active at all in the sales picture or would even permit his name to be used, we could have a 'president's Club' such as many of the companies like, Avon, Fuller, and Real-Silk have . . . since we don't have that kind of President we make do with other gimmicks."[63]

Despite the unparalleled accomplishments of Brownie Wise's direct sales approach, Tupper had grown tired of her gimmicks and expenditures and the increasing inseparability of her personal life and corporate career. In March 1958 Brownie's demise, referred to as "semi-retirement," was celebrated in a memo (marked "Extremely Confidential") written by Tupper. "I am getting more and more enthusiastic about the future of THP now that B.W. is out . . . I can see ourselves becoming as big as Sears, Roebuck and if we can get that big then we ought to be able to get bigger."[64] With the departure of Wise, Tupper aimed to refocus attention on the significance of the Tupperware designs as a boost for sales; he also recognized that Wise's business acumen might just as easily benefit a rival company. "BW will, of course, be out for any kind of a deal that can be worked with a competitor. We can best upset their applecart and [stall] competition by moving fast on a well-planned program with all these new items," he exclaimed. During the initial negotiations regarding Brownie Wise's departure from THP, her "semi-retirement" package offered a one-time payment of $30,000, provided she refrain from seeking employment with Tupperware's competitors. In February 1958, however, she formed a company specializing in sales consultation and public relations in association with former THP executive Charles McBurney. Wise organized a press release describing her departure from THP as a "resignation" and advertising herself as "one of the most dynamic sales leaders in America," responsible for building "Tupperware to a multi-million dollar corporation in the span of seven years."[65] The copy also used this opportunity to emphasize her unique and exceptional accomplishments as a woman. "She is the first woman member of the Board of Advisors for American Salesman magazine, and was the first woman to be selected as a member of the board of the National Association of Direct Selling Companies." When Earl Tupper learned of this press release, he summoned the newly appointed THP leaders, Hamer Wilson and Gary McDonald, to discuss Wise's future; notes of the meeting recorded how Tupper planned to re-taliate by letting her "potential hirers . . . know that she was removed and did not resign."[66]

The cancellation of Wise's initial "semi-retirement" agreement led her to sue for damages against the Tupper Corporation in March 1959. In the six months following her dismissal, and after a brief stint in real estate dealing, Wise had become president of a direct sales organization called the "Cinderella International Corporation," based in Kissimmee, Florida, which featured her on the front pages of its in-house magazine, *Cinderella Coach Line*. The company, which distributed cleaning products and cosmetics, had been established for at least ten years, but unlike Tupperware it lacked innovative products and a nationally high profile. Just months before her move for litigation against THP, Wise organized a flamboyant "Christmas Cinderella Parade" a couple of miles from the Tupperware headquarters, which included "beauteous floats," with women in strapless, white ball gowns, gliding down the main street to promote her new direct sales venture.

Brownie Wise attempted to sue Tupperware Homes Parties for breach of contract and conspiracy damages to the sum of $160,000; she failed. The entire proceedings regarding Wise's dismissal were shrouded in mystery and never formally announced to the Tupperware sales force. According to the amount of personal correspondence received by Wise, cards and letters of affection lamenting her demise, her presence was sorely missed. "Dear Brownie," wrote a former Tupperware manager, "whatever your reason was for leaving Tupperware Inc.—accepting another position or retiring to enjoy your home and family, it should have been announced in the Sentinel [house organ] . . . does anyone think you can just vanish and we won't be concerned?"[67]

• • •

# "Tupperware—Everywhere!"
## The Globalization of Tupperware

After the dismissal of Brownie Wise in 1958, Earl Tupper promoted Hamer Wilson (head of marketing) and Gary McDonald (sales promotion manager) to the positions of president and vice president, and the Tupperware enterprise (still largely dependent on the promotional schemes and dealership system initiated by Wise) continued to boom. Tupper, freed from what he perceived as the constraints of Wise's megalomaniacal sales leadership, put the Tupper Corporation and its sister company THP up for sale. Also that year he sought a divorce from his wife, Marie, effectively consigning to the past the two most important relationships and the two most important women associated with the construction of Tupperware as a multimillion-dollar empire. Throughout the 1930s Marie had contributed considerably to Tupper's endeavors as a fledgling designer, and without the efforts of Brownie in the 1950s the Tupperware party would have been but a fleeting and ineffectual sales concept. As founder, president, and principal stockholder, Earl Tupper stood to gain substantially from the flotation of his company; he was also eager to preserve a sense of autonomy in the face of a burgeoning corporate organization. The introduction of punitive taxation measures also prompted major misgivings regarding his relationship with the company, a fear that ultimately led to his renunciation of U.S. citizenship in the 1960s.

# Tupperware

In September 1958 the Tupper Corporation and its subsidiaries were purchased for the sum of $16 million by Rexall Drug Company, a business eager to develop its association with plastics manufacture. Tupper was precluded from pursuing independent commercial houseware design in the United States and Canada for a ten-year period following the Rexall take-over.

"In the field of direct selling to the consumer," announced Rexall President Justin Dart, "the Tupperware Home Parties Division has established a position of national leadership in the plastics industry through its nationwide network of distributors . . . and we believe this operation has outstanding growth potential."[1] That Dart chose to retain the exclusivity of the Tupperware sales scheme, despite Rexall's established distribution to around 11,000 drugstores and the growing national retailing tendency toward the sale of plastic products from similar outlets, reveals how effective the party plan system was perceived to be in securing the product's success.[2] Although, in addition to the cash payment, Earl Tupper received 175,000 Rexall shares and a position as chair on the newly owned Tupper Corporation board, privately he did not share Dart's optimism regarding the growth of the Tupperware venture. According to oral histories he instinctively felt that the Tupperware phenomenon had reached its sales peak, and most significantly that it had grown unwieldy and increasingly divorced from the "one-man" operation he had originally conceived.

Tupper's retrospective accounts of the "Tupperware Story" provided an entirely revisionist history, one that sought to eradicate the impact of Wise's marketing skills. An autobiographical profile written in 1970, for instance, charted his business success: "I bought 750 acres [300 hectares] of land in Osceala County, Florida and built there my international Sales Headquarters for Tupperware Home Parties Inc. A sales organization I had built to sell one special line of our products on the Home Party Plan." Tupper failed to make even a passing reference to Wise. The same autobiographical excerpt, written with the benefit of hindsight, described the sale of the Tupperware Corporation at a "sacrifice price" motivated by pending tax liabilities that would have "eaten everything."[3]

Sorely disillusioned with his country of birth and what he described as the degenerative nature of the rat race, Earl Tupper sought a place where he could "wheel and deal . . . without breaking any laws" and have "freedom just as did my old ancestors from Sussex, England, when in the 1630s [they] left their homeland for the fresh new frontiers of America." In

1967, he gave up U.S. residency, thus setting himself free, in his own words, "to work toward citizenship and ownership of an Island."[4] Tupper had harbored this desire for isolation and seclusion since his earliest diary entries in the 1930s, stating prophetically that after getting his "millions" he would never again be forced to live "within a mile of another neighbor."[5] He moved to Costa Rica in 1973, pursuing his humanitarian vision through contributions to charitable foundations and the engineering of medical contraptions. In 1976, he was inducted into the Plastic Hall of Fame by the Society of the Plastics Industry. During the latter part of his life, an idyllic island existence inspired a typically pragmatic vision of the ultimate "adult village." Retirees, he told a relative, might while away their days in a haven of creative activity, living on "an island dream land where there would be no rude awakening; only peace and happiness" and, of course, a "well staffed hospital."[6] In 1983, Earl Tupper died from a heart attack at the age of seventy-six.

As for Brownie Wise, following her brief presidency with the Cinderella International Corporation, in 1961 she took on a more glamorous role as leader of Viviane Woodard Cosmetics, taking THP executive Charles McBurney with her as vice president. "Viviane Woodard," she announced, "is going to be the biggest cosmetic company in the world — soon!"[7] After only minor success with the company, in the late 1960s Wise became a marketing consultant for the Sovera Company, another direct sales cosmetics firm, which, benefiting from the contemporary appeal of natural health products, was using aloe vera as the basis of its ingredients and marketing focus. The Cinderella, Woodard, and Sovera ventures sought to utilize the unique charisma Wise had imparted as the general manager of THP.[8] Ironically, however, by the 1960s the home party plan, as refined by Wise herself in the 1950s with its elaborate corporate rituals and premium campaigns, had become a highly competitive and less exceptional mode of distribution, used to sell everything from hosiery to wigs. Consequently, despite her ardent career attempts, Wise was destined never to relive the celebrity of her former THP glory; however, she did maintain an unerring ability to impart enthusiasm and continued to develop her interest in positive thinking.[9] In 1968, she attended one of the many women's organizations as a speaker. On this occasion, a decade after her departure from Tupperware, she addressed her audience about "a brand new psychology," called "psycho-cybernetics," in which self-image and thinking "outside one's self" played a crucial role. "Love is only effective when given freely," she concluded, telling her audience to relax and "Go slow, don't blow."[10] Vacating the Water's Edge mansion in 1965, after her retirement in the 1970s Wise lived with her son, Jerry, in the Kissimmee area of Florida. She worked as an artist in ceramics and textiles and pursued her interest in church affairs until her death in December 1992 at the age of seventy-nine.

## "As Soft Sell Steals into Suburbia"
### Consolidating the International Market

The dynamic, if contentious, relationship between Tupper's invention and Wise's sales techniques created a legacy that continues today in the form of the thriving Tupperware corporate empire. The assimilation of the product and sales system into an international market actually began as early as 1952, when the THP slogan "Tupperware—Everywhere" took on a new meaning as a growing number of dealers from Puerto Rico demanded their own unit manager team.[11] The dynamism of the party plan meant that individual dealers often opened up entire sales networks single-handedly. In 1957, for example, dealers Audrey Snyman and Jane Bakke, traveling to South Africa and Iran, respectively, took with them collections of Tupperware to establish local sales schemes. Between 1952 and 1956, largely through the efforts of individual dealerships, Tupperware developed markets in Africa, Canada, France, Germany, Hawaii, India, the Bahamas, Guatemala, and Mexico. In 1955, according to *Tupperware Sparks,* the Tupperware party even proved popular among the Inuit population of Alaska.[12]

Despite this largely piecemeal approach to international growth, Tupperware formally expanded to a European market in the early 1960s. Initial market research, exploring the introduction of Tupperware parties to other English-speaking nations, concluded that the uniquely American phenomenon of the sales system could not be readily transposed to another culture. But in defiance of the 1960 report, the corporation made a bid for the British market. Led by the long-established Tupperware executive Elsie Mortland (described by the British press as a "charming, warm-hearted American housewife"), a Tupperware promotional campaign introduced the product and sales system to the suburban housewives of England with a notably mixed reception. Although numerous tabloid newspapers rallied against the divisive American marketing technique, others focused on the novelty of a sales system that offered social benefits

Guatemalan Tupperware dealers, ca. 1964, pose behind a hand-embroidered textile that they designed for the display of Tupperware items and made as a gift to honor pioneering THP executive Elsie Mortland. Courtesy of Elsie Mortland.

alongside consumer goods. An article titled "The Soft Sell with the Social Service," for example, described the Tupperware notion of homemaking as "a skilled task and most worth-while career" and recommended the party system as an antidote to isolation, loneliness, and
frustration of new housewives. The contemporary growth of new housing estates and suburban developments created the ideal environment for
the British debut of Tupperware, when the National Housewives' Regis-
ter featured Tupperware parties as part of the "getting to know you"
schemes. However, press reaction, including the *Daily Mail*'s feature "As
Soft Sell Steals into Suburbia," revealed an inherent suspicion regarding
the invasion of commercial activity into the sanctity of the domestic
sphere. Similarly, in 1965, *Which?* magazine, the popular and highly regarded mouthpiece of the Consumer Association, assessed the validity of
Tupperware and its sales system by drawing comparison with less expensive "off the shelf" plastic containers. The report concluded that equivalent products purchased at lower cost from Woolworth's, without the

elaborate sales scheme, proved better value for the money. The rational, performance-based test, which took little account of style, design, or the contemporary appeal of the Tupperware party, aimed to demystify Tupperware as a product that had gained considerably in status and popularity since its first introduction to England in 1960.

Despite the rather dismissive tone of the Consumer Association report, Tupperware continued to thrive in a British context. Plastic in 1960s Western Europe, in the form of shiny miniskirts and inflatable transparent furniture, had become emblematic of a thrusting, youthful, modern lifestyle. *Queen* magazine, a contemporary high-style publication exemplifying fashionable living, lauded Tupperware as "the greatest revolution in household consumer goods since the Phoenicians invented glass."[13] In the same edition, Tupperware containers were shown as ideal accessories for the busy 1960s fashion photographer, keeping films and chemicals airtight on a glamorous location shoot. As many of the first British Tupperware parties took place in the prestigious suburbs of London, they took on kudos manifest by an association with contemporary living and social mobility. Notably, despite the initial media coverage, few women actually identified the product or the party system as an American phenomenon, because of the ease with which it became assimilated into British culture, from picnics to packed lunches and seaside visits.

Contrary to the limitations imposed by major cultural differences in food storage, preparation, and associated domestic rituals, the Tupperware product, it seemed, could be easily appropriated and reinterpreted according to localized customs and specific social worlds. Tupperware unarguably provided a useful, functional form of storage; ultimately, the global, mass consumption of Tupperware highlights the cross-culturally recognizable position of women as an economically disenfranchised group, performing labor ostensibly undervalued in a capitalist system.

Just as British housewives embraced a form of sales that seemingly contradicted the national propensity for privacy, by 1965 Japanese housewives, traditionally understood as cloistered and shy, gathered together on bamboo mats to share lively gossip at Tupperware parties. Even with average per capita income estimated at one-sixth of that of the U.S. housewife, during this period Japanese women purchased twice as much Tupperware as their American counterparts. Products such as Econo-Canisters were redefined as "Kimono-Keepers," deemed ideal for protecting ceremonial garments from insects and humidity. So effective were the Tupperware parties in Japan that Tupperware designers began to re-

# The Globalization of Tupperware

By 1965 the Tupperware party had expanded to an international market. Japanese women, here seated on tatami and enjoying a product demonstration, wholeheartedly embraced the Tupperware phenomenon. Reprinted from the 20 November 1965 issue of *Business Week* by special permission. © 1965 by McGraw-Hill Companies.

spond directly to the local demands of new consumers. *Business Week* showed workers in rice paddies drinking from Tupperware tumblers and reported how the Tupperware design team was creating a prototype for a "bentobako," a traditional Japanese lunch box to store rice, raw fish, and seaweed.[14]

By the 1970s, as well as catering to the Americas, Tupperware was selling in fifteen European countries, Asia Pacific, the Middle East, and South Africa, with corporate divisions reflecting the needs and policies of each region. The product line expanded to include Tupperware toys, such as the primary-color Shape 'O' Ball, which was designed to be a safe and educational item with cross-cultural appeal.[15]

In its country of origin, the increasing globalization of Tupperware led to a more nationalistic corporate identity grounded in a renewed pride in America's manufacturing and marketing prowess. In 1975 the configuration of an American flag constructed from 76,325 red, white, and blue Tupperware bowls on the grounds of the Florida headquarters signaled one of many future sales competitions initiated between Tupperware Europe and Tupperware US.[16] Direct selling and the accomplishments of Tupperware distributors were aligned once again with the patriotic belief in the democracy of free enterprise. An article in *Salesman's Opportunity,* "Direct Selling: The Frontier of Unlimited Opportunities," compared "early explorers who traded with Indians" to the new sales pioneers of the 1970s, and the country's historical "quest for 'Independence'" with the need to liberate the American housewife "from a drab and dreary existence."[17]

While many countries outside North America were embracing Tupperware as a symbol of modernity, within the United States in the 1970s it began to appeal to advocates of an "alternative economy." "Switch to the Good Life" announced an article that urged disillusioned waiters, social workers, librarians, clerks, nurses, and receptionists to "Switch to Positive Direct Selling." Although direct selling had always provided self-determined employment outside the strictures of the formal workplace, in the 1970s organizations such as the Direct Selling Association began to promote direct sales culture as the means to an alternative lifestyle, freed from the constraints of corporate bureaucracy and time-keeping. Ironically, whereas direct sales in the early to mid-twentieth century had been inextricably bound to the pursuit of the American Dream, albeit through the back door, by the 1970s direct sales opportunities thrived on the notion of an abandoned American Dream. "Are you tired of fighting the landlord, the tax collector, the utility companies and others who constantly want your hard-earned dollars?" asked *Speciality Salesman*. "Maybe it's time to stop fighting." Instead of settling for inadequate wages, "nonstop inflation" and fighting "that big bad wolf who has taken permanent residence at your door," it might be time to join many other "unhappy and underpaid workers [and] switch . . . to the highly profitable field of direct selling."[18] Similarly, with the increasing popularization of the women's movement, direct selling — and its opportunities for employment outside the "normal" labor market — took on a renewed significance and allure.

## "Sisters Are Doing It for Themselves"
### The Home Party and the Women's Movement

Despite the apparently radical shift in women's positions, both socially and economically, since the inception of Tupperware in the 1940s through the 1950s, the appeal of the home party has remained intrinsically unchanged. As one journalist commented in 1973, "for those who attend [Tupperware] parties, it is a break from the monotony of housework, a time to play silly games, a respite from family, an hour with 'the girls.'" Certainly, a growing popularization of feminist politics caused Tupperware management policy to become more attuned to the issues of women's labor and social standing. In the early 1960s, publications with titles such as *How Women Can Make up to $1000 a Week in Direct Selling* and *The Selling Power of Women* clearly acknowledged direct selling as a potentially feminine domain; and by the 1970s, academic and popular articles alike seriously considered the home party as a potentially empowering experience for women.[19] Tupperware, it was argued, provided employment for pregnant women, those on short-term maternity leave, and those with relatively inflexible child-care responsibilities. "The Tupperware Company," wrote one journalist, "has 50,000 women, traditionally considered unemployable" by the majority of companies reluctant to give them even "a second look."[20] The academic journal *Radical America* advocated Tupperware parties as a possible arena of consciousness raising. And an African-American community activist, belonging to a feminist organization called "Big Sisters," recommended selling homemade goods on the party plan as a route to independent economic success.[21] Aware of the company's unique position in negotiating the contradictions of women's changing historical roles, in 1975, Joe Hara, then-president of Tupperware, was quizzed by *Ms.* magazine on the company's policy toward female employment and responded, "We are constantly telling women they can better their best and we are constantly hearing them say, 'No one ever patted us on the back for polishing the kitchen floor.' I know of no business where a woman has more of an opportunity to use her ability to a fuller extent."[22]

During this period, however, the conservative notion of women's fulfillment through home- and beauty-based activity persisted in the form of companies such as Mary Kay Cosmetics and Mary C. Crowley's Home Interiors and Gifts. As contemporaries of Brownie Wise, both Mary Kay Ash and Mary Crowley had worked as Stanley Home Products saleswomen in the late 1940s, and their use of distinctly feminine incentive schemes and "Cinderella gifts" (as Mary Kay referred to premiums such as mink coats and diamond rings) owed much to Wise's initiatives with THP in the 1950s. The corporate philosophies of Ash and Crowley both embraced religion and domestic subordination in a far more orthodox fashion than Tupperware had. In her autobiography, *Mary Kay — You Can Have It All,* Ash (who introduced pink as her corporate hallmark more than a decade after Wise's widespread use of and reference to the color) describes the means to "having it all" as "24-hour-a-day" commitment to God and family and the positioning of career as a final consideration. "My purpose for writing this book," she announced, "is to assure today's working woman that she need not abandon her cherished values. If doing so were a prerequisite to her success, gains made in the workplace would be offset by personal losses."[23]

Similarly, Mary C. Crowley's autobiography, *Think Mink!* (revealingly subtitled, "How you can achieve the self-confidence, excellence and dynamic faith that motivate this remarkable Christian businesswoman") justified women's entrepreneurial activity in the home party plan, through an understanding of the moral significance of the household and its objects. Promoting the spiritual nature of home decoration, Crowley began her autobiography with an account of a woman's redemption reached through a home demonstration of porcelain figurines, scented candles, and whimsical plaques. Depressed and isolated, Betty, a reluctant party hostess and lapsed Christian, had let her homemaking chores, like her faith, fall to the wayside. "As I carried my two heavy sample cases up the walk," recounted Crowley, "I could spot fingerprints advertising their message of dirt and neglect around the doorbell . . . I wanted to set out my pictures, plaques, figurines, and candles on top of her TV in an attractive arrangement. But first I had to gather up a collection of unpaid bills and try to keep from sneezing as I removed a dusty doily."[24] Inspired by the home demonstration, Betty revamps her home interior and in so doing rediscovers her faith in God and a renewed belief in the American home as "a place of refuge, peace . . . harmony" and beauty.

Whereas in the United States Mary Kay Ash and Mary C. Crowley divested the party plan system with a conservative, Christian zeal, in Britain, by the late 1970s, a new form of distinctly risqué merchandise was popularized using the home party plan. Far removed from the benign domesticity associated with normal home parties, the Ann Summers versions used the exclusively female environment to sell sex toys and erotic lingerie. These underwear parties, which customized Tupperware party games with the introduction of ribald jokes and sexually explicit references, developed following the success of Pippa Dee clothing parties, which sold mother- and child-oriented products to British women in the 1970s. Tupperware and Pippa Dee typified the safely domesticated pitch of the party plan, but Ann Summers created all-women parties (that welcomed the inclusion of alcoholic beverages and uninhibited behavior) as a potentially anarchic interpretation of women's shared domestic and consumer activities.[25] Although arguably conservative in their stereotypical depictions of women as availing sex objects, Ann Summers parties reflected changing sexual relations in which women could explore a world of erotica, with other women, which, in the form of retail outlets, had previously been a predominantly male arena. As the flip side to the perceived conformity and safe domesticity of the original Tupperware parties, the Ann Summers versions continue to thrive.

Throughout the 1980s and into the late 1990s, Tupperware consistently evolved, in terms of its product design and party plan, in keeping with social and cultural change. Its sale and its success remain tied exclusively to the home party plan.[26] The 1980s saw the introduction of a luxury line of Tupperware aimed at a new, upwardly mobile generation of consumers (dubbed "Yuppieware" by some observers). Recognition of the growing number of working women led to the development of "rush-hour" Tupperware parties organized at nominated homes along the route of women's commuter journeys.[27] Although the expansion of shopping malls, and the treatment of these sites as places of sociality and leisure, signaled major changes in shopping behavior, Tupperware parties continued. New products such as the Rock 'N' Serve for freezers and microwaves, the Legacy tabletop serving range, and Magic Tupper (made under the license of the Walt Disney Company) reflect the Tupperware Corporation's expansion. Ecological concerns have heightened the company's recycling awareness and, fortuitously, echoed one of the product's earliest promotional campaigns, which encouraged women to use Tupperware as a positive alternative to disposable packaging.

By the year 2000, the Tupperware Corporation anticipates expanded markets in China, India, and Central Europe; according to the 1996 annual report, Tupperware responds ideally to geographical and demographic areas with "large emerging middle classes, undeveloped retail infra-structure and shortages of jobs for women who want to work."[28] Peru, Columbia, and Central America are considered to offer further possibilities for global "Tupperization."

Tupperware's relation to shifts in gender politics continues. In 1996, pseudo–drag queen Pam Teflon (adorned with bouffant platinum pageboy wig, glittery gloves, and false eyelashes) became all the rage at gay Tupperware parties and won the award for best-selling salesperson of Tupperware's Los Angeles franchise.[29] Since its inception in the 1940s Tupperware has accrued status as a mundane yet extraordinary artifact, receiving numerous accolades ranging from celebrity consumers to design awards. Elizabeth Taylor lent Tupperware the ultimate glamour by hosting a Tupperware party on board her yacht in the 1960s, and at the turn of the twenty-first century the Museum of Modern Art continues to exhibit the product as an exemplary object born of "distinctive design." Although there have been numerous changes in the Tupperware designs and terminology over the fifty years of its existence (with the famous Tupperware "burp" reinvented as a more refined "whisper" in the 1970s), its status as a globally recognizable generic product endures.

In the late 1990s, Tupperware is poised to infiltrate yet another cultural landscape as the multifaceted market of the worldwide web beckons. Virtual Tupperware parties, where "no coffee is served and there are no demonstrations of the products' notorious 'burp,'" have brought together guests from places as far flung as Japan, Singapore, Germany, and the Netherlands. As a means of technological retailing that denies "face-to-face" contact, direct sales opponents of the internet believe it will "undermine the shoe-leather efforts of their human sales force." However, independent salespeople, in defiance of corporate policy, have begun to use the internet as the ultimate social network, "the next generation of old-fashioned door-to-door sales."[30]

● ● ●

# Conclusion

production-led understanding of Tupperware as a "design classic" born of formal technical research, clever engineering, and adherence to strict aesthetic principles is clearly inadequate in explaining the cultural meaning of this product. Contrary to the rationale behind modernist exhibits of the Museum of Modern Art, Tupperware is not simply a functional object or a neutral commodity operating as a blatant manifestation of rational market economy and twentieth-century aesthetics. Like all products of mass consumption, Tupperware embodies the complex social relations of everyday life, where commodities circulate beyond the realms of utility, status, and individualized desire.

In Tupper's own rural New Hampshire household of the 1930s, everyday provisioning revolved around the informal exchange of goods and services with neighbors and kin. With barely two nickels to rub together, the family constantly sought to remedy their hardship through thrift and prudence. Yet as diary accounts in 1933 reveal, the Tupper family also took part in window-shopping jaunts to local towns and invested in many of the latest fashionable products, chosen from the pages of the Sears and Roebuck catalog. The purchase of apparently luxurious items, strangely incongruous with the Tupper family's life of plain living and restricted income, seemingly substantiates theories of emulative and conspicuous consumption popularized by early market economists.[1] However, these artifacts of a newly burgeoning mass consumer culture did not merely offer a material escape from the harsh realities of the Depression; their acquisition represented a commitment to a shared vision of modernity and social advancement.

In a similar way, Tupperware in the 1950s anchored modern customs, manners, and social roles and instigated changes as well. As one historian explains, the profusion of new consumer goods is "intimately associated with new sensibilities and new social taxonomies." And in this way consumption acts as a form of "cultural orientation."[2] As households and gender relations shifted from social and economic contexts of the interwar to postwar period, Tupperware encapsulated the contradictions of modern living. It "guarded food values" and endorsed thrift while also promoting conviviality and excess in the form of designs devised to "add glamour to a simple snack" and accessories for the "hostess who wants . . . the 'soupçon' of gay informality." The Tupperware party celebrated the pursuit of a new idealized domesticity while thriving on the mundane realities of isolated domestic labor and the limitations of women's social and economic positions. The postwar suburban homes of North America, though engaged in a culture of increased household expenditure, did more than use new commodity forms such as Tupperware as superficial props in the construction of inauthentic worlds. In addition to creating and contesting social identities, goods operated in the realms of moral economies negotiating the intersection of private and public worlds and values.

Of course, in an instrumental sense, Tupperware offered consumers a perfectly utilitarian product. Indeed corporate literature encouraged dealers to limit their demonstrations, when they were addressing "the very poorest" consumers, to literal and functional explanations of the product's worth. "Word-pictures," for example, were used to illustrate to housewives the wastefulness of throwing away even the last two slices of a loaf. These demonstrations, corporate literature reiterated, proved "particularly effective in Birmingham and in the Pittsburgh area" during steel strikes and showed that "the closer the household budget is shaved, the more attentively a woman will listen when you tell her how to conserve the food she buys."[3] But for the majority of homemakers, Tupperware embodied a relation to consumption that far exceeded a simple, rational equation of price and economy.

The Tupperware party, unlike conventional forms of marketing and retailing, addressed an exceptionally diverse range of consumers, adapting as it did to the divergent and localized interests of its dealer networks. But ultimately it thrived on what Brownie Wise acknowledged as "the medium class" market—a new middle class described by Wise as providing a "picnic ground for Home Demonstration companies."[4] Since the publication of Veblen's classic work, *The Theory of the Leisure Class* (1899), the relationship between the emergence of new middle classes and consumer goods in the United States has prompted widespread commentary and debate. In the postwar period the notable rise in the standard of living, enabled by a ready supply of consumer goods and services, inspired the term "consumer citizen." As historian Lizabeth Cohen asserts, "Mass consumption not only shaped the economy, but also altered the political realm, becoming a new vehicle for delivering the traditional American promises of democracy and egalitarianism."[5]

Though Tupperware flourished in the postwar era of economic prosperity, the phenomenon was firmly embedded in broader social and political debates initiated in the 1930s, when the notion of the "consumer" became a crucial facet of the modern state. As Cohen argues, "In the process of constructing the New Deal state during the 1930s, a wide range of people—from ordinary citizens to policy makers—began to recognize for the first time that consumer interests and behavior had central economic and political consequences for American society."[6] In a popularist context, Earl Tupper's writings and diary entries of the 1930s, informed by Roosevelt's radio addresses and the commentaries of contemporary magazines, referred consistently to the importance of the modern consumer and mass consumption in securing America's future prosperity and civic life. Tupper's aim to "be a better social friend" through the design of desirable goods was directly informed by a belief in the transformative power of consumerism.

Similarly, throughout the 1920s and 1930s, the notion of consumption as part of a broader humanitarian and nationalistic vision was promoted by direct sales concerns that viewed their service to the American consumer as a patriotic endeavor. Because they bore the brunt of much trade legislation (because of the precariousness of their door-to-door business), direct sales companies developed a keener interest in consumer politics than many formal retail outlets.[7] By the 1950s, acutely aware of the power of the consumer, Tupperware Home Parties Incorporated nurtured its reputation as a direct sales concern through constant reference to the sanctity of the "consumer public." In 1954, a brass plaque donned the headquarter grounds, inscribed with the words: "Dedicated to Tupperware Dealers, Managers and Distributors, whose sincere regard for the consumer public is reflected in the purposeful progress of Tupperware Home Parties Incorporated. Their accomplishments have proven the soundness of their philosophy that greater growth brings greater service."

Interventionist policies of the New Deal and the activities of wartime government regulatory bodies impacted on postwar understandings of political economy. Organizations such as the Office of Price Administration, in the pursuit of rationalized consumption strategies, raised the status of the housewife as a powerful force within broader political economy. Such bodies largely represented women's relation to consumption in terms of thrift, value for money, and accuracy of trade descriptions.[8] Although New Deal rhetoric and World War II rationing policies accentuated the cross-class politics of women's roles as consumers, after the war bodies such as the National Consumer League ostensibly came to represent the interests of the educated, middle-class housewife. Though historically the provisioning of the home has never been a purely rational or economically driven activity, in the postwar period defined by mass purchasing power (if unevenly distributed) it took on a new significance. The "rationalized" approach to consumption advocated by many consumer's groups held minimal relevance to women whose "work" as consumers increasingly involved the negotiation of less tangible issues of taste and style in the chaotic world of postwar consumer goods.

In this context, the flamboyant displays of conspicuous consumption, offered through the gifts, commodities, rituals, and customs of THP, embraced consumption as a thoroughly valorized and culturally based activity. As housewives, women occupied a historically established but trivialized relation to the provisioning of the home and the acquisition of household appliances, but with Tupperware these roles were transformed into significantly powerful positions worthy of celebration and expansion. Many working-class and newly middle-class women precluded from mainstream social and economic worlds received adulation and recognition. Elaborate displays of gift giving, in which women were awarded everything from fifty-seven pairs of shoes with matching handbags to a safe playground for their children, transformed commodities and their consumption into meaningful and collectively understood displays of affection and worth. As vice president of THP, Brownie Wise represented conspicuous consumption as an ethically informed practice that held a direct corollary with women's personal self-empowerment and increased productivity. "Use yourself freely," she urged Tupperware women, "for you'll never, never, never use yourself up!"

## Conclusion

The Tupperware phenomenon is inextricably bound to these shifting discourses of consumption in the twentieth-century United States. Although this study has premised cultural over technical or business history, it does not mean to construct these forces as separable considerations. The "success" of a specific design cannot be traced to one monolithic process but is the result of a multitude of frequently conflicting forces and agents that make up the dynamic between production and consumption. Mass-produced artifacts do not neatly follow technically determined or predestined pathways to mass consumption, despite the efforts of manufacturers and marketers. Artifacts are bound by complex and interactive social contexts; their consumption is not merely a market-driven response to values of production. The constraints and interests of commerce, profit, manufacturing, design, advertising, and marketing are inseparable from broader discourses of consumption, through which consumers "manipulate the meaning of . . . forms through differential selection, placement, use and association."[9] Through this process Tupperware became a generic branded product design.

The enduring significance of Tupperware resides in its integral association, through design and direct sales, to the social relations and continued economic marginalization of women. Consumers attending Tupperware parties in Peru in the twenty-first century (as the Tupperware Corporation proposes) will not be imitating the kaffeeklatsches and suburban Round Robin get-togethers of their 1950s American predecessors. Tupperware will undoubtedly continue to hold resonance as an object of modernity, with particular appeal to an emerging middle class and a female population precluded from mainstream employment, but it will also be appropriated as part of an entirely different, and historically specific, discourse of consumption and gender politics.

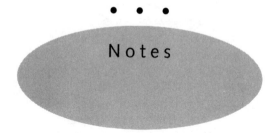

# Notes

Materials deposited at the Archives Center of the National Museum of American History, Smithsonian Institution, Washington, D.C., such as the papers of Earl Tupper and Brownie Wise, are identified as "NMAH" plus a collection number and a series number.

## Introduction

1. *Tupperware: The Growing Opportunity* (Middlesex: Tupperware UK and Ireland, 1994).

2. "A Worldwide Success Story," Tupperware corporate web site, http://www.tupperware.com, June 1998.

3. The term "Tupperization" was commonly used within the Tupper Corporation. See, for example, Brownie Wise to Earl Tupper, interoffice memo, 21 November 1953, Tupper Papers, NMAH 470, series 3.

4. "Tupperware Ladies Dig for Treasure," *Business Week,* 17 April 1954.

5. Rex Taylor, "Marilyn's Friends and Rita's Customers: A Study of Party Selling as Play and as Work," *Sociological Review* 3, no. 26 (1978): 574.

## one
## Designing for a Moral Economy

1. See Jeffrey Meikle, *Twentieth Century Limited: Industrial Design in America* (Philadelphia: Temple University Press, 1979).

2. The term "jobber" refers to a wholesaler who works on a small-scale level selling directly to independent retailers, salesmen, and institutions. As manufacturing distribution changed with the rise of a mass market at the turn of the century, such definitions changed. According to Susan Strasser, in her book *Satisfaction Guaranteed: The Making of the American Market* (New York: Pantheon Books, 1989), 59: "The term 'jobber,' originally applied to merchants who broke down lots of imported goods and distributed them to retailers, was by 1870 used interchangeably with 'wholesaler' to refer to a new kind of middleman that had become dominant."

3. The term "moral economy" is understood mainly by historians (as derived from the work of British social historian Edward P. Thompson) to describe a competing force pitted against the alienating market economy of capitalism. A particularly useful summary of its relevance to consumption studies and technologies is provided by Roger Silverstone, Eric Hirsch, and David Morley, "Information and Communication Technologies and the Moral Economy of the Household," in *Consuming Technologies: Media and Information in Domestic Spaces,* ed. Roger Silverstone and Eric Hirsch (London: Routledge, 1992). The authors emphasize the moral economy of the household as "both an economy of meanings and a meaningful economy," which most significantly "stands in a potentially or actually transformative relationship to the public, objective economy of the exchange of goods and meanings," 18.

4. See Thomas P. Hughes, *American Genesis: A Century of Invention and Technological Enthusiasm, 1870–1970* (New York: Viking, 1989) for extensive discussion of American and European interpretations of modernism during the 1920s and 1930s.

5. Earl Tupper, notes, "Have the Courage of Your Convictions," ca. 1937, NMAH 470, series 1.

6. Joseph J. Corn, ed., epilogue to *Imagining Tomorrow: History, Technology, and the American Future* (Cambridge: M.I.T. Press, 1986), 228.

7. Tupper Corporation advertisement, "An institution is but the lengthened shadow of one man" (Farnumsville, Mass.: Tupper Corporation, 1949), NMAH 470, series 4.

8. For use of biography as a commercial device, see Karal Ann Marling, "Betty Crocker's Picture Cook Book: The Aesthetics of Food in the 1950s," in *As Seen on TV: The Visual Culture of Everyday Life in the 1950s* (London: Harvard University Press, 1994).

9. "I am determined that my career should be in inventing and designing to that end and that I shall be a better social friend, I'm pledging my relentless drive," Tupper diary, 1 January 1936, NMAH 470, series 2.

10. Tupper, invention journal and sketchbook, opening page, "My Purpose in Life," 1937, NMAH 470, series 2.

11. Lawrence Alan Rosenwald describes the significance of the diaries and almanacs of Puritans and transcendentalists exemplified by "The Journal or Diary of a Faithful Christian," written in 1656 by John Beadle, a work that typified the

Puritan custom of recording and accounting the arduous labor endured to reach an appropriate level of self-consciousness and atonement, in *A Companion to American Thought*, ed. Richard Wightman Fox and James T. Kloppenberg (Oxford: Blackwell, 1995), 179–80. For a contemporary cultural analysis of "success" in the United States, see Jeffrey Louis Decker, *Made in America: Self-Styled Success from Horatio Alger to Oprah Winfrey* (Minneapolis: University of Minnesota Press, 1997).

12. Tupper, notes connected to correspondence course work, "Thoughts," in which Tupper describes the importance of perseverance, ca. 1932, NMAH 470, series 1.

13. *Physical Culture* magazine to Tupper, 12 June 1923, in response to an inquiry; NMAH 470, series 1.

14. Tupper diary, 28 February and 16 March 1933, discusses bodybuilding regime and reading list, which includes Harold Bill, *The Calling of Dan Matthews*, and Peter B. Kyne, *Outlaws of Eden;* NMAH 470, series 2.

15. "Tupper's Cosmopolita," a project completed for the "International Correspondence Schools Course in Advertising as a Business Force," 1932, NMAH 470, series 1.

16. Tupper worked briefly at an advertising agency on 14th Street, New York City, shortly after graduation from high school in 1925. Tupper personal records, NMAH 470, series 1.

17. Charles R. Hearn, *The American Dream in the Great Depression* (London: Greenwood Press, 1977), offers an extensive discussion of the changing notion of the American Dream and the onset of the Depression as expressed through contemporary literature.

18. In "Tupper's Cosmopolita," 1932, within the context of a written exercise to advertise a hypothetical publication for the promotion of advertisers and advertising, Tupper included a section titled "Put New Machines to Work"; NMAH 470, series 1.

19. See Harry D. Kitson, *The Mind of the Buyer: A Psychology of Selling* (New York: Macmillan, 1921); Hazel Kirk, *A Theory of Consumption* (Boston: Houghton Mifflin, 1923); Roy Sheldon and Egmont Arens, *Consumer Engineering* (New York: Harper & Brothers, 1932).

20. See Leland J. Gordon, *Economics for Consumers* (New York: American Book, 1939).

21. David A. Hounshell, *From the American System to Mass Production, 1800–1932* (Baltimore: Johns Hopkins University Press, 1984), 322.

22. International Correspondence Schools, Scranton, Pa., to Tupper, 13 September 1932, with accompanying introductory literature titled "Branches of Advertising Work That Beginners Have Taken up Successfully," NMAH 470, series 1.

23. Ibid., 3.

24. Roland Marchand, *Advertising the American Dream* (Berkeley and Los Angeles: University of California Press, 1985), xxi.

25. Tupper, "Practice What You Preach," work notes regarding correspondence course, 1932, NMAH 470, series 1.

26. Tupper, notes regarding advertising ideas for the correspondence course, including the following: "The difference in character and future usefulness between the self educated and the college pampered person is the difference between the baby who can sit up and feed himself, and the one who has to be held and have the food spooned into him," 1932, NMAH 470, series 1.

27. Ibid., "Be Santa Claus, and A Friend."

28. Tupper diary, 25 June 1932, NMAH 470, series 2.

29. See F. E. and F. P. Manuel, *Utopian Thought in the Western World* (Cambridge: Harvard University Press, 1979).

30. Tupper, "The Cardinal Points of Good Advertising," written for correspondence course, 1932, NMAH 470, series 1.

31. See Howard P. Segal, "The Technological Utopians," in *Imagining Tomorrow* (Corn, ed.), 131.

32. Tupper, 1932, NMAH 470, series 1.

33. Kenneth Roemer, "Technology, Corporation, and Utopia: Gillette's Unity Regained," *Technology and Culture* 26 (July 1985): 560–70.

34. Tupper diary, 25 September 1937, entry made after Tupper's visit to the colonial craft section of Brockton Fair, NMAH 470, series 2.

35. Tupper diary, 27 January 1933, NMAH 470, series 2.

36. Tupper diary, 30 February 1933, NMAH 470, series 2.

37. Tupper diary, 15 May 1937, NMAH 470, series 2.

38. Tupper, sketchbook and journal, 17 May 1937, NMAH 470, series 2.

39. Tupper, miscellaneous product notes, 1937, NMAH 470, series 2.

40. "The radio informed us, tonight, that president Roosevelt plans to address the public at least twice a month from now on. That's a good idea. Both will profit socially and materially from the intelligence given out, and it will cement bonds of friendship and cooperation." Tupper diary, 14 March 1933, NMAH 470, series 2.

41. Tupper diary, 1 January 1933, NMAH 470, series 1.

42. Under the title "Value of a Good Book," Tupper described his admiration for authors able to utilize a principal or single idea to great effect; notes written for correspondence course, 1932, NMAH 470, series 1.

43. "I am determined that my career should be in inventing and designing to that end and that I shall be a better social friend, I'm pledging my relentless drive." Tupper diary, 1 January 1936, NMAH 470, series 2.

44. Tupper diary, 25 November 1934, NMAH 470, series 2. Tupper perceived Mr. Winthrop Sheedy as a role model during this period. He spoke of Sheedy's admirable ascent from his humble beginnings as the son of a railroad gang section leader to a successful life as a benevolent businessman. Sheedy arranged loans for a couple of Tupper's (unsuccessful) designs, and in 1944 Tupper was proudly able

to reward his support by informing him that one of his plastic designs had appeared in an edition of *Bakelite Review.* Tupper also forwarded a poem, "The New Dealer," but was advised by Sheedy, "[Y]ou better stick to Plastics and forget the poetry. Make some money while the going is good and provide for the family." Winthrop Sheedy, Groton Leatherboard Company, West Groton, Mass., to Tupper, Farnumsville, Mass., 8 August 1944, NMAH 470, series 2.

45. David Shi, *The Simple Life: Plain Living and High Thinking in American Culture* (New York: Oxford University Press, 1985), 242. See also Leo Marx, *The Machine in the Garden: Technology and the Pastoral Ideal in America* (Oxford: Oxford University Press, 1967).

46. Shi, *Simple Life,* 228.

47. "I'm sure I'll never again live in an apartment house or within a mile of a neighbor after I get my million dollars (?)." For Tupper, rural living was an ideal rather than a necessity; a brief experience of urban apartment life left him adamant to pursue a more isolated existence. Tupper diary, 6 January 1933, NMAH 470, series 2.

48. Tupper diary, 11 June 1933, NMAH 470, series 2.

49. Tupper diary, 27 September 1937, NMAH 470, series 2.

50. Tupper diary, 25 December 1934, NMAH 470, series 2.

51. F. T. Kihlstedt, "Utopia Realized: The World's Fairs of the 1930s," in *Imagining Tomorrow* (Corn, ed.), 100.

52. Marie Tupper's notes in Tupper diary, 25 September 1939, NMAH 470, series 2.

53. Tupper diary, 18 December 1933, NMAH 470, series 2.

54. Tupper, sketchbook and invention journal, opening pages of "How to Invent," 1937, NMAH 470, series 2.

55. Joseph J. Corn, "Educating the Enthusiast: Print and the Popularization of Technical Knowledge," in *Possible Dreams: Enthusiasm for Technology in America,* ed. John L. Wright (Deerfield, Mass.: Henry Ford Museum, 1992), 29.

56. Don Slater, "Integrating Consumption and Leisure: 'Hobbies' and the Structures of Everyday Life," paper presented at European Sociological Association Conference, University of Essex, 30 August 1997.

57. See Steven M. Gelber, "'A Job You Can't Lose': Work and Hobbies in the Great Depression," *Journal of Social History* 24 (June 1991): 741–66.

58. Corn, "Educating the Enthusiast," 24.

59. Tupper diary, 12 March 1937, includes records of prototypes made for Sears; NMAH 470, series 2.

60. Stephen Bryce, manager of National Automobile Chamber of Commerce to Tupper, 27 June 1933, in reply to inquiry of 21 June 1933, NMAH 470, series 2.

61. Tupper diary, 18 June 1933, NMAH 470, series 2.

62. Hearn, *American Dream in the Great Depression,* 156.

63. Tupper diary, Marie Tupper's notes, 5 April 1936, NMAH 470, series 2.

64. Tupper diary, 20 August 1938, with the addition of Marie Tupper's notes, NMAH 470, series 2.

65. Jeffrey I. Meikle, *American Plastic: A Cultural History* (New Brunswick: Rutgers University Press, 1995), 82–83.

66. Quote from Robert Friedel, *Pioneer Plastic: The Making and Selling of Celluloid* (London: University of Wisconsin Press, 1983), 108–9. For analysis of Du Pont's prominence in experimentation during this period, see Meikle, *American Plastic,* and David F. Noble, *America by Design: Science Technology and the Rise of Corporate Capitalism* (Oxford: Oxford University Press, 1979).

67. The Chamber of Commerce in Leominster proposed "Pioneer Plastic City" as a more flattering title than "Comb City." See paper presented by the Chamber of Commerce to the Historical Society of Leominster, Mass., 15 February 1974, NMAH 470, series 3.

68. Meikle, *American Plastic,* 92.

69. The agreement struck with the Doyle factory meant that the manufacture of any patentable product under Tupper's name would be assigned to Du Pont, with a maximum royalty of 5 percent given to the designer.

70. Tupper diary, 10 December 1937, records the delivery of a new box of headed stationery pertaining to Tupper's newly acquired status as an "Industrial Inventor/Designer," NMAH 470, series 2.

71. Meikle, *American Plastic,* 133.

72. Tupper diary, 17 September 1937, NMAH 470, series 2.

73. Tupper diary, 3 December 1937, NMAH 470, series 2.

74. Tupper diary, 18 September 1937, NMAH 470, series 2.

75. Tupper, sketchbook and journal, 13 February 1937, NMAH 470, series 2.

76. Tupper diary, 25 September 1938, NMAH 470, series 2.

77. Tupper diary, 8 September 1937, NMAH 470, series 2.

78. Tupper diary, 14 October 1937, NMAH 470, series 2.

79. Tupper, sketchbook and journal, 16 July 1937, NMAH 470, series 2.

80. See Kathy Peiss, *Hope in a Jar: The Making of America's Beauty Culture* (New York: Metropolitan Books, 1998), 146–48.

81. Tupper, sketchbook and journal, 14 August 1937 (design dated as 1935), NMAH 470, series 2.

82. Tupper diary, 4 October 1937, NMAH 470, series 2.

83. Tupper, sketchbook and journal, 4 October 1937, NMAH 470, series 2.

84. Tupper diary, 19 September 1937, NMAH 470, series 2.

85. Audrey frequently hand painted designs for Tupper. Tupper diary, 23 August 1937, NMAH 470, series 2.

86. Tupper diary, 28 July 1939, featuring Marie Tupper's notes, NMAH 470, series 2.

87. Tupper, sketchbook and diary, 24 September 1937, NMAH 470, series 2.

88. Tupper, notes, "Have the Courage of Your Convictions," ca. 1937, NMAH 470, series 1.

89. *Syndicate Store Merchandiser,* December 1940, 8. In 1940, a selection of Tupper's earliest mass-produced designs were marketed under the trademark of the Earl S. Tupper Company of Leominster. The *Merchandiser* magazine advertised the Nautical Necktie Rack, plastic coat hangers, and a novelty Kamoflage comb available to gift shop retailers.

90. The careful negotiation of the relationship between manufacturers and chemical companies proved vital to the functioning of the plastics industry during this period. For example in 1950 the Bakelite Division of Union Carbide and Carbon Corporation informally advised the Tupper Corporation that because of government intervention, a priority system would favor military uses for the polyethylene development, thus creating shortages for up to five years. Therefore it was, according to Frank Fisher, production manager of the Tupper Corporation, "essential that Bakelite know what their customers are going to do with their resin allocations." But because of "the feeling of personal relationship" between the Bakelite Division and Tupper, it was suggested that together they could "focus on certain future activities that will put the [Tupper Corporation] in line to get a big TONNAGE of polyethylene as Bakelite's capacity increases." Tupper Corporation, interoffice memo, 22 December 1950, NMAH 470, series 3.

91. Tupper diary, 4 September 1949, NMAH 470, series 3.

92. In 1950 Mr. Intemann, head of the Bakelite Division, indicated "that he didn't think the potential market for Tupperware was large enough," recommending instead that "the [Tupper Corporation] get into the bottle business." Tupper Corporation, interoffice memo, 22 December 1950, NMAH 470, series 3.

t w o
## The Creation of a Modernist Icon?

1. Arthur Drexler and Greta Daniels, eds., *Introduction to Twentieth Century Design* (New York: Museum of Modern Art, 1959), 75.

2. Tupper to John C. Healy (advertising manager), interoffice memo, 14 September 1949, NMAH 470, series 3. In this memo Tupper prepares an entry describing the development of Tupperware for the "Modern Plastics Story," a publication for the Society of the Plastics Industry.

3. See Meikle, *American Plastic,* 86. Du Pont in the United States and Imperial Chemicals Industries in Great Britain signed an agreement to share world markets, patents, and research data. Despite this agreement they continued to explore substances such as acrylics, unbeknownst to each other. Later, in 1952, ICI and Du

Pont lost control over polyethylene, resulting in a drastic price decline and a steep increase in its mass production; see Meikle, 189.

4. *Modern Plastics Encyclopedia* (Bristol, Conn.: Society of the Plastics Industry, 1948), 165.

5. "For Lasting Service!" *Bakelite Review,* October 1946, 8.

6. "Leftovers Can Be Tasty!" *Good Housekeeping,* no. 118 (January 1944): 89, cited in Meg Jacobs, "'How about Some Meat?': The Office of Price Administration, Consumption Politics, and State Building from the Bottom up, 1941–1946," *Journal of American History* 84, no. 3 (December 1987): 910–41.

7. "Tupperware helps to tie-in housewares with Labor Day sales of sporting goods, beach wears, lawn and porch fittings, outing gear," pull-out section of a Tupper Corporation pamphlet (Farnumsville, Mass., 1949) promoting Tupperware for outdoor activities. This pamphlet included diagrams explaining Tupper seals.

8. John Craig Healy, Tupper Corporation, to Miss Frances Troy Schwab, Boston, Mass., 11 May 1950, re: syndicated article describing the 50-ounce (1.5-liter) Tupperware canister, NMAH 470, series 3.

9. "Earl S. Tupper of Upton Granted Valuable Patent," *Milford (Mass.) Daily News,* June 1947, NMAH 470, series 3.

10. Meikle, *American Plastic,* 155.

11. Elizabeth Gordon, "Fine Art for 39 Cents," *House Beautiful,* October 1947, offprint, NMAH 470, series 3.

12. Meikle, *American Plastic,* 172–73.

13. *Tupperware Product Catalogue-C* (Farnumsville, Mass.: Tupper Corporation, 1949).

14. "'Flying Disc' Appears at Logan Airport," *Boston Post,* 17 July 1947.

15. "Tumblers That Make Light of a Heavy Foot: Made of Du Pont Polyethylene . . . They're Unbreakable!," advertisement circulated to houseware buyers by C. A. Jackson, sales manager, Tupper Corporation, June 1948; offprint, NMAH 470, series 3.

16. "Better by Far than Can or Jar!" (Farnumsville, Mass.: Tupper Corporation, 1947).

17. Examples taken from press clippings featuring Tupper products and comparable items: *House Furnishing Review,* February 1947, 148, and "Refrigerator Helps," *Farm Journal,* March 1947. NMAH 470, series 3.

18. Bill Fahey, taped interview with author, Orlando, Fla., December 1989. Fahey worked closely with John Ansley in product development.

19. Sears, Roebuck and Co., catalog (n.p.: Sears, Roebuck and Co., 1941–42), 886.

20. Harriet Morrison, "Subject to Change: Canisters of Metal, Glass, Plastic Are Improved in Design, Come in Gay Colors," *Herald Tribune,* 29 August 1948.

21. Harriet Jean Anderson, "For Cold Storage: There's a 'New Look' to Refrigerator Containers," *Herald Tribune,* 15 February 1948, section 8.

22. In 1947 numerous publications including *Farm Journal, New York Post, Hardware Retailer,* and *House Beautiful* showed Tupper Wonder Bowls as ergonomically distinctive plastic wares.

23. Tupper to Healy, interoffice memo, 14 September 1949, re: "Modern Plastics Story," NMAH 470, series 3.

24. Thomas Hine, *Populuxe* (London: Bloomsbury London, 1990), 3.

25. Ibid.

26. Russell Lynes, *The Tastemakers* (New York: Dover, 1980; reprint of 1955 edition with an afterword including illustrated chart), 348–49.

27. For a summary of this debate see, for example, Richard H. King, "Modernism and Mass Culture: The Origins of the Debate," in *The Thirties: Politics and Culture in a Time of Broken Dreams,* ed. Heinz Ickstadt, Rob Kroes, and Brian Lee (Amsterdam: Free University Press, 1987).

28. "An Exhibition for Modern Living," 11 September–20 November 1949, and exhibition catalog by the same title, ed. A. H. Girard and W. D. Laurie Jr. (Detroit: Detroit Institute of Arts, 1949).

29. Harold Van Doren, *Industrial Design: A Practical Guide to Product Design and Development* (New York: McGraw-Hill, 1954).

30. John Heskett, *Industrial Design* (London: Thames and Hudson, 1987), 156.

31. Vance Packard, "The Short Sweet Life of Home Products," in *The Waste Makers* (London: Longmans, 1960), 107.

32. Roland Barthes, "Plastics," in *Mythologies* (London: Paladin, 1988), 99.

33. Ibid., 98.

34. Dick Hebdige, "Towards a Cartography of Taste, 1935–1962," in *Hiding in the Light,* ed. Dick Hebdige (London: Comedia, 1988).

35. Meikle, *American Plastic,* 255.

36. Van Doren, *Industrial Design.*

37. Elsie Mortland, former THP executive, taped interview with author, Kissimmee, Fla., 2 December 1989. During the 1950s Elsie Mortland acted as an informal product tester, advising Earl Tupper of the potential uses for and defects in the Tupper Corporation's product designs. The leaking coffee cup was remembered fondly by numerous dealers as an inexplicably popular and best-selling, yet badly designed, product.

38. Daniel Miller, *Material Culture and Mass Consumption* (Oxford: Blackwell, 1987), 142.

39. Throughout his invention notebook, diaries, and sketchbook, Tupper consistently referred to contemporary automobile design, product innovations, exhibitions, and world fairs.

40. Tupper pasted the images of illustrious men such as Thomas Jefferson in

his notebook with comments beneath, to remind himself of the ingredients of their "genius"; Tupper sketchbook, 7 February 1937, NMAH 470, series 2.

41. Tupper, invention diary and sketchbook, opening page, "My Purpose in Life," 1937, NMAH 470, series 2.

42. See Ruth Schwartz Cowan, *More Work for Mother: The Ironies of Household Technology from the Hearth to the Microwave* (London: Free Association Books, 1989), 196.

t h r e e
## A Gift of Modernity

1. Mary Douglas and Baron Isherwood, *The World of Goods: Towards an Anthropology of Consumption* (London: Routledge, 1979), 69.

2. Claude S. Fischer, *America Calling: A Social History of the Telephone to 1940* (Berkeley and Los Angeles: University of California Press, 1992), 16.

3. "With All Best Wishes," *Herald Tribune,* 6 June 1948, NMAH 470, series 3.

4. *Tupperware Product Catalogue-C* (Farnumsville, Mass.: Tupper Corporation, 1949).

5. Arthur J. Pulos, *The American Design Adventure* (Cambridge: M.I.T. Press, 1988), 153.

6. See, for example, Sacvan Bercovitch, *The Puritan Origins of the American Self* (New Haven: Yale University Press, 1975); Colin Campbell, *The Romantic Ethic and the Spirit of Modern Consumerism* (Oxford: Blackwell, 1995); and Ann Kibey, *The Interpretation of Material Shapes of Puritanism* (Cambridge: Cambridge University Press, 1986).

7. Rodris Roth, "The New England, or 'Olde Tyme,' Kitchen Exhibit at Nineteenth Century Fairs," in *The Colonial Revival in America,* ed. Alan Axelrod (Winterthur, Del.: Norton, 1985), 161.

8. Melinda Young Frye, "The Beginnings of the Period Room in American Museums: Charles P. Wilcomb's Colonial Kitchens, 1896, 1906, 1910," in *Colonial Revival* (Axelrod, ed.).

9. *Tupperware Product Catalogue-C,* 1949, 6.

10. On domestic Protestantism see Colleen McDannell, *The Christian Home in Victorian America, 1840–1900* (Bloomington: Indiana University Press, 1986).

11. See Carolyn M. Goldstein, "Part of the Package: Home Economists in the Consumer Products Industries, 1920–1940," in *Rethinking Home Economics: Women and the History of a Profession,* ed. Sarah Stage and Virginia B. Vincenti (Ithaca: Cornell University Press, 1997), 276.

12. Items such as the Silent Partner Poker Chips, the King Cigarette Case, and the Tupper Ice Cracker and Muddler constituted at least a quarter of the product collection; *Tupperware Product Catalogue-C,* 1949, 6.

13. Goldstein, "Part of the Package," 274.

14. See Regina Lee Blaszczyk, "'Where Mrs. Homemaker Is Never Forgotten': Lucy Maltby and Home Economics at Corning Glass Works, 1929–1965," in *Rethinking Home Economics* (Stage and Vincenti, eds.), 164. The firms included "the Kraft-Phenix Cheese Company, Ball Brothers Manufacturing Company, Sears, Roebuck and Company, Piggly-Wiggly Stores, and the Aluminum Goods Manufacturing Company."

15. Ibid., 177.

16. The rapidly expanding cosmetics industry during this period also courted the "woman's viewpoint" with, for example, the assignment of women to beauty accounts in advertising agencies. See Peiss, *Hope in a Jar*, 119: "As a more self-conscious notion of the woman consumer took hold, it became axiomatic among mass-market manufacturers and advertisers that 'if you are selling to women, nothing succeeds like a woman's viewpoint.'"

17. See Victoria de Grazia, ed., with Ellen Furlough, *The Sex of Things: Gender and Consumption in Historical Perspective* (Berkeley and Los Angeles: University of California Press, 1996).

18. Peiss, *Hope in a Jar*, 135.

19. Ellen Wiley Todd, "Art, the 'New Woman' and Consumer Culture: Kenneth Hayes Miller and Reginald Marsh on Fourteenth Street, 1920–40," in *Gender and American History since 1890*, ed. Barbara Marsh (London: Routledge, 1993), 140.

20. See, for example, Kathy Peiss, *Cheap Amusements: Working Women and Leisure in Turn-of-the-Century New York* (Philadelphia: Temple University Press, 1986).

21. Todd, "Art, the 'New Woman' and Consumer Culture."

22. Peiss, *Hope in a Jar*, 3–4.

23. For a brief and useful summary of arguments regarding the politics of consumption in relation to feminist discourse and historical perspective, see Victoria de Grazia, "Empowering Women as Citizen-Consumers," in *Sex of Things* (De Grazia, ed.), 275–86.

24. Tupper, invention journal, June 1935, sketches recording inventions of a gypsy moth gun, a double-bladed hatchet, and a double cigarette holder, NMAH 470, series 2.

25. Tupper diary, 25 September 1937, entry made after his visit to Brockton Fair, NMAH 470, series 2.

26. See Warren Leon and Margaret Piatt, "Living-History Museums," in *History Museums in the United States: A Critical Assessment,* ed. Warren Leon and Roy Rosenzweig (Chicago: University of Illinois Press, 1989), 66–67.

27. Quoted in Leon and Piatt, "Living History Museums," 67.

28. Karal Ann Marling, "Of Cherry Trees and Ladies Teas: Grant Wood Looks at Colonial America," in Axelrod, *Colonial Revival,* 296.

29. Jeanne S. Rymer, "Arthurdale: A Social Experiment in the 1930s," in *Colonial Revival* (Axelrod, ed.), 326.

30. Ibid., 328.

31. Tupper diary, 25 September 1937, NMAH 470, series 2.

32. Tupper's discussion with Fred Hastings, product manager at Doyle Works, regarding the introduction of the plastic kits to children's clubs across North America; Tupper diary, 27–28 September 1937, NMAH 470, series 2.

33. Steven M. Gelber, "A Job You Can't Lose: Work and Hobbies in the Great Depression," *Journal of Social History* 24 (June 1991): 741–66.

34. Fred Margaretten, "Physicians and Their Hobbies," *Avocations* 2 (June 1938): 228; quoted in Gelber, "A Job You Can't Lose," 745.

35. Ruth Schwartz Cowan, *More Work for Mother: The Ironies of Household Technology from the Open Hearth to the Microwave* (New York: Basic Books, 1983), 180, describes the addition of a chapter in a revised edition of Emily Post's *Etiquette: The Blue Book of Social Usage* (New York, 1937), in which Post discusses the problem of a new generation of women expected to maintain high standards of entertainment and hospitality without domestic help.

36. Schwartz Cowan, *More Work for Mother,* 205.

37. See Ruth Schwartz Cowan, "Coal Stoves and Clean Sinks: Housework between 1890 and 1930," in *American Home Life, 1880–1930: A Social History of Spaces and Services,* ed. Jessica H. Foy and Thomas J. Schlereth (Knoxville: University of Tennessee Press, 1992), 218.

38. *Tupperware Product Catalogue-C,* 1949, 5.

39. Ibid., 6.

40. Ibid., 223.

41. Ibid., 72.

42. Hearn, in *American Dream in the Great Depression,* Chapter 5, discusses the move from a narrative of material success and publicly laudable achievements to a reemphasis on family life, love, and relationships, and the home as a haven for spiritually invigorating pursuits.

43. Laura Lee Burroughs, *Flower Arranging: A Fascinating Hobby,* vol. 2 (Toronto: Coca-Cola, 1941), 1.

44. Ibid.

45. Ibid.

46. Douglas and Isherwood, *World of Goods,* 69.

47. For challenges to the classical anthropological polarization of gifts and commodities, see James Carrier, *Gifts and Commodities: Exchange in Western Capitalism since 1700* (London: Routledge, 1995); Annette B. Weiner, *Inalienable Possessions: The Paradox of Keeping-While-Giving* (Berkeley and Los Angeles: University of California Press, 1992); Caroline Humphrey and Stephen Hugh-Jones, eds., *Barter, Exchange and Value: An Anthropological Approach* (Cambridge: Cambridge University Press, 1992).

48. See, in particular, David Cheal, *The Gift Economy* (London: Routledge, 1988).

49. John Davis, *Exchange* (Minneapolis: University of Minnesota Press, 1992), 53.

50. "Tupperware," *Time,* 8 September 1947, 92.

51. *Premium Practice,* December 1948, offprint, NMAH 470, series 3.

52. Ibid., 26.

53. "Hang your stocking this Christmas Mr. Manufacturer . . . but don't take down your 'sock' when it's over!" (Farnumsville, Mass.: Tupper Corporation, 1947).

54. *Gift Preview: The Buyer's Guide to What's New in Gifts and Decorative Accessories* 1, no. 1 (June 1946), NMAH 470, series 3.

55. *Tobacco Jobber,* ca. 1947, offprint, NMAH 470, series 3.

56. *Sports News,* May 1947, 43.

57. Ben Fine and Ellen Leopold, in *The World of Consumption* (London: Routledge, 1993), apply the term "system of provision" to suggest a useful framework in which commodities can be viewed in multiple perspective, taking account of production and consumption. This approach acknowledges the specificity and interrelated nature of commodity forms; food has a historically bound system of provision that differs, for example, from that of clothing. However, as this study of Tupperware reveals, commodities frequently defy such bounded frameworks according to the specificity of their cultural consumption.

58. Michael Schudson, *Advertising, the Uneasy Persuasion: Its Dubious Impact on American Society* (New York: Basic Books, 1984).

59. Cited in Schudson, *Advertising, the Uneasy Persuasion,* 183; Benno Milmore and Arthur Canover, "Tobacco Consumption in the United States, 1880–1955," appendix to William Haenszel, Michael B. Shimkin, and Herman P. Miller, *Tobacco Smoking Patterns in the United States,* Public Health monograph no. 45 (Washington, D.C.: U.S. Government Printing Office, 1956), 107.

60. For a definitive discussion of this concept from a social anthropological perspective, see Arjun Appadurai, ed., *The Social Life of Things: Commodities in Cultural Perspective* (Cambridge: Cambridge University Press, 1986).

61. Tupper to Healy, interoffice memo, 14 September 1949, re: "Modern Plastics Story," NMAH 470, series 3.

f o u r
## The Origins of the Home Party Plan

1. "Tupperware," *Time,* 8 September 1947, 92.

2. Guaranty Bank and Trust Company, Worcester, Mass., to Tupper, statement of accounts, 7 June 1948. The working capital increased from a deficit of $11,000 to a net working capital of $72,000 between 31 December 1946 and 31 March 1948. NMAH 470, series 3.

3. Bernard G. Preistley, "Tupperware Makes Whirlwind Debut via Big Store Demonstrations," *Sales Management,* 15 April 1948, offprint, NMAH 470, series 3.

4. Advertising executives of the Chambers and Wiswell agency personally pro-

moted the new houseware in an attempt to capture, and convert, the attentions of an inquisitive consumer audience.

5. "Sales Policy for Tupper Corporation Self-Merchandising Sales Display Stand," 1947, NMAH 470, series 3.

6. See Earl Lifshey, *The Housewares Story: A History of the American Housewares Industry* (Chicago: National Housewares Manufacturers Association, 1973).

7. "550 Exhibitors at Atlantic City Show Expect Big Auditorium to Be Busy as Beehive," *Home Furnishing Review,* May 1948, NMAH 470, series 3.

8. See, for example, G. S. McLellan, *The Consuming Public* (H. W. Wilson: New York, 1968).

9. In "Sales Policy for Tupper Corporation Self-Merchandising Sales Display Stand," Tupper Corporation mentions home demonstration companies as one of eight forms of merchandise outlets, 1947, NMAH 470, series 3.

10. Tupper diary, 23 October 1933, NMAH 470, series 2.

11. "Sales with Tupper Products" (Farnumsville, Mass.: Tupper Corporation, 1947), front cover.

12. Norman W. Squires to "Reggie," Queens Village, New York, 23 June 1928; Damigella Collection, NMAH 583, series 4.

13. "The Birth of the Hostess Party Plan," typed manuscript by Norman W. Squires, NMAH 583, series 4. Squires wrote that at the suggestion of a female sales team, Beveridge responded, "If you're bringing any women into the Stanley Company, see that transom Norman[?] I'm going to put you right through it." This manuscript was written retrospectively as a testament to his role as the originator of the party plan sales scheme, since in 1950 Tupper accused him of creating a copy-cat direct sales company after their business relations failed.

14. In 1932, the legacy of the Green River Ordinance, based on legislation formulated in Green River, Wyo., prohibits unsolicited sales presentations, making the invitation of the homeowner a prerequisite of doorstep sales. See Nicole Woolsey Biggart, *Charismatic Capitalism: Direct Selling Organizations in America* (Chicago: University of Chicago Press, 1989), 32: "Green River laws, as they are generally known, were vigorously opposed by NADSC [National Association of Direct Selling Companies] wherever proposed, and they continue to be opposed by its successor, the Direct Selling Association."

15. "A Nice, Friendly Time," *Fortune,* November 1947, 144–47.

16. Peiss, *Hope in a Jar,* 81.

17. Ibid.

18. Ibid., 82.

19. Alfred Carl Fuller, *A Foot in the Door* (New York: McGraw-Hill, 1960), 57.

20. During the period 1918–23 recruitment of the unsalaried, commission-paid Fuller Brush sales force grew several fold, and it was estimated that a salesman making fifty calls per day could earn, on average, fifteen to thirty dollars a week. See Fuller, *Foot in the Door,* 138.

21. Extract from comments of 1920s Realsilk dealer C. Clair Cox, in Morris L. Mayer, *Direct Selling in the United States: A Commentary and Oral History* (Washington, D.C.: Direct Selling Education Foundation, 1995), 21.

22. *Stanley Pilgrim,* Michigan Area, 22–25 August 1948, refers to a speech given by Stanley Home Product's "First Lady," Catherine O'Brien, executive vice president, in which she estimates sales for 1948 at $50 million; Wise Papers, NMAH 509, series 2.

23. Fuller, *Foot in the Door,* 188.

24. Ibid.

25. Ibid., 197.

26. Ibid., 192.

27. *Stanley Pilgrim,* 22–25 August 1948.

28. "The Brush Man," *Time,* 6 January 1950, 80.

29. Tina Manko, "Fuller Brush Men and Avon Ladies," seminar paper presented at the University of Delaware, Newark, November 1995.

30. Timothy B. Spears, *Hundred Years on the Road: The Traveling Salesman in American Culture* (New Haven: Yale University Press, 1995), 145.

31. "Sustaining Interest and Closing," in *Instructions for General Agents* (New York: California Perfume Company, 1915), 10, cited in Manko, "Fuller Brush Men and Avon Ladies."

32. Biggart, *Charismatic Capitalism,* 186.

33. Fuller, *Foot in the Door,* 128.

34. Ibid., 143.

35. Ibid., 196.

36. *Stanley Pilgrim,* Michigan Area, 22–25 August 1948, 7.

37. Ibid., 8.

38. Ibid., 6.

39. Quoted in Mayer, *Direct Selling in the United States,* 37.

40. Tom and Ruth Macy formed one of the earliest exclusively Tupperware distributorships. In their correspondence to the Tupper Corporation they wrote of the public's anticipation of new designs and the ability of fresh products to "stimulate business." Tom and Ruth Macy, Egypt, Mass., to Tupper Corporation, 22 November 1949, NMAH 470, series 3.

41. Anne Brittain, San Diego, Calif., to Tupper Corporation, 6 November 1949, in response to questionnaire regarding distribution of Tupperware through direct sales, NMAH 470, series 3.

42. John Howzdy to Tupper, interoffice memo, 2 February 1951, "re: copies of revisions made in the sales outline discussed with Mr. Squires," NMAH 470, series 3. The document reveals how Tupper is conducting negotiations with Norman Squires regarding implementation of the hostess plan.

43. "Tupper Corp. Buys N.Y. Concern's Assets," unidentified newspaper clipping, 24 August 1950, NMAH 583, series 4.

44. The origins of the party plan system and the Squires's version of events regarding the Tupper Corporation take-over are still hotly contested. In 1984 Daniel T. Squires (son of Norman) wrote to the editor of the *Wall Street Journal* following the misattribution of the party plan system to Mary Kay Ash. He wrote, "The party plan sales concept was originated by my father, Norman W. Squires, when he was the leading national producer for Wearever Aluminum Cooking Products. . . . My father formed his own company in 1945, Hostess Home Accessories, Inc., which was merged into Tupperware in the late 1940's. He then headed the 'Hostess Division' of Tupper, Inc." See "Letters to the Editor," *Wall Street Journal,* 17 April 1984, NMAH 583, series 4.

45. In an article featured in the Tupperware corporate magazine, Thomas and Ann Damigella describe the financial hardship that drove them to join the party plan sales system as dealers. Ann Damigella worked with her husband to build up a successful Tupperware distributorship; her son highlights the appeal of Tupperware dealing in the 1950s to women with limited career opportunities: "Mom saw the potential for women in free enterprise. She held parties and recruited people. She knocked on doors and ran the office. She saw the future in the Tupperware business for women. You could write your own ticket for financial success and fulfillment"; see "Necessity Became the Parent of Adventure," *Our World,* July 1981, 10–16.

46. Thomas Damigella, interview by Neil Osterweil, 16 September 1988, NMAH 470, series 4. As a former Stanley Home Products distributor, Damigella was chosen by Earl Tupper to take part in think-tank sessions regarding the inception of THP. Damigella continued in the Tupperware business into the 1980s.

47. *Go-Getter,* 23 February 1948, NMAH 509, series 2.

48. *Go-Getter,* 5 September 1949, and *Dear All-of-You* sales bulletin, 14 May 1949, NMAH 509, series 2.

49. John Howzdy to Tupper, interoffice memo, 2 February 1951, a "sales outline" for the establishment of a national direct sales organization solely responsible for the distribution of Tupperware, NMAH 470, series 3.

50. "To put all his life, his dream . . . into something like this [the party plan] . . . we're not business people, we're little home party people in a lot of people's minds and this took vision to do it," T. Damigella, interview, 16 September 1988, NMAH 470, series 4.

51. Ibid. Damigella commented that Earl Tupper became "his own market researcher."

52. Though it might be assumed that farmers would have been a logical target market for the Tupper Corporation's functional containers, it was in fact items of overt novelty and modernity, such as the "50-cent Non-Breakable Tupper Comb" in assorted colors, that were directed toward this rural segment of the population; Stan Nowak, head of advertising and promotions, memo, news release on Tupper Comb, issued to all Tupperware distributors, 3 August 1953, NMAH 470, series 3.

53. "'Sunny' featherweight hair dryer" advertisement clipping, NMAH 509, series 2.

54. Exceptions were made for branch and area managers who, in negotiation with the company, were allowed minimal monthly compensations for essential business expenses in accordance with high sales volume.

55. Quoted in Mayer, *Direct Selling in the United States,* 69.

56. Biggart, *Charismatic Capitalism,* 11.


f i v e
**The Ascent of the Tupperware Party**

1. William G. Damroth, "How to Find, Hire, Train, Keep the All-Women Direct Sales Force," *Sales Management,* 1 May 1954.

2. "We're 20,000 Strong!" *Tupperware Sparks* 3, nos. 21–22 (October–November 1954), front cover.

3. *Tupperware Sparks* 3, no. 23 (December 1955), front page.

4. This information is compiled from a combination of oral histories, photographic evidence, and references throughout contemporary corporate literature.

5. *Tupperware: The Nicest Thing That Could Happen to Your Kitchen,* product catalog (Orlando, Fla.: THP, ca. 1958), 6.

6. Ibid.

7. Prominent staff in 1954 included Jack Marshall (general sales manager), Gary McDonald (sales promotion manager), Charles McBurney (director of advertising and public relations), Don Fuhr (director of premium purchases), Glen Bump (public relations), C. David Serafine (head of IBM operations), and Joe Hara, Herb Young, and Hamer Wilson (sales counselors), among others.

8. "The Lush New Suburban Market," *Fortune,* November 1953, 129.

9. Department stores such as B. Altman of New York and Hecht's of Washington, D.C., created suburban branches.

10. "Lush New Suburban Market," 230.

11. Ibid., 231.

12. Ibid., 130.

13. See Elaine Tyler May, *Homeward Bound: American Families in the Cold War Era* (New York: Basic Books, 1988), 169. For in-depth discussion of American suburbanization, see Kenneth T. Jackson, *The Crabgrass Frontier: The Suburbanization of the United States* (New York: Oxford University Press, 1985); Dolores Hayden, *Redesigning the American Dream: The Future of Housing, Work and Family Life* (New York: Norton, 1984); and Gwendolyn Wright, *Building the Dream: A Social History of Housing in America* (New York: Pantheon, 1981).

14. Tyler May, *Homeward Bound,* 165.

15. "Lush New Suburban Market," 131.

16. Ibid., 230.

17. Victor P. Buell, "Door-to-Door Selling," *Harvard Business Review,* May–June 1954, 113; according to this report, Avon had a net profit of $7 million before taxes.

18. C. Claire Cox, *How Women Can Make up to $1000 a Week in Direct Selling* (New Jersey: Van Nostrand, 1960).

19. Buell, "Door-to-Door Selling."

20. Cox, *How Women Can Make up to $1000 a Week,* 1.

21. Veronica Strong-Boag, "Their Side of the Story: Women's Voices from Ontario Suburbs, 1945–60," in *A Diversity of Women: Ontario, 1945–80,* ed. Joy Parry (Toronto: Toronto University Press, 1995), 59.

22. Harry Henderson, *Harper's,* November 1953, 26.

23. Tyler May, *Homeward Bound,* 163.

24. Vice President Richard Nixon and Soviet Premier Nikita Sergeyevich Khrushchev, upon visiting the American Exhibition in Moscow in 1959 (which featured a model home and numerous household appliances), entered into a lengthy debate focusing on access to mass consumer goods as an indicator of true democracy. See "Nixon in Moscow: Appliances, Affluence and Americanism," in Marling, *As Seen on TV,* and "The Commodity Gap: Consumerism and the Modern Home," in Tyler May, *Homeward Bound.*

25. *Tupperware Sparks* 2, no. 3 (March 1952): 1.

26. Brownie Wise, "Welcome," rough draft of speech given at the 1955 Homecoming Jubilee, Orlando, Fla., NMAH 509, series 2.

27. *Tupperware: The Nicest Thing That Could Happen,* 1.

28. *Tupperware—A Household Word in Homes Everywhere!,* product catalog (Orlando, Fla.: THP, 1957), 3.

29. *Tupperware Sparks* 4, nos. 3–4 (March–April 1955): 4.

30. *Tupperware Party Games* (Orlando, Fla.: THP, 1956).

31. *Speciality Salesman,* March 1960, 7.

32. *Dorothy Dealer's Dating Diary* (Orlando, Fla.: THP, 1959).

33. "Check List: Whom Do You Know?," ca. 1951, NMAH 509, series 2.

34. The "Tupperware Club Plan" (all members present) and "Round Robin" (parties conducted individually with group members) used demonstrations as the focal point of charitable meetings and gave the dealer access to a high percentage of potential party recruits.

35. Gary McDonald, *A Timely Reminder,* THP pamphlet, 11 June 1952, and "Prospecting and Previewing," transcription from 1953 second managerial convention, NMAH 509, series 2.

36. Susan Strasser, *Never Done: A History of American Housework* (New York: Pantheon, 1982), 133.

37. Donald Smalley and Frances Trollope, eds., *Domestic Manners of the Americans* (New York: Vintage, 1960), 281–82.

38. *Tupperware—A Household Word,* 24.

39. Ibid., 23.

40. *Know-How* (Orlando, Fla.: THP, 1955), 44.

41. *Tupperware Sparks* 3, nos. 12–13 (January–February 1954): 6.

42. *Will You Be My Gold Key Hostess?* (Orlando, Fla.: THP, 1955), 1.

43. Anonymous "mall-walker," one of a group of retirees interviewed by the author, 18 November 1989, in a shopping mall in Osceola, Fla., that local walkers frequent for their early morning exercise.

44. *Tupperware Sparks* 2, nos. 6–7 (June–July 1952): 3.

45. *Market Basket Demonstration,* brochure (Orlando, Fla.: THP, 1956), 2.

46. *The Tupperware Story—A Story of Opportunity* (Orlando, Fla.: THP, 1956), 4.

47. *Dealer Guide to Demonstration* (Orlando, Fla.: THP, 1951), 8.

48. *The Tupperware Home Party Way,* promotional pamphlet (Orlando, Fla.: THP, 1952).

49. McDonald, "Prospecting and Previewing."

50. *Tupperware—A Household Word,* 5.

51. *Tupperware Sparks* 5, no. 9 (September 1956): 2.

52. *Tupperware—A Household Word,* 15.

53. *How to Guard Food Values in Your Refrigerator or Freezer* (Orlando, Fla.: THP, 1957), 1. The booklet also reveals how the growth of refrigeration and freezer storage played an integral part in the success of Tupperware.

54. The keenness to present Tupperware as a way of protecting food from contamination was expressed by many former corporate employees as an integral part of the product image, thus substantiating the tone of the corporate literature; Joe Hara, taped interview with author, 12 December 1989.

55. Tyler May, *Homeward Bound,* 20.

56. *Tupperware Product Catalogue* (Orlando, Fla.: THP, 1958), 7.

57. *Tupperware—Guards Food Flavor . . . Freshness* (Orlando, Fla.: Rexall, 1959), 15.

58. See Harvey Levenstein, *Paradox of Plenty: A Social History of Eating in Modern America* (Oxford: Oxford University Press, 1993); Sylvia Lovegren, *Fashionable Food* (New York: Macmillan, 1995); and Sidney W. Mintz, "Choice and Occasion: Sweet Moments," in *The Psychobiology of Human Selection,* ed. L. M. Baker (Westport, Conn.: Avi Publishing, 1982).

59. "Marie was first to demonstrate Tupperware for Betty Crocker," *Tupperware Sparks* 5, no. 6 (June 1956): 3.

60. Elsie Mortland, taped interview with author, 2 December 1989, Kissimmee, Fla.

61. *Tupperware Sparks* 5, no. 9 (September 1956): 3.

62. *Market Basket Demonstration,* brochure, 4.

63. *Tupperware Sales Sentinel* 1 (February 1957): 1.

64. Rex Taylor, "Marilyn's Friends and Rita's Customers: A Study of Party Selling as Play and as Work," *Sociological Review* 3, no. 26 (1978): 574.

65. Leila J. Rupp and Verta Taylor, *Survival in the Doldrums: The American Women's Rights Movement, 1945 to 1960s* (New York: Oxford University Press, 1987); Marty Jetzer, *The Dark Ages: Life in the United States, 1945–1960* (Boston: South End Press, 1982).

66. Rochelle Gaitlin, *American Women since 1945* (London: Macmillan, 1987), 54.

67. Hine, *Populuxe,* 3.

68. Gaitlin, *American Women since 1945,* 54.

69. Stuart Ewen, *Captains of Consciousness* (New York: McGraw-Hill, 1976), 178.

70. Ibid., 54.

71. Glenna Matthews, in *"Just a Housewife": The Rise and Fall of Domesticity in America* (Oxford: Oxford University Press, 1987), describes the enhanced prewar "possibility for self-respect on the part of the housewife" as having "dissolved by the mid-twentieth century," 222.

72. Tyler May, in *Homeward Bound,* links postwar domestic subordination with reactionary politics of the cold war and McCarthyism. Betty Friedan, in *The Feminine Mystique* (London: Pelican, 1982), described the alienation and malaise of feminine domesticity under the heading "The Problem That Has No Name."

73. Jennifer Kalish, "Spouse-Devouring Black Widows and Their Neutered Mates: Postwar Suburbanization—A Battle over Domestic Space," in *Women, Gender, and History* 14, special issue, *UCLA Historical Journal* (Los Angeles: Regents of the University of California, 1994), 149, citing Friedan, *Feminine Mystique,* 202.

74. Joanne Meyerowitz, in "Beyond the Feminine Mystique: A Reassessment of Post-war Mass Culture, 1946–1958," *Journal of American History* (March 1993), 1458, challenges Friedan's passive domestic construct of the postwar American woman and reassesses popular feminine literature as a potentially active force that drew on "the tension between domestic ideals and individual achievement." In her edited volume, *Not June Cleaver: Women and Gender in Postwar America, 1945–1960* (Philadelphia: Temple University Press, 1994), Meyerowitz brings together selected essays to challenge the typical textbook subheadings of the period: "The Suburban Family," "Life in the Suburbs," "Domesticity," and "Back to the Kitchen." This volume offers histories of other women, such as political activists, single mothers, immigrants, and lesbians. Similarly, Rochelle Gaitlin, in *American Women since 1945,* considers women's involvement in countercultures and labor, race, and class activism.

75. Meyerowitz admits that *Not June Cleaver* does not offer a comprehensive history and that it aims instead "to subvert the persistent stereotype of domestic, quiescent, suburban womanhood, and to generate new histories of a complicated era"; introduction, 11.

76. Strong-Boag, "Their Side of the Story," 48.

77. *Tupperware—A Household Word,* 23.

78. Wini Breines, "Domineering Mothers in the 1950s," *Women's Studies International Forum* 8, no. 6 (1985): 603–4.

79. Kalish, "Spouse-Devouring Black Widows," 139.

80. Pat Jordan (active Tupperware distributor throughout the 1950s), taped interview with author, 18 November 1989, Kissimmee, Fla.

81. Elsie Mortland (official Tupperware hostess throughout the 1950s and initiator of Tupperware in Europe during the 1960s), taped interview with author, Kissimmee, Fla., November 1989.

82. Tommy Jasionowski (1950s Tupperware dealer and graphic designer for THP International in the 1980s), taped interview with author, Orlando, Fla., December 1989.

83. Scott Donaldson identifies the "kaffeeklatsch" as a commonly pilloried symbol of "mock" friendliness in suburbia: "Left to themselves during the day, the neighborhood ladies get in the habit of sitting around drinking coffee and exchanging lies," *The Suburban Myth* (New York: Columbia University Press, 1969), 12, 23, 111. Classic contemporary critiques of suburbia include William Whyte, "The New Suburbia," in *The Organization Man* (London: Cape, 1957); David Riesman, "The Suburban Sadness," in *The Suburban Community,* ed. William Dobriner (New York: Putnam's, 1958); and John Keats, *The Crack in the Picture Window* (Boston: Houghton Mifflin, 1956). Richard E. Gordon, Katherine K. Gordon, and Max Gunther, in *The Split-Level Trap* (New York: B. Geis, 1961), describe "Disturbia," a neurosis brought about through suburban living.

84. John R. Seeley, R. Alexander Sim, and Elizabeth W. Loosley, *Crestwood Heights* (New York: Constable, 1956), 42–43, 50.

85. Thorstein Veblen, *The Theory of the Leisure Class: An Economic Study in the Evolution of Institutions* (London: Macmillan, 1899; reprint, Allen and Unwin, 1925); the notion of "Pecuniary Emulation" continued until comparatively recently to underlie the assumptions of many critiques of consumption.

86. Lewis Mumford, *The City in History* (New York: Harcourt Brace, 1961), 486.

87. Donaldson, "Onslaught against the Suburbs," *Suburban Myth,* 9.

88. Robert C. Wood, *Suburbia: Its People and Their Problems* (Boston: Houghton Mifflin, 1958), 131. Wood draws parallels between suburban conformity and socialization and pioneering communities of old.

89. Hine, *Populuxe,* 36.

90. Mary Beth Haralovitch, "Sitcom and Suburbs: Positioning the 1950s Homemaker," *Quarterly Review of Film and Video* 11, no. 1 (1989): 71.

91. Ibid.

92. See Charles Fishman, "Is the Party Over?" *Orlando (Fla.) Sentinel,* 15 March 1987.

93. Gaitlin, *American Women since 1945,* 54.

94. Lizabeth Cohen, "A Middle-Class Utopia? The Suburban Home in the 1950s," in *Making Choices: A New Perspective on the History of Domestic Life,* ed. Janice Tauer Wass (Springfield: Illinois State Museum, 1995), 10.

95. Ibid.

96. Oral histories provide the most substantive evidence to support this claim, which requires further investigation. One African-American woman described organizing her first black Tupperware party in 1952, after discovering Tupperware containers when she was working as a maid for a white family. In the Osceola, Fla., mall-walkers group interviewed by the author, retirees from New York recalled predominately Jewish Tupperware parties in that era. Hispanic women in a similar group of retirees spoke of using their large social networks to generate essential income. Single women and divorcées frequently featured in *Tupperware Sparks* as top achievers; obviously for many of these women it was their only viable means of employment.

97. Janet Foster (Tupperware dealer and hostess, 1952–53), taped interview with author, 24 October 1989, Winter Park, Fla.

98. Joe Hara (president of Tupperware US, responsible for worldwide operations, 1966–86), taped interview with the author, Orlando, Fla., 12 December 1989, in which Hara recounts his memories of the early 1950s Tupperware parties.

99. Jolene Richards (former Tupperware hostess), taped interview with author, 13 November 1989, Miami, Fla.

100. Pat Jordon (former Tupperware dealer), taped interview with author, 18 November 1989, substantiated by interview with Elsie Mortland and transcriptions of McDonald, "Prospecting and Previewing."

101. Elayne Rapping, "Tupperware and Women," *Radical America* 6, no. 14 (1980).

s i x
## The Feminization of Positive Thinking

1. "Help Yourself to Happiness," *Woman's Home Companion,* August 1954, 34.

2. Ibid.

3. Brownie Wise avidly followed and documented the preaching of America's key proponents of positive thinking. For a historical analysis of the popularization of this movement, see Carol V. R. George, *God's Salesman: Norman Vincent Peale and the Power of Positive Thinking* (Oxford: Oxford University Press, 1993).

4. Meyerowitz, "Beyond the Feminine Mystique," 1455.

5. "Help Yourself to Happiness," 96.

6. "Direct Selling the Magic Field—Where Dreams Come True," *Salesman's Opportunity,* February 1958, 38.

7. Ibid., 52.

8. "Help Yourself to Happiness," 96.

9. Though the rags-to-riches biography of Brownie Wise might initially be interpreted as corporate myth making, in fact, according to personal documents, accounts of her hardship and endurance were not exaggerated; NMAH 509, series 1.

10. *Tupperware Sparks* 4, no. 1 (January 1955).

11. See Peiss, *Hope in a Jar,* 80.

12. Marling, *As Seen on TV,* 38.

13. From the 1960s onward, Mary Kay Ash, following Brownie Wise, also recognized the importance of gifts and incentives that referred to a popular feminine culture: "We [Mary Kay Cosmetics] give Cinderella gifts . . . I decided that where women are concerned you should give them things they would not normally go out and buy for themselves, like a pink Cadillac, a mink coat, a diamond ring— the things we wait around for that guy on the white horse who never shows up to bring us." Quoted in Mayer, *Direct Selling in the United States,* 37.

14. "Help Yourself to Happiness," 34.

15. Ibid.

16. According to figures circulated in the press, women constituted 95 percent of the Tupperware workforce; "Tupperware Ladies Dig for Treasure," *Business Week,* 17 April 1954, 35.

17. Ibid., 35.

18. "The Tupperware Success Story," *Success Unlimited,* October 1954, 7.

19. Receipts, corporate memos, and personal letters reveal how Brownie Wise personally responded to correspondence and used her own personal shopping sprees as a means of acquiring gifts for Tupperware women. NMAH 509, series 1.

20. According to historian Kathy Peiss, in *Hope in a Jar,* 81, "The projection of personality and expertise was central to the sales strategies women entrepreneurs adopted." In this sense Wise was following a precedent set by women working in the early-twentieth-century feminine industries of beauty culture.

21. Wise filed this note securely among her business and personal papers; NMAH 509, series 1.

22. *Tupperware Sparks* 3, no. 5 (June 1953): front cover.

23. *Success Unlimited,* October 1954, 4.

24. Ibid.

25. Ibid.

26. Ibid., 15.

27. *Tupperware Sparks* 2, nos. 6–7 (June–July 1952): 2.

28. Ibid., 7.

29. Ibid.

30. *Tupperware Sparks* 3, nos. 6–7 (July–August 1953).

31. The headquarters, which commenced construction in February 1952, were finally completed in spring 1955.

32. *Orlando (Fla.) Sentinel,* 18 January 1952, 91.

33. Wise, "Welcome," rough draft of a speech given at the 1955 Homecoming Jubilee, Orlando, Fla., NMAH 509, series 2.

34. *Tupperware Sparks* 3, no. 2 (March 1953): 4.

35. *Tupperware Sparks* 3, no. 20 (September 1954): 3.

36. Wise, "Welcome."

37. Ibid., 4.

38. For a thorough analysis of the popularization of "art" in 1950s North America, see Marling, *As Seen on TV.*

39. The presentation took place at the Art Institute of Chicago, 11 June 1954, as recorded in numerous press releases; NMAH 509, series 2.

40. *Tupperware Sparks* 3, nos. 17–18 (June–July 1954): 3.

41. Gary J. McDonald, sales promotion manager, "Sparko-Gram," 4 March 1954, NMAH 509, series 2.

42. Ibid.

43. McDonald, "Sparko-Gram," 12 March 1954, NMAH 509, series 2.

44. "There's Gold for Me thru '53," July 1953 conference for distributors and subdistributors, Orlando, Fla.

45. Ibid.

46. The "Gold Digger Trail" was aligned to a seven-stage sales progression scheme: (a) 20 parties dated during August; (b) $1,000 retail Tupperware sales and one dealer recruited during September; (c) $1,200 retail Tupperware sales and two dealers recruited during October; (d) $1,500 retail Tupperware sales during November; (e) 30 cemented January parties dated during December; (f) $1,000 retail Tupperware sales and two dealers recruited during January; and (g) $1,000 retail Tupperware sales during the first two weeks of February.

47. *Tupperware Homecoming Jubilee News,* 9 April 1954, NMAH 509, series 2.

48. "Life Goes on a Big Dig," *Life,* 3 May 1954, 172.

49. "Plastic Houseware Maker Dedicates New Headquarters," *Speciality Salesman,* June 1954, 15.

50. McDonald, "Sparko-Gram," 12 March 1954.

51. *Jubilee News,* also quoted in *Kissimmee (Fla.) Gazette,* 9 April 1954.

52. *Speciality Salesman,* June 1954, 15.

53. "Jubilee Celebration Song," ca. 1957, personal collection of former Tupperware executive Elsie Mortland, Kissimmee, Fla.

54. J. M. George, president of the National Association of Direct Selling Companies, to Brownie Wise, letter of confirmation, 6 December 1957, mentions the keynote address and praises Wise for her inspirational leadership of THP; NMAH 509, series 2.

55. "American Women at Work," *Newsweek,* 27 February 1956, 76–77.

56. Pat Jordon, taped interview with author, concerning her work as an early Tupperware distributor active in the 1950s, 18 November 1989, Lake Mary, Fla.

57. *Jubilee Movie* preview, courtesy of Tupperware US, Orlando, Fla.

58. *Miami Herald,* 24 April 1955, 19-E.

59. Katherine Allen, "Accent Your Own True Self," *Your Psychology,* July 1954, 19.

60. Ibid., 17.

61. Brownie Wise, "Tupperware Is the Way," draft of a rally speech, ca. 1955, NMAH 509, series 2.

62. Ibid., 10.

63. *Know-How* (Orlando, Fla.: THP, 1955), 38.

64. Ibid.

65. Ibid.

66. Brownie Wise, "Write Your Own Ticket," address to the Winter Convocation, Jackson College for Negro Teachers, Jackson, Miss., 2 February 1955, NMAH 509, series 2.

67. Arlie Hochschild, *The Managed Heart: The Commercialization of Human Feeling* (Berkeley and Los Angeles: University of California Press, 1983).

68. Nicole Woolsey Biggart, "Rationality, Meaning and Self-Management: Success Manuals, 1950–1980," *Social Problems* 30, no. 3 (February 1983): 308.

69. Dorothy E. Peven, "The Use of Religious Revival Techniques to Indoctrinate Personnel: The Home-Party Sales Organizations," *Sociological Quarterly* 9 (1968): 97–106.

70. Ibid., 98.

71. Eugenia Kaledin, *Mothers and More: American Women in the 1950s* (Boston: Twayne, 1984), 13.

72. Herbert Gans, *The Levittowners* (London: Allen Lane, 1967), 264–65.

73. Will Herberg, *Protestant, Catholic, Jew: An Essay in American Religious Sociology* (New York: Doubleday, 1960), 102; also R. Laurence Moore, *Selling God: American Religion in the Market Place of Culture* (New York: Oxford University Press, 1994).

74. "If you believe in a thing[,] you work for it. . . . You are *active* in it. You participate"—a call for positive thinking and increased productivity; Brownie Wise, *Tupperware Sparks* 2, no. 4 (April 1952): 2.

75. Correspondence to Betty Friedan, deposited in the Schlesinger Library and cited in Wendy Simonds, *Women and Self-Help Culture: Reading between the Lines* (New Brunswick: Rutgers University Press, 1992), 94.

76. Ibid., 93.

77. Simonds, *Women and Self-Help Culture,* 222.

78. Wise, "Write Your Own Ticket," 8.

79. Ibid., 12.

80. Ibid., 13.

81. Although THP courted the business of what it described as the "negro market," it was clearly seen as a potentially problematic area of recruitment, in light of a document aimed at new distributors that read, "Section 27: Recruiting Negro Dealers: Should they work under white managers? How to recruit the first ones? The problems"; New Distributors Conference draft paper, 1956, NMAH 509, series 2.

82. *Tupperware Sparks* 3, no. 4 (May 1953). Although the feature concerning

Artie Watts reveals a public acknowledgment of African-American Tupperware dealers, such representations proved the exception rather than the rule.

83. Kathy Peiss, "Making Up, Making Over: Cosmetics, Consumer Culture, and Women's Identity," in *Sex of Things* (De Grazia and Furlough, eds.), 330.

84. Brownie Wise, opening speech for Fourth THP Sales Conference, January 1953, NMAH 509, series 2.

85. Biggart, *Charismatic Capitalism*, 10.

s e v e n
## The Politics of Consumption

1. De Grazia and Furlough, eds., in introduction to *Sex of Things*, 2.

2. Numerous well-established cultural histories identify consumer culture and the rise of advertising in the nineteenth and twentieth centuries as crucial elements of American history: Richard W. Fox and T. J. Jackson Lears, *Culture of Consumption: Critical Essays in American Culture* (New York: Pantheon, 1983); Simon J. Bronner, ed., *Consuming Visions: Accumulation and Display in America, 1880–1920* (New York: Norton, 1989); Daniel J. Boorstin, *The Americans: The Democratic Experience* (New York: Random House, 1973); William Leach, *Land of Desire: Merchants, Power, and the Rise of a New American Culture* (New York: Random House, 1993); Stuart Ewen, *Captains of Consciousness: Advertising and the Social Roots of the Consumer Culture* (New York: McGraw-Hill, 1977); and David Morris Potter, *People of Plenty: Economic Abundance and the American Character* (Chicago: University of Chicago Press, 1954).

3. For a broader discussion regarding the limitations of economic theory, see Daniel Miller, *Capitalism: An Ethnographic Approach* (Oxford: Berg, 1997).

4. Vivianna A. Zelizer, *The Social Meaning of Money* (New York: Basic Books, 1994), 211.

5. Andrew R. Heinze, *Adapting to Abundance: Jewish Immigrants, Mass Consumption and the Search for American Identity* (New York: Columbia University Press, 1990).

6. Cohen, "A Middle-Class Utopia?"

7. See, for example, Schwartz Cowan, *More Work for Mother*.

8. Zelizer, *Social Meaning of Money*, 211.

9. See Peiss, "Making Up, Making Over," for an excellent historical account of feminine identity, consumption, and "glamorization" in North American culture. See also Stevi Jackson and Shaun Moores, eds., *The Politics of Domestic Consumption: Critical Readings* (London: Prentice Hall, 1995).

10. Tyler May, *Homeward Bound*, 164.

11. Wise to Tupper, memo, 27 October 1953, re: "Press Party in New York,"

NMAH 470, series 3. Editors present at the press party included those from *Business Week, American Journal of Commerce, Mademoiselle, Glamour, Opportunity,* and *Newsweek.*

12. Wise sponsored the hybridization of a Tupperware rose by a horticulturist responsible for creating what she described as "the only truly thorn-less rose."

13. Cited in "An Open Letter to All Distributors and Dealers," 21 August 1955, NMAH 470, series 3.

14. *Wishes Can Come True with Tupperware,* pamphlet (Orlando, Fla.: THP, 1954). Wise mentioned the usefulness of wishes in numerous public addresses throughout her involvement with THP, culminating in her autobiography, *Best Wishes, Brownie Wise: How to Put Your Wishes to Work* (Orlando, Fla.: Podium Publishing, 1957).

15. Insurance records and photographs of household contents, December 1956, show details of Tupper's house on Mowry Road, in Smithfield, R.I., with value of contents estimated at $75,000; NMAH 470, series 3.

16. "Inside the Home of the Week," *Orlando (Fla.) Sentinel,* 25 April 1954, 5-D.

17. Rough draft of letter to "Experience" column, *Detroit News,* ca. 1938, Wise Papers, NMAH 509, series 1.

18. Nancy Brown, *Home Edition* (Detroit: Detroit News, 1939), 239.

19. As a young woman, Brownie Humphrey also belonged to sororities and women's reading groups. See high school scrapbook (1928) and personal papers, NMAH 509, series 1. For a contemporary interpretation of women's relation to fantasy and romantic literature, see Janice A. Radway, *Reading the Romance* (New York: Verso, 1984).

20. Throughout the 1940s and 1950s, Wise fastidiously kept and filed her collection of dressmaking patterns and swatches of chosen fabric; NMAH 509, series 1.

21. "What a Woman," *Orlando (Fla.) Sentinel,* 9 January 1955; the editorial to the cover story read, "Inspiration—Jerry Wise is the reason his mother works so hard. He's also her companion on late afternoon horseback rides and hikes to their lake for angling. Together the two of them enjoy reading and relaxing in the evening. Asked about his famous mother, 16-year-old Jerry replied, 'She's not famous. Famous people are movie stars and people like that. She's just my mother.'"

22. See Susan Strasser and Charles McGovern, eds., *Getting and Spending: European and American Consumption in the Twentieth Century* (Cambridge: Cambridge University Press, 1998); Victoria de Grazia, "Empowering Women as Citizen-Consumers," in *Sex of Things* (De Grazia and Furlough, eds.), 275–86.

23. Wise, "Things We Should Use," NMAH 509, series 2.

24. "The Tupperware Success Story," *Success Unlimited,* October 1954, 18.

25. Ibid.

26. "Help Yourself to Happiness," August 1954, 34.

27. "A Letter from Brownie," *Tupperware Sparks* 2, no. 10 (October 1952): 3.

28. De Grazia and Furlough, eds., in introduction to *Sex of Things,* 5.

29. Front cover, *Tupperware Sparks* 5, no. 6 (June 1956).

30. *Tupperware Wish Party: Wishes Do Come True!,* the program for event held in Spokane, Wash., 6 May 1957, NMAH 509, series 2.

31. *Tupperware Wish Party Extra* 1, no. 1 (April 1957): 2.

32. *Sales Sentinel,* July 1957, 7.

33. Zelizer, *Social Meaning of Money,* 65.

34. The use of incentives and gifts, although greatly elaborated, did not originate with the direct sales concern of THP. Annie Turbo Malone, founder of the "Poro" hair care business and contemporary of Madam C. J. Walker, used incentives for the reward of top-selling agents from the early 1900s. This included "bestowing diamond rings, low price mortgages and public accolades for recruiting new agents," Peiss, *Hope in a Jar,* 77.

35. *Sales Sentinel,* July 1957, 10.

36. Ibid., 9.

37. Mr. and Mrs. Weber, Wheatheart [Kans.] Sales Tupperware Distributors, to THP, 6 December 1957, NMAH 509, series 2.

38. *Tupperware Sparks* nos. 6–7 (July–August 1953): 3.

39. *This 'N' That,* THP publication, 1957, NMAH 509, series 2.

40. *Teen* 4 (June 1960): 39.

41. *Co-Ed: The Magazine for Career Girls and Homemakers of Tomorrow* 5 (May 1960).

42. *Tupperware Sparks* 3, no. 20 (September 1954).

43. Film addressed to a Wally Taver, ca. 1957, viewed by the author at Tupperware World Headquarters, Orlando, Fla., December 1989.

44. Wise, "Preview Parties," a 1955 manuscript used to address a Homecoming Jubilee sales seminar, "Prospecting Preview Parties," in which Wise compares the Tupperware party with informal systems of exchange: "When you're selling Tupperware or selling a Tupperware Party you are bartering, you're trading — you don't just sell." NMAH 509, series 2.

45. Wise, "How Tupperware Uses Incentives," 21 September 1954, NMAH 509, series 2.

46. Ibid., 4.

47. Wise to Tupper, interoffice memo, 21 November 1953, NMAH 470, series 3.

48. "The Tupperware Galaxy of Heavenly Gifts," THP in-house publication, January 1954, NMAH 509, series 2.

49. "As Brownie Introduced the Vanguard," *Tupperware Sparks* 4, no. 5 (May 1955): 6.

50. Alta Reutten to Wise, 16 August 1957, NMAH 509, series 2.

51. Cleo Mohiman to Wise, 3 August 1957, NMAH 509, series 2.

52. *Tupperware Sparks* 5, no. 5 (May 1956): 7.

53. Ibid., 8.

54. Wise, "Research on Birthdays," NMAH 509, series 2.

55. See "THP reimbursed clothing expenses, 1950–56," NMAH 509, series 1.

56. Tupper to Wise, interoffice memo, 8 June 1957, NMAH 470, series 3.

57. Tupper to Wise, interoffice memo, 12 November 1957, NMAH 470, series 3.

58. An internal memo reveals that, even at this early stage in THP's organization, Wise's dictatorial attitude caused concern. "If an idea is not hers, it is no good," commented THP executive Elliot to Creiger, and the memo described how she was "surrounded by 'yes men'"; NMAH 470, series 4.

59. Wise, *Best Wishes, Brownie Wise.*

60. Wise to Tupper, "Re: The Book 'Best Wishes' from Brownie Wise," 26 May 1957, letter in response to correspondence from Earl S. Tupper, NMAH 509, series 2.

61. Tupper occasionally acknowledged Wise's outstanding organization and distribution abilities. See correspondence to the distributor Evans Enterprises, St. Petersburg, Fla., 4 August 1952: "At last we have someone (in the person of Brownie Wise) who has the knowledge, ability and character to handle the difficult job of liaison between the factory, upon which you depend." NMAH 470, series 3.

62. Wise to Tupper, interoffice memo, 21 November 1953, NMAH 470, series 3.

63. Wise also brought to Tupper's attention the fact that THP actually incurred fewer costs than all top-ranking direct sales companies on incentive schemes and premiums: "I am confident that you will find the cost of our Sales Program is surprisingly low compared with that of other Home Party Plan companies. I was told, for instance, by McPherson of Stanley in July, that 35 percent of their growth goes into direct sales promotion and by this he meant the entire selling program. Mr. Graves of Avon made the statement that last year's, '52, was his most economical year and it took 28 percent. I was grateful that during this particular conversation no one turned the spotlight on me, because I would not have wanted to answer truthfully, and even if I had, doubt if they would have believed me." Ibid.

64. Typed notes pertaining to a meeting held between Tupper, Gary McDonald, and Hamer Wilson, 18 March 1958, NMAH 470, series 4.

65. Press release, McBurney Public Relations Associates, Winter Park, Fla., 22 February 1958, NMAH 470, series 4.

66. Minutes of meeting held 24 February 1958; present were Tupper, Wilson, and McDonald, NMAH 470, series 4.

67. Modella Markwardt, Sturgeon Bay, Wisc., to Wise, 7 August 1958, NMAH 509, series 2.

eight
**The Globalization of Tupperware**

1. Press release re: Rexall takeover, 17 September 1958, NMAH 470, series 4.

2. "The Corner Druggist Turns Manufacturer," *Business Week,* 11 October 1958, 132–38.

3. Manuscript written by Tupper in May 1970, in preparation for a proposal application for Hong Kong residency, NMAH 470, series 4.

4. A manuscript contained in Tupper's personal papers describing the reasons for his departure from American life, ca. 1970, NMAH 470, series 4.

5. Tupper diary, 6 January 1933, NMAH 470, series 2.

6. Manuscript, "The Vision of Earl S. Tupper," by Harriet Woods Holden, 1984, written in response to a request from Tupper's sister Gladys, 1 December 1983, after Tupper's death, for "memories of a close friend." NMAH 470, series 4.

7. "Who's Who in Viviane Woodard Cosmetics: Meet the People Who Assure Your Success," pamphlet (California: Viviane Woodard Corporation, 1961).

8. Wise worked as a marketing consultant for various home party and direct sales companies during this period, including Viviane Woodard, Cinderella, Carissa, Sovera, and Artex.

9. Numerous journalists interviewing Wise in her later years comment on her charismatic demeanor; see Charles Fishman, "How the Party Bowled America Over," *Orlando (Fla.) Sentinel,* 15 March 1987, 10–18. Even at the age of seventy-six, Wise consistently sought to reassure those around her by imparting positive-thinking philosophy; in a telephone interview with the author in December 1989, Wise advised, "Reach for the stars and make your dreams come true."

10. *Kissimmee (Fla.) Gazette,* 28 March 1968, 5.

11. *Tupperware Sparks* 1, no. 2 (February 1952): 2. Throughout the 1950s the Puerto Rican market for Tupperware thrived and was a much-coveted territory for potential distributors. Rose Humphrey, Wise's mother, operated the "Gardenia Sales" distribution unit for Puerto Rico from the early 1950s until her death in 1960; NMAH 509, series 2.

12. "Tupperware—Everywhere: Even the Eskimos Have Tupperware Parties," *Tupperware Sparks* 4, no. 12 (December 1955): 6. An excerpt from this article: "One Eskimo Housewife gave Syd an order for $52.12. Two of her parties over $100.00 last week were held in Eskimo homes. Syd said she is having a little trouble getting around because of the snow."

13. *Queen,* February 1965.

14. "Tupperware Brings Home Party to Japan," *Business Week,* 20 November 1965, 162–64.

15. By 1983, Tupperware, then a division of Dart & Kraft Industries, operated factories in Argentina, Australia, Belgium, Brazil, Canada (in Cowansville, Quebec, and in Morden, Manitoba), England, France, Greece, Guatemala, Japan,

Mexico, New Zealand, the Philippines, Portugal, South Africa, Spain, and Venezuela, in addition to its four U.S. plants (in Idaho, Rhode Island, South Carolina, and Tennessee). See *Tupperware Topics* 22, no. 10 (October 1983): front page (Smithfield, R.I.: Tupperware, 1983).

16. Dee Wedemeyer, "There's a Tupperware Party Starting Every 10 Seconds," *Ms.,* August 1973, 71–85.

17. *Salesman's Opportunity,* February 1976, 35–108.

18. Roger R. Russell, "Switch to the Good Life—Switch to Positive Direct Selling," *Speciality Salesman,* November 1975, 16.

19. Cox, *How Women Can Make up to $1000 a Week;* Dottie Walters, *The Selling Power of a Woman* (Englewood Cliffs, N.J.: Prentice Hall, 1962).

20. Wedemeyer, "There's a Tupperware Party Starting Every 10 Seconds," 74. This article does also draw attention to the fact that the majority of distributorships are husband and wife teams and therefore the support of women's families provided THP with the added benefit of their "invisible," unpaid labor.

21. Elayne Rapping, "Tupperware and Women," *Radical America* 6, no. 14 (1980); Margo Harakas, "There's Money in Your Talent: You, Too, Can Go into Business," article, ca. 1976, in Direct Selling Association archives, Washington, D.C.

22. Wedemeyer, "There's a Tupperware Party Starting Every 10 Seconds," 74.

23. Mary Kay Ash, *Mary Kay—You Can Have It All: Lifetime Wisdom from America's Foremost Woman Entrepreneur* (Rocklin, Calif.: Prima Publishing, 1995), xii–xiv.

24. Mary C. Crowley, *Think Mink!* (Old Tappan, N.J.: F. H. Revell, 1976), 12–13.

25. Ann Summers Parties are thriving into the late 1990s. See Jacqueline Gold, *Good Vibrations: The True Story of Ann Summers* (London: Pavilion Books, 1995). Mary Kay Cosmetics also continue to thrive in Europe and the United States.

26. Premark International, a spin-off of Dart & Kraft, took over Tupperware in 1988 and mentioned experimentation with catalog sales and new products, including a range of preschool toys and "knickknack holders." See *Forbes,* 14 November 1988, 76–80. Certainly the temptation of introducing Tupperware to retail outlets has loomed large over the years. A *Business Week* report in 1985, for example, considered eroded U.S. sales figures as a sign of "busy working women, who don't have time for parties . . . shifting to cheaper plastic containers available at supermarket and discount stores"; *Business Week,* 25 February 1985, 108–9.

27. Tupperware's major growth, however, lies in the international market including Asia, Mexico, and Latin America, partly because of changing U.S. demographics, more women in the workplace, and retail competitors such as Rubbermaid offering undercutting, discount prices; "Premark Discloses Plan to Spin off Tupperware Unit," *Wall Street Journal,* 28 March 1996, 1.

28. *Tupperware Corporation Annual Report,* 1996.

29. "Wong Foo, Thanks for the Tupperware," *L.A. Times Magazine,* 21 January 1996.

30. "Direct-Pitch Stalwarts Reluctant to Sell Online," *New York Times,* 22 February 1998.

## Conclusion

1. See, for example, Leland J. Gordon, *Economics for Consumers* (New York: American Book, 1939).

2. Paul Glennie, "Consumption within Historical Studies," in *Acknowledging Consumption,* ed. Daniel Miller (London: Routledge, 1995), 182.

3. Wise to Tupper, interoffice memo, 21 November 1953, NMAH 470, series 3.

4. Ibid.

5. Lizbeth Cohen, "The New Deal State and the Making of Citizen Consumers," in *Getting and Spending: European and American Consumption in the Twentieth Century,* ed. Susan Strasser and Charles McGovern (Cambridge: Cambridge University Press, 1998), 112.

6. Ibid.

7. For an in-depth review of the direct selling industry's relation to consumer movements, see Thomas R. Wotruba, *Moral Suasion: Development of the U.S. Direct Selling Association Industry Code of Ethics* (Washington, D.C.: Direct Selling Education Foundation, 1995).

8. Jacobs, "How about Some Meat?," 910–41.

9. Daniel Miller, *Material Culture and Mass Consumption* (Oxford: Blackwell, 1987), 158–59.

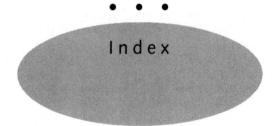

# Index

# Index

# Index

Malone, Annie Turbo, 85
Marchand, Roland, 15
marketing. *See* advertising; Tupperware marketing
Marling, Karal Ann, 132
Marshall, Jack, 134, 141
Mary Kay Cosmetics, 132, 193
Masiello, Frank, 138
mass consumption. *See* consumption
mass production, 52, 71, 72, 75, 156, 201; modernity of, 51; of plastic products, 52; Tupper's view of, 13, 67
McBurney, Charles, 183, 187
*McCall's,* 147
McDonald, Gary, 98, 183, 185
Meikle, Jeffrey, 27, 28, 42, 52–53
men: in direct sales, 83–84, 87, 89; as Tupperware dealers, 123, 146–47; as Tupperware Home Parties managers, 135, 147
*Merchandiser,* 34–35
Meyerowitz, Joanne, 120, 129
Mills, C. Wright, 154
modernity: consumer product designs, 53–54; contrasted with traditional values and styles, 17–18, 20–21, 60–62; mass culture and, 49–50; symbols, 23, 66; Tupper's affinity for, 16, 21–22, 23; Tupperware as icon of, 10–11, 36, 42–43, 45, 49, 50–51, 53, 158–59, 175, 201
Mohiman, Cleo, 177
MOMA. *See* Museum of Modern Art
Mortland, Elsie, 103, 116–18, 142, 188
Mumford, Lewis, 124
Museum of Dishes, 138–39, 174
Museum of Modern Art (MOMA), 3, 36, 49, 196

National Housewares Manufacturers Association (NHMA), 80–81
New Deal, 66, 67–68, 199, 200
New England colonial kitchens, 61
*Newsweek,* 146
New York World's Fair, 23, 66
Nixon, Richard, 106

O'Brien, Catherine, 83, 89
Orlando (Florida), Tupperware Home Parties headquarters, 103, 137–41, 178

Packard, Vance, 51–52
*Parents,* 118, 122
party plans, 82–86, 91–92, 93, 94, 96; benefits for women, 136; criticism of, 118–20, 150; erotic merchandise in Britain, 194–95; expansion in 1960s, 187; feminism and, 192–93; historical precedents, 109–10; sociability, 85, 88–89, 106; Stanley Home Products, 83–84, 87, 88–89, 90; success in suburbs, 106. *See also* Tupperware parties
Patio Parties, 94, 95–96
Peale, Norman Vincent, 129, 135, 150–51, 181
Peiss, Kathy, 64, 85, 154
Peven, Dorothy E., 150
plastic products, 51–52; designs, 27, 52–53; direct sales of, 82; dog dishes as negative image for Tupper, 76–77, 180–81; housewares, 44; industry, 26–28, 52; innovations, 28; mass consumer market for, 27, 45; public perception of low quality, 41–42, 45, 76–77
polyethylene, 36–38, 45; properties, 38, 41; use in Tupperware, 3, 9, 35; use promoted by Tupper, 37, 44
Poly-T material, 9, 36, 38, 41, 42–43, 44
*Popular Mechanics,* 24
popular psychology, 91, 129, 136, 148–50, 151
positive thinking, 22, 129, 135–36, 145, 148, 181, 187
postwar American society: corporate culture, 154–55; economy, 114, 156, 157–58; hierarchies of taste, 49–50; kitchen debate, 106; material culture, 133; popular psychology, 148–50, 151; religion, 150–51; repression of housewives seen, 118–20, 122. *See also* consumption; modernity; suburbs

# Index

# Index

# Index

191; tumblers, 46, 48, 53, 73, 81; Wonder Bowls, 8, 46, 47, 53, 58, 112, 115

Tupperware Rose, 132, 158

Tupperware sales incentive schemes, 103, 133, 142, 165–67, 168–73, 176–78, 200; romantic and luxurious products, 152, 168; Wise's personal belongings given in, 134, 171–73

*Tupperware Sparks,* 101, 111, 133, 162, 166, 171, 172, 174, 188

TWA (Trans World Airlines), 44–45

Tyler May, Elaine, 115, 157

utopianism, 16–18, 19, 22–23

Van Doren, Harold, 50–51

Victoria and Albert Museum, 3

Walker, Madam C. J., 85, 154

Watts, Artie, 153–54

Wearever Aluminum Cooking Products, 82, 83

Welsh, Frank, 22

Whyte, William, 154

Wilson, Hamer, 183, 185

Wise, Brownie: autobiography, 145, 181, 182; background, 160; *Business Week* cover story on, 2–3, 128, 130; charisma as leader, 3, 127, 132, 133, 134, 145; clothing, 134, 171–73, 178; death, 188; departure from Tupperware Home Parties, 180, 183, 184; direct sales companies, 94, 95–96, 183–84, 187, 199; eating habits, 133; emotional investment in Tupperware Home Parties, 131, 134; gift-giving research, 178; glamour associated with, 133, 158, 170–73; home, 159, 162, 171, 178, 188; at Homecoming Jubilees, 142; management team, 103, 135, 147; positive thinking and self-

improvement encouraged, 129–31, 135–36, 145, 148, 151, 153, 163, 181, 187–88; preference for pink, 132, 133; public image, 133, 159–60, 162, 178–79; relationship with Tupper, 3, 103, 134, 158, 159–60, 179–83; as role model, 134, 147–48; sales incentives given by, 134, 152, 171–73; speeches at African-American colleges, 126, 153; spending habits, 134, 178–79; as Stanley Home Products dealer, 93–94, 161; support for women in business, 129–32, 146; Tupperware Art Fund, 140–41; at Tupperware Home Parties, 2–3, 95–96, 125, 128–29, 132; Tupperware Home Parties headquarters and garden, 137, 138, 178; view of consumption, 159, 163–65, 175–76, 200; as writer, 160–62, 163–65

Wise, Jerry, 160, 162, 163, 179, 188

Wolfe Products Company, 46

*Woman's Home Companion,* 128–29, 163, 164

women: in business, 129–32, 146; cigarette smoking, 75; conservative, 193–94; as consumers, 62, 63–65, 200; in direct sales, 88–91, 106, 131, 193; discrimination against, 153; economic power, 168; feminism, 120, 129, 151–52, 192–93; mothers, 122, 131; New Woman, 64, 65; pin money, 164–65, 168; politicized, 120, 127; in postwar period, 118–20; siren stereotype, 64; Tupper's inventions for, 30–33, 64–65. *See also* housewives

Wonder Bowls, 8, 46, 47, 53, 58, 112, 115

Wood, Robert C., 124

Wright, Richardson, 70–71

Zelizer, Vivianna, 156, 157, 168